Wild Africa

Wild Africa

exploring the African habitats

Patrick Morris, Amanda Barrett, Andrew Murray
and Marguerite Smits van Oyen

Contents

COASTS   **Marguerite Smits van Oyen   8**

Africa's coastline represents its most diverse habitat, in terms of extreme temperatures, land-form and wildlife. At 29,000 km (18,000 miles), it is also one of the largest, a zone where familiar land animals make the most of the ocean's riches and creatures from the sea pioneer some of the continent's most hostile environments.

MOUNTAINS   **Patrick Morris   44**

Ever since its creation, Africa has been folded, squeezed and torn at by massive subterranean forces, lifting great mountains high into the sky. Some, like Kilimanjaro, are so tall that permanent ice fields crown their summits. This chapter explores how wildlife copes with the harsh physical demands of altitude, and how climate, geology, age and isolation have all played a significant role in shaping the ecology of this unusual world above the clouds.

LAKES AND RIVERS   **Amanda Barrett   80**

Without water there would be no life on Earth as we know it today and, despite the aridity of Africa, there are diverse lakes and rivers providing homes for an exuberant mix of wildlife. There are tumbling, ice-cold mountain springs and the longest river in the world; and lakes that vary in colour from jade green to blood red soda. There is Lake Victoria, the second largest freshwater lake on the planet. And between these extremes are swamps and flood-plains that provide fertile grazing ground for a host of antelope.

DESERTS

Patrick Morris   116

Deserts cover more of Africa than any other environment. With their burning temperatures, intense solar radiation and shortages of water, food and shelter, they seem the most inhospitable places to live. This chapter reveals the intriguing ways in which animals and plants survive in the desert, and examines the different influences on life in Africa's four mightiest deserts – the Sahara, Kalahari, Karoo and Namib.

JUNGLES

Andrew Murray   154

Across Africa's Equator is a vast green swathe of tropical rainforest. This endless, hot, humid, plant world is the most mysterious and unexplored of Africa's habitats. Since the age of the dinosaurs, it has been a bubbling cauldron of evolution, a central hotspot of Africa's rich diversity. This chapter explores the rainforest's infinite web of life and discovers the origins of some of the continent's most remarkable creatures.

SAVANNAHS

Amanda Barrett   192

Twenty-five million years ago, Africa became drier and rainforests shrank to a shadow of their former selves. The way was open for the birth of a new world – savannahs – a potent combination of woodland, thicket and grassland, which even today still supports the largest herds of herbivores on Earth as well as a magical mix of social and solitary carnivores. This is the land where buffalo vote and hyaenas engage in power politics; where grasses and trees thrive; and where one primate gained the upper hand.

Foreword

Seen from space, Africa resembles a giant heart, splashed with all the colours of the spectrum, and bounded by every shade of blue. Moving closer, these textured patterns become great swathes of forest and desert, interrupted by giant mountain ranges and savannahs, and cut by swamps, lakes and rivers. Ocean currents pulse around the coastline, generating life-giving clouds that drift across the land. Moving closer still, the African landscape stirs. A line of elephants wanders across a shimmering sea of sand dunes. High on a snow-capped mountain, a plant unfurls its frozen leaves to greet the warmth of the sun. In the savannahs, a giraffe stretches tall to pluck the leaves from the crown of an acacia tree.

A land of dazzling beauty, Africa is also a land of surprise, from baboons that feast on shark eggs to the fur seals that crowd on to baking desert shores. But the magnificent diversity of life we see in Africa today is no coincidence. It is the culmination of more than 100 million years of climatic, geological and biological change since the continent first emerged from an ancient supercontinent known as Gondwana. Like flints carved from a rock, South America, Australia, India, the Middle East, Southeast Asia and Antarctica were all scattered across the southern hemisphere. Africa was the largest and least mobile fragment that remained – the mother continent – turning on its axis and drifting slowly north and east until about 30 million years ago, when it first collided with Eurasia. Crucially, these long periods of isolation from other continents allowed African wildlife to flourish without regular interference from invaders. The gently shifting climate, cushioned by the warm Equator, promoted change but prevented catastrophe. And Africa's sheer size – a quarter of the world's total land mass – meant that life could find a foothold in a bewildering variety of habitats.

The animals and plants of Africa are spread among six key environments – the coastal margins, mountains, wetlands, deserts, forests and savannahs. By their very nature, each of these worlds presents different challenges to wildlife, both physical and biological. Africa's coasts are the most diverse habitat of all, encompassing coral reefs and mangrove swamps, desert shores, forested creeks and storm-battered cliffs. Inland, mountains of all ages raise their heads above the clouds. There are mighty young volcanoes, like the famous Kilimanjaro, along with many ancient peaks formed by the warping and upthrust of the land. Home to some of Africa's hardiest and most unusual plants and animals, mountains are also vital interceptors of rain-clouds and the source of much of the continent's fresh water. Four giant rivers, the Nile, Congo, Zambezi and Niger – and a host of smaller waterways – drain the continent. In places, enormous inland lakes, deltas and floodplains sustain the most prolific and colourful gatherings of wildlife of all.

The Equator spans more of Africa than any other continent, and here copious amounts of sunshine, rainfall and warmth fuel a vast green carpet of rainforest. This tangled world, dominated by plants, has

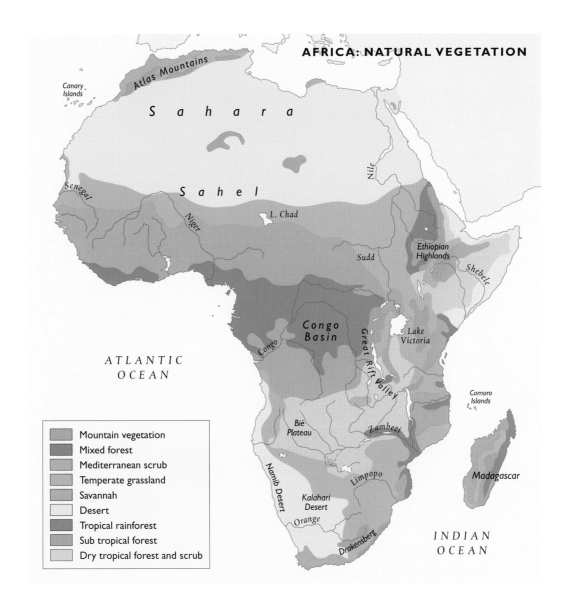

AFRICA: NATURAL VEGETATION

Mountain vegetation
Mixed forest
Mediterranean scrub
Temperate grassland
Savannah
Desert
Tropical rainforest
Sub tropical forest
Dry tropical forest and scrub

long been a hotbed of evolution, steadily adding new species to the African mix. Although the tropics receive ample rainfall, most of Africa is starved of moisture and dominated by desert. These include the world's largest expanse of arid land, the Sahara, and the most ancient, the Namib. Yet these hostile expanses are far from lifeless – some ingenious animals and plants manage to get by on the most meagre amounts of food and moisture. Trapped between the margins of deserts and forests, savannahs snake their way across the continent. They are the newest environment in Africa – a dynamic, energy-rich world of woodlands and short grassy plains, fed by seasonal rains and bathed in sunshine. Today, this brave new world supports the most impressive concentrations of large mammals in Africa, and historically, it was a setting very similar to this that was so crucial to our own development as a species.

1

COASTS

ISLAND AFRICA

The coastline of Africa was born out of geological violence. The great shifting processes of the landmasses, which occurred more than 100 million years ago in the southern seas, as the supercontinent Gondwana wrenched apart into the continents we know today, were some of the most dramatic changes that the surface of the earth has witnessed.

One of the largest islands to break away was already recognizable. While its coastal scars were still fresh, the familiar shape of Africa was born.

As the new lands travelled further apart over the southern hemisphere, literally floating over the liquid mantle beneath the earth's crust, they left in their wake widening bodies of water. On either side of Africa, two new, vast oceans emerged: the South Atlantic and the Indian Ocean, two giants that to this day work to shape, break and heal the fringes of Africa's great continent.

Previous page: Bottlenose dolphins enjoy riding the surf at Africa's southernmost point. They time their leaps from the backs of the waves moments before they are thrown onto the beach.

1. The ragged and desolate coast of Djibouti, at the entrance to the Red Sea. Geological activity is still wrenching these young shores apart at a rate of 2 cm (1 inch) per year.

A MOMENT IN TIME

Following the break-up of Gondwana (▷ pp. 18–19), Africa continued to shift, but very slowly compared to the other fragments. It spent more than 100 million years as an island hugging the Equator, long enough to develop communities of animals and plants unlike any other on Earth. By 30 million years ago it had progressed far enough north to collide with Europe and Asia, closing in on a body of water that used to be the Tethys Ocean, and today is called the Mediterranean – a sea in the midst of land. In contrast, the youngest of Africa's seas was born only 3 million years ago, as the Great Rift opened along the eastern side of the continent. Today, the Red Sea fills with warm waters from the Indian Ocean.

Flanked by two of the world's largest oceans and topped by two seas, Africa's coastline bathes in the most extreme currents, from cold upwellings to warm monsoon carriers, currents that have a determining effect on the continent's ecology. The result is a patchwork of climates and habitats, ranging from arid desert to lush, tropical forest, which nurture an incredible variety of animals and plants on Africa's beautiful shores.

After this turbulent past, a look at Africa today is just like a snapshot, a moment in time; the geological forces that have shaped her thus far are, of course, still continuing and will continue well after our passage on the planet. A closer look at this picture reveals an immense linear habitat, 29,000 km (18,000 miles) of coastline, from the Mediterranean to the tip of South Africa, through the steamy shores of the tropics. However different these habitats are, what remains consistent is the influence the great ocean currents, and the winds that push them, have on life on shore. They determine what can live there, and what cannot.

1

1. Winds race uninterrupted across the South Atlantic, lifting the seas to gargantuan scale. The action of these fierce waves along much of the southwestern shores has moulded a hostile and rocky world where only the toughest and best-adapted creatures can survive.

1

WINDS

Looking at the Earth from space, one can see that our planet is in fact much more water than land, with about 70 per cent of its surface covered by oceans and seas. The oceans and the atmosphere form one system that is never still, moving continuously around and above the landmasses.

This movement is driven partly by the rotation of the Earth and partly by the heat of the sun, which promotes circulation in the atmosphere, i.e., it generates winds, which push currents across whole ocean basins.

Trade winds

All along the Equator, hot air rises and atmospheric pressure is low. Since winds blow from areas of high pressure to areas of low pressure, the Equator draws in air both from the north and the south; these are the 'trade winds'.

Because of the deflection due to the Earth's rotation (Coriolis Force), the trade winds actually blow from the northeast in the northern hemisphere, and the southeast in the southern one. As well as significantly influencing marine life, they have changed the face of Africa as people used them to traffic to and from the continent.

These winds are a constant over water, like the Atlantic, which is mirrored north and south of the Equator. In contrast, the Indian Ocean does not have a northern counterpart but instead is topped by a gigantic landmass extending from Europe to Asia, which generates a unique wind pattern.

Monsoon

The word 'monsoon' is derived from an Arab word meaning 'winds that change seasonally'. In winter, the vast continental mass of Eurasia cools the air above it faster than the ocean does, because land cools down and heats up faster than water. This dense and heavy cool air produces an area of high pressure over the continent and pushes a flow of air from Eurasia to the Equator. With the deflection to the right in the northern hemisphere due to the Earth's rotation, it actually blows from a northeasterly direction. It is the *northeast monsoon*. In the northern summer this situation is reversed, generating the stronger *southwest monsoon*, also the carrier of heavy rains.

This trade wind reversal is unique to the Indian Ocean (▷ Somali Current, p. 16).

OCEAN CURRENTS

Winds generate surface currents so it comes as no surprise that their patterns are almost perfectly matched. Near the Equator the trade winds drive the ocean surface waters to the west; nearer the poles the westerly winds drive the waters back towards the east. The combined effect of these winds is to create a broadly circular system of currents known as gyres.

Gyres

To Africa, the North Atlantic gyre brings in the cold Canaries Current from the north and the South Atlantic gyre generates the Benguela Current. Both come to meet the coasts of Africa with dramatic effect, as nutrient-rich upwelling currents meet deserts.

The Indian Ocean only has a southern gyre, which pushes warm equatorial waters into the Agulhas Current, while the north part of the Indian Ocean is unique in having a current pattern that changes twice during the year under the influence of the monsoon winds (▷ pp. 12 and 16).

Upwelling currents

Currents are not only moving bodies of water that can travel horizontally, they can also flow up or down. Coastal upwellings are most marked in areas of gyres and trade winds: the winds drive a surface current along the coastline and the deflection due to the Earth's rotation forces it to the right in the northern hemisphere, and to the left in the southern one. As the water is pushed offshore, it leaves a depression along the coastal boundary, which can only be filled with waters coming in from the deep. This is called a coastal upwelling.

Deep waters are cold and rich in nutrients, since there are no plants down in the unlit waters to absorb the accumulated particles. So by the time they reach the surface, these waters are a banquet of untouched nutrients. Here, the minute plants, or 'phytoplankton', can proliferate under the light of the sun and this rich resource forms the basis of a bountiful food chain. These regions thus typically support an enormous population of fish which in turn feed a host of predators, including humans.

Although there are some upwellings in the Indian Ocean, it is those on the western sides of continents that are most spectacular and of incredible biological importance, like the Benguela upwelling off Namibia and South Africa, and the one that occurs off the coast of Mauritania. These waters sport some of the best fishing grounds in the world and are of high economic value.

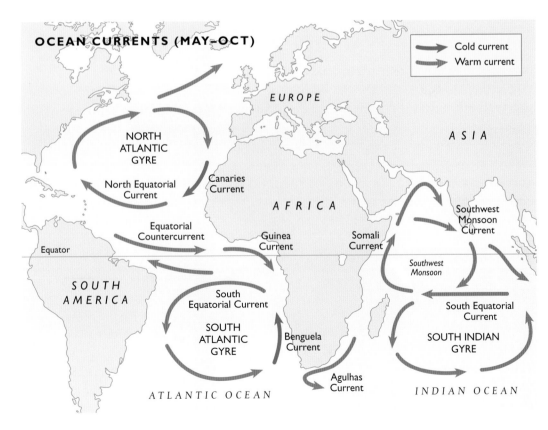

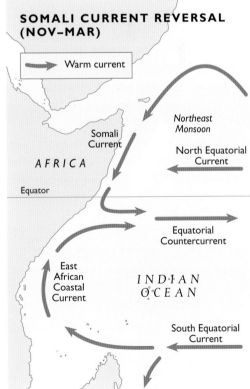

TIDES

Tides are created by the gravitational effects of the moon, the sun and the Earth on large bodies of water. The ebb and flow of the oceans is a familiar pulse on any shore, and life along the African coastline beats to its twice-daily rhythm. From communities of fish and crabs in mangroves, to wading birds and hordes of invertebrates, this inexorable rise and fall of water is one of the most tangible influential forces on coastal creatures.

Worlds of change

It is likely that since life originated in the oceans, the large shallow areas under tropical regime that were present over three hundred million years ago would have provided ideal opportunities for animals to develop air breathing, both in marine and in fresh waters, and led to the conquest of the land.

A look at today's tropics may give some insight as to how this might have worked. In mangrove swamps, tides expose large areas of mud and sand flats twice a day and offer a platform for marine animals to adapt to an existence above water. Today, fish like mudskippers seem to be on the cusp of change, able to breathe air yet no longer good at swimming, and many crabs have already completely or partially adapted to terrestrial life.

Other animals, like the limpets on Africa's southern shores, batten down their hatches when exposed to the air, and when the tide is high they graze on the narrow, but immensely rich, gardens of algae that persist on intertidal rocks. One limpet even depends on the action of the tide to get to its favoured food. As the tide drops and brushes strands of kelp past it, the Argenville's limpet of South Africa waits with its shell raised high and slams it down at the right time to slice off a chunk of kelp frond. With the rising tide, its food source is taken out of reach once more.

This narrow band of coast, the intertidal zone, is one of the most demanding environments on Earth. To survive here, animals and plants must be able to withstand wildly fluctuating extremes of temperature, salinity, violent water and air. But, for the specialists the rewards are high, often bringing more or less exclusive access to natural resources.

This zone is also an interface between creatures of the land and those of the sea, and is utilized by both according to the state of the tide. These include jackals that patrol the strandline and some specialized primates, such as baboons, that have learned that the seashore can provide rich pickings.

 A CURRENT LIKE A WALL

Superficially, the seas around Africa appear to be one continuous mass, a great soup of life that washes randomly around its shores. But nothing could be further from the truth. Currents, winds, coastlines and seabed together form as complex a habitat as any savannah or mountain on land. In addition, temperature separates the two warm currents on Africa's east and west coasts. The warm Agulhas Current is never able to meet the warm Guinea Current, as they are separated by a stretch of cold water in the form of the Benguela upwelling. Where cold waters meet warm an invisible barrier is created. The cold, stormy waters on the southwest coast of the continent are as hostile and foreign to a tropical clownfish (right) as a desert is to a hippopotamus.

This tip of cold water effectively separates the animals and plants of the Indian Ocean from those of the Atlantic and prevents them migrating across. Though the habitats are alike, no mangrove species is shared between the two sides of Africa. Sea mammals like dugongs and manatees share a common ancestor that once lived on land and took to the sea. Today, the dugong is restricted to the Indian Ocean, and the manatee to the Atlantic.

1

AFRICA'S OWN CURRENTS

Africa's coasts are characterized by oceanic influence, but it is perhaps the currents that have the most significant effect on life as a whole. On the southeast coast the dominant flow is known as the Agulhas Current. Like a powerful river in the sea, it sweeps warm waters from the Indian Ocean down Africa's east coast, meeting the wall of cold water to the south and west and twisting back to the east. It provides a highway that is used by a host of marine creatures, including one of the planet's most remarkable concentrations of fish. Each year, vast shoals of sardines (or pilchards) swim against this flow from their breeding grounds in the south to feed on the riches carried by the current. Ironically, these cold-water fish must wait for winter, when the surface waters cool, to make their pilgrimage. The shoals are sometimes caught in the turbulent waters close to shore in their search for a meal. Inevitably, they are followed by attendant hordes of hunters: dolphins, whales, fur seals, Cape gannets and sharks, which patrol the warm channel year round. The 'sardine run' is just one of the many mass movements of creatures governed by Africa's pattern of oceanic currents.

1. When under attack, huge shoals of anchovies bunch tightly together to confuse predators, behaving like one huge, shimmering organism.

Each year, evaporation removes more than 110,000 cubic km (26,000 cubic miles) of water from the surface of the oceans.

The Somali Current

Further north off Africa's east coast the currents are more fickle. In the northern winter, waters are carried south along the Somali coastline due to the effects of the north-east monsoon. This flow persists until spring, when temperature changes result in the south-west monsoon (▷ p. 12), affecting the ocean to such an extent that the current does a 180 degree turn, and starts to flow north and east.

This annual shift has been exploited by animals and people alike to aid progress around the Indian Ocean and the Arabian Sea. Much of Africa's trading past was fuelled by the forces of this reversing Somali Current, as Arab traders sailed down to fill their boats with timber, ivory and other exotic goods, only to sail back six months later with a full load, aided by the shifting current.

Further north again, the sea takes on an altogether different character, with the relatively infant Red Sea and the all but land-locked Mediterranean.

Atlantic shores

A very different world from the east coast, Africa's west coast is battered by waves that have rolled unhindered across thousands of kilometres of open water. Beneath the turbulent surface the Canaries Current promotes a cold upwelling, bringing an explosion of phytoplankton and its attendant food chain. Although the land in this region is desert-like, the shoreline provides sustenance for millions of resident and migratory birds (▷ Banc d'Arguin, p. 40).

Rounding the western tip, Africa's coasts change character once again. With the energy of the wave action dissipated by the run of land and the increased temperature due to proximity to the equator, the seas become typically tropical. Warm equatorial waters are swept against the shores by the Guinea Current and this more sedate action, added to the constant run of fresh water into the ocean from the forested and rain-filled West African mainland, has created vast areas where sand and other sediments have been deposited. This region is typified by mangrove forest, sandbars, deltas and lagoons, and includes some of the wettest places on Earth. Some of the most extensive mangrove forests flourish here, with bands 50 km (30 miles) wide from the sea to the landward face. There are over 25,000 sq km (9650 sq miles) of mangroves stretching from Senegal to Angola alone.

But, further south, the actions of wind and water combine to bring an unexpected effect

 ## A PENGUIN IN AFRICA

Africa's only penguin lives at the tip of Africa, thanks to the cold Benguela Current. These birds are more associated with frozen seas, but the African penguin (left) is endemic to the inshore seas of Southern Africa. This excellent swimmer thrives on the riches of fish in the current system, and can dive as deep as 100 metres (330 feet) to hunt its main prey, pilchard or sardine.

But like all birds they have to come ashore to breed and they do so in large colonies on rocky islands, safe from land predators. The parents share looking after the two chicks, one parent shading them from the African sun or warming them in the cold fog, while the other is out at sea hunting.

They normally nest in ancient burrows dug in guano deposits, but since this 'white gold' was mined as a profitable fertilizer in huge quantities during the nineteenth century, penguins have nothing left to dig in to. Many pairs are now forced to nest on bare rock, exposing the eggs or young to solar radiation and kelp gull predation. The chicks especially, but also the adults, suffer from overheating on summer days with no wind. Only a few thousand birds remain in the wild today, largely due to overfishing of penguin food and the massive consumption of penguin eggs in the past.

1

that involves the cold Benguela Current. One might expect the sea to be warm at this latitude, but this rise of icy waters from the ocean's depths creates a paradox of conditions – on land, the searing heat of the Namibian desert; at sea, cool waters rich with vast shoals of fish feasting on the nutrients stirred up by the upwelling.

Some creatures endure great hardships to reap this marine bounty. Fur seals, penguins, cormorants and others, all better suited to temperate climes, jostle for space on the baking shoreline and surrounding islands so that they might raise families close to the ocean's harvest. Inevitably, the sun takes its toll on some, but the rewards from the sea far outweigh the hardships faced on land.

Two oceans at the tip of Africa

Further south again one meets the greatest paradox of all, where the cold Benguela Current meets the warm Agulhas one. Because Africa's southern tip finishes much closer to the Equator than its closest ecological equivalent, South America, which extends almost into the Antarctic, the two currents on either side of Africa meet at the Cape peninsula. The result is a head-on collision of cold and warm water species at Africa's southern tip. The point at which these waters meet shifts with season and conditions, but the shoreline in this region hosts one of the most diverse and fascinating communities of marine life to be found on the planet.

1. A testament to the fruitful influence of the Benguela Current, thousands of Cape cormorants rest between fishing trips on the roasting Namibian shore. The sea is the sole provider for a huge community of animals.

⭐ The 'cold Benguela Current' is not cold because it comes from the South Pole, as is often said, but because it originates from the deep sea. It is an upwelling current.

GONDWANA

From space, the Earth seems to show a fixed pattern, with all the continents and oceans firmly in place. Europe and Asia, the Americas, Australia and Africa all show very familiar and constant shapes. Yet nothing could be further from the truth. The continental plates that form the surface of our planet are in continual movement, either bumping against each other or moving further apart. The oceans wax and wane between gaps in the landmasses, while mountain chains arise where two plates collide.

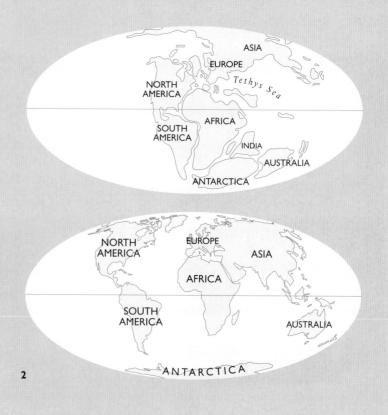

2

1

1. The inexorable march of sands towards the ocean is escorted by flamingos on the western shores. The birds find a rich supply of tiny crustacea in the shallow waters of lagoons and salt marshes.

2. After the break-up of Pangea about 180 million years ago, the world's continents first appeared as we know them now. The continents are still shifting today.

3. Tropical paradise? Perhaps, for a human visitor, but the warm seas along Africa's coastline cannot support the same level of life as the colder waters.

Continental drift

In 1915, the German geophysicist Alfred Wegener suggested a revolutionary idea! He observed the similarity between the South American and West African coastlines and proposed that at one time in the Earth's history, all the continents had been joined. But it was only in the 1960s, with the help of fossil evidence (Antarctica for example shares many fossils with southern Africa) that his ideas were widely accepted. Today, we know that the positioning of the continents is due to the movements of the continental plates over the last few hundred million years.

Most of these movements happened well after life evolved on the planet, so the changes in ocean sizes and climates that these movements provoked had a profound effect on the evolution of plants and animals.

Pangea

So between 290 and 250 million years ago, all the continents of the Earth were fused

together in a single landmass called Pangea. This was a time when ichthyosaurs and giant ammonites dominated the ocean, and reptiles already roamed the land.

When Pangea split into two, North America, Europe and Asia formed Laurasia and to the south emerged the supercontinent Gondwana. Between the two, the new Tethys Ocean opened up and, this was the first time warm equatorial waters were able to circulate around the globe. They brought moist, warm air with them, greatly influencing life on Earth and preparing the planet for the explosion of the reptiles to come.

Gondwana – the primordial continent

The supercontinent Gondwana began to split apart 145 million years ago and all the southern continents appeared, Africa the biggest fragment of them all. Today, animals such as the unique lungfish of Africa, South America and Australia exhibit features that reveal their common Gondwanan ancestry.

During the Cretaceous, 145–70 million years ago, the development of flowering plants changed the face of the Earth. This key period in evolution laid the foundations for modern ecosystems, paving the way for the dramatic development of birds and mammals from reptilian ancestors.

When all the southern continents moved away, 100 million years ago, Africa began a long period of isolation, still straddling the Equator. Rainforests dominated the land, reaching coast to coast, and this tropical climate favoured the rapid evolution of a massive diversity of unique animals.

Africa meets Eurasia – today

Finally, about 22 million years ago, Africa moved far enough north to establish a land-bridge with Eurasia via Arabia. Many ungulates and carnivores flooded into Africa, while primates and elephants moved out to conquer new lands. This movement trapped the ancient Tethys Ocean to form the

Mediterranean, altering the climate dramatically. The environment on land became drier and more seasonal. The Great Rift erupted and separated Africa's forests for good.

By 18 million years ago the union of Africa and Eurasia was complete. Hippos first appeared in fossils from East Africa at this time, and many other animal groups followed, including our own ancestors!

TROPICAL SHORES

To most people, tropical beaches represent the ultimate idyll – white sands, palm trees and clear, blue, warm waters. For a holidaymaker this may well be Utopia, but for the resident creatures, tropical shores represent a survival challenge. The usual problems associated with tidal exposure are further aggravated by the high temperatures that prevail here; salinity may increase through rapid evaporation. Animals and plants face a daily battle. Where the shoreline is rocky the challenges are at their greatest, but even the relative calm of sandy, muddy shores poses a unique set of problems that must be overcome to ensure success.

Yet the waters between the tides are slightly richer in food and oxygen than the adjacent shallow areas, qualities that some hardcore pioneers have found hard to resist. Mangrove forests and armies of amazingly adapted animals abound in these conditions and cope with the hostile world caught between land and sea.

MANGROVES – GREEN PIONEERS

As people have colonized the tropical coast-line they have had to contend with mangrove forests. Development companies wishing to 'reclaim' coastal flats see the tangle of trees as nothing more than an inconvenience, but this is truly a hostile place for people, with its deep, foul-smelling mud, mosquitoes and other biting insects, and an impenetrable tangle of roots and trunks. But it is precisely this wooden fortress that has protected much of the tropical African coastline from erosion, which ultimately would result in a barren, wasted world.

The mangrove forest is a marvel of evolution. Mangroves are the only trees that can tolerate these extremes of saltwater and scorching air, and their adaptation to this environment provides a habitat integral to the survival of a plethora of marine species. To the creatures of the tropical coastline, mangroves represent nursery, larder, sea wall and shelter, all rolled into one.

Distribution and biogeography

Mangrove forests thrive only on sheltered tropical shores, away from direct wave action and where the sea temperature does not drop below 20°C (68°F), except where warm currents, like the Agulhas in the southeast, allow them to spread beyond the tropics (▷ 1.1 Island Africa).

1. One of the richest habitats along the warmer shores is mangrove swamp. The combination of tidal mudflats, an abundance of sediments, a meeting of fresh and salt waters, and thick forest hosts a most diverse fauna. **1**

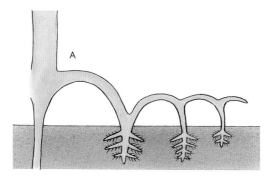
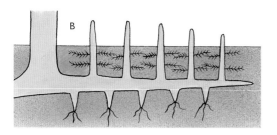
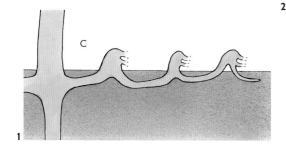

1. The root systems of African mangroves: 'prop roots' of Rhizophora (A); pneumatophores of Avicennia (B); 'knee roots' with secondary shoots of Bruguiera (C).

2. Rhizophora's prop roots move in and anchor trees in the mud. Mangroves are floral pioneers, stretching their roots and stems to the very limit of terrestrial plant types. Their spread and demise shapes the very coastline of tropical Africa.

⭐ Mangroves are very salt-tolerant, but when there is some freshwater input, such as from rivers or predictable rainfall, they can grow up to 20–30 m (65–100 feet) high!

Although there are some 54 mangrove species worldwide, there are only nine species in East Africa and five in West Africa. This is because the cold waters around the southern tip of Africa prevent contact between the tropical waters of the Indian Ocean and the Atlantic, as we saw earlier. What is more, the species on either side of the continent are different, with the Indian Ocean side holding the bulk of them. This reinforces the theory that they first originated in the Indo-Pacific region and later spread to the Atlantic side via the then huge and warm Tethys Ocean (▷ p. 19). Once this sea was closed, Africa effectively created a land barrier between the two oceans and mangroves continued evolving in isolation, which accounts for the differences between species on either side of the continent today.

Harsh world, hard tree!

Mangrove trees survive where no other tree is able. This is in part thanks to a unique root system, one of their most striking adaptations. There is hardly any oxygen in the dense mud and the small amount that does exist is consumed by bacteria. Normal trees have roots branching off the main trunk underground to absorb oxygen and nutrients, but in mangrove trees a special aerating device is deployed. In Rhizophora species, roots shoot out from the main tree trunk as much as 2 m (6½ feet) above ground and penetrate the mud some distance away. There, a series of finer roots, which can absorb nutrients, spread into the soil; there may also be secondary roots that loop off and ground themselves further from the main trunk.

The aerial part of the root is covered in minute pores or 'lenticels', through which air penetrates. These tiny vents respond to incoming water by closing, making the roots impermeable to water at high tide. The impressive arching roots are in fact the real support of the tree and prevent it from sinking into the mud, as the main trunk peters out as it reaches the ground. They are aptly named 'prop roots' or 'stilt roots'. Each tree has many of these out-shoots, and they criss-cross with those of neighbouring trees. The resulting tangle of roots is impenetrable

and gives the Rhizophora forests an intimidating appearance at low tide.

Just as uninviting is the peculiar root architecture of Avicennia trees. Their woody snorkels, or 'pneumatophores', stick straight up out of the mud up to 30 cm (12 inches) above the surface. A single tree can have as many as 10,000 pneumatophores, and each is covered in lenticels. In this way, they satisfy their requirement for oxygen when the tide is out. For anyone walking barefooted in an Avicennia forest at low tide, the saving grace is that the pneumatophores are actually quite soft, otherwise it would be a very painful experience. Sonneratia trees have tough, strong pneumatophores and Bruguiera forms knee-roots, by folding over the main root, giving them a knobbly appearance.

Enemy salt

The various mangrove species cope differently with high salinity and deploy a variety of means to deal with the excess salt – some eliminate it by excretion, others do not allow it through their roots and bark. Several mangrove species deposit salt in the bark of stems and roots (Avicennia, Rhizophora, Sonneratia and Xylocarpus). Some trees use their leaves rather as we use our kidneys, filling a leaf with excess salt and toxins and then simply dropping it.

Most mangroves have thick leaves with a heavy, waxy cuticle on the outside; the stomata (breathing holes) are on the underside to reduce the loss of water and hence prevent a build-up in the concentration

 ## COASTAL FOREST: RESERVOIRS OF LIFE

The African continent has been an ever-shifting range of habitats over the millennia. Deserts have spread and shrunk, mountain ranges risen, rifts widened. One of the few consistent influences over the past 30 million years has been that of the Indian Ocean. Throughout this time it has provided predictable rain on Africa's eastern seaboard.

As the forests that once reached coast to coast shrunk under the advancing drier regime inland, a string of coastal forests were preserved, thanks to the nurturing moisture from the ocean.

In effect, each of them has become an island and, as such, life within forests bears many similarities with that found on true islands. Many species of animal and plant are unique to a single stretch of forest, particularly those that are restricted by the risk of desiccation should they venture away from the forest domain. Tree frogs, chameleons and a host of invertebrates all show variation across the region, but many variants are completely restricted to their own forest island, like the red colobus in Zanzibar (right). Other creatures are more widespread, including elephant shrews, which scurry around the leaf litter, sniffing out their invertebrate prey with their long, mobile noses. Though isolated from each other, many of these forests have provided highways for animals and plants to spread inland to the nearby mountain ranges, acting as reservoirs of life.

⭐ As one claw of fiddler crab males is enlarged for sexual display, they spend twice as long feeding as females, which use both 'hands' to collect micro-algae from the mud floor.

of salt. In addition, a number of mangrove species have salt glands on their leaves through which salt is excreted. The lower leaf surface of Avicennia is covered with a dense carpet of hairs that keeps the droplets of salty water away from the leaf surface. All mangrove species are tolerant to some degree of high salt concentrations in their tissues. *Avicennia marina* is the most salt-tolerant, capable of growing in places where the water is three times as salty as seawater, although in such conditions the trees are stunted.

With leaves laden with salts and toxins it seems unlikely that any animal would be able to use the mangrove forests as a food resource. But, as is so often the case where there is a meal to be had, there is an army of diners prepared to do battle with the hazards to reach it.

Crabs, whelks and a fish out of water

With the leaves of the mangrove acting as a waste disposal unit for the trees, you would be forgiven for thinking that each leaf that fell could be processed only by bacteria. Though minute organisms do play a vital role in the recycling process of organic matter within a mangrove forest, an army of creatures waits for every precious leaf or other products to come their way.

Of all the species that live here, crabs have taken the best advantage of this leaf-fall, some taking the leaves as they hit the mud, others filtering through the soil for minute edible particles. Then there are a few species that have adapted to life in the trees themselves (▷ pp. 26–7) and still more that hunt other crabs, lying in wait beneath the canopy, such as the 'forceps' crab. In addition, molluscs such as the small littorian whelks make a slow-motion charge across the mud, once the tide is out, to collect leaf matter and break it down into its useful components. All this must occur whilst the water is absent from the floor of the forest, since with the returning tide comes a new army of swimming predators. ▷▷

1. Mudskippers may afford a glimpse at the influences that once encouraged life to move out of the oceans and on to the land.

2. (opposite) Some clans of vervet monkeys have changed their mainly vegetarian diet to encompass proteins that may be gleaned from the shores.

CLIMBING CRABS OF THE MANGROVES

The productivity of mangroves is such that they have been called the rainforests of the sea. But there is fierce competition on the mud floor as animals wait for the leaves to fall – so much so that hardly any leaf litter accumulates. Colourful crabs shoot out of their burrows to wrestle for the fallen bounty, and whelks congregate by a leaf and devour it piecemeal.

Life is not easy for the leaf eaters, but there is one way to keep competition at bay and have the fresh leaves of the forest to yourself: all it takes is the ability to climb trees and reach the canopy before the leaves fall. The climbing crabs of East Africa do this twice a day, every day.

2

1. Nothing is wasted in the mangroves. Every fallen leaf is consumed by an army of mud-dwellers. Here, *Neosarmatium meinerti* pulls its prize to the safety of a burrow.

2. Every day, twice a day, climbing crabs may reach a height of up to 20 m (65 feet), the equivalent of a man climbing well over 1000 m (3280 feet).

3. A climbing crab in heaven: by rising above its competitors at the top of the canopy, *Sesarma leptosoma* can enjoy an undisturbed meal of fresh leaves.

1

An upwards marathon twice a day!
Every morning at dawn a line of small, dark crabs starts the slow, long climb to the top of the trees, which can be up to 20 m (65 feet) high. One after the other they scale familiar routes, often in huge numbers. Each tree may provide for 300 or 400 crabs, an optimum number, it seems, because this little community will remain remarkably faithful to its host tree. If one is removed by an accident of the tide or an untimely fall it usually finds its way back to its favourite mangrove, even from some distance. Once in the canopy, the crabs graze on the soft undersides of the leaves, but their mealtimes are not long.

The first movement into the canopy takes place in the early morning and is overwith by

3

mid-morning, when they migrate back down the trunk. If the crabs were to stay at height through the heat of the day they would risk the drying effects of sun and wind, and suffocate (these semi-terrestrial crabs need water on their gill chambers to breathe). Then, as the afternoon cools, they make their way back up to the leaves for supper and some may stay there overnight.

Avoid being eaten

Surprisingly perhaps, these crabs do not find sanctuary in the water, but remain in the aerial root system of the mangrove, even when resting. In this way they avoid the predatory attention of the many fish that invade the mangroves at high tide, while keeping cool and damp in the algae-covered roots. Even when the tide is out, this species (*Sesarma leptosoma*) does not venture onto the mud. Thus, it avoids contact with the hustle and bustle of the other crab species that vie for the bounty of fallen leaves, and the attention of the crab plover which, as its name suggests, is a bird that specializes in taking these little crustaceans from the mudflats. Perhaps the greatest threat to these tiny specialists is a close cousin. The predatory *Epixanthus dentatus* (or 'forceps' crab) is not as competent a climber as its potential prey, but it is able, none the less, to make its way up into the root system and lower trunk of the mangrove. Here it waits, claws widespread, for a hapless crab to stumble into its vice-like grip, before eating it alive.

The remarkable synchrony of this vertical mass migration is impressive and unique, as is the crabs' fidelity to their tree, which may have to do with predator pressure. Being amongst a large group, danger is diluted and there are, of course, advantages in knowing your tree inside out in case a rapid escape is needed.

Sesarma leptosoma is the only crab known to have this peculiar habit. Other crab species, in the Caribbean for example, also climb trees but they tend to spend all their adult lives in the canopy, only returning to water level to release their eggs into the sea. Others only climb up a few metres. Our sporty tree-climbing crab lives only on the western edge of the Indian Ocean.

Fish in their thousands invade the tangle of roots, some to hide from other fish, others to seek a meal. Crabs, small whelks and other invertebrates seek shelter until the mud is exposed once again, when, apart from danger from avian predators, they are able to move around in relative safety. The irony is that all depend on the sea to survive on a day-to-day basis. Crabs need to keep their gill chambers moist in order to breathe and are dependent on the sea for releasing their larvae. Yet it is the sea that brings with it the greatest threat to the crabs in a flow of predatory fish.

And it is not only fish that prey on the crabs. In both East Africa and West Africa, vervet monkeys have developed skilful techniques to hunt crabs, carefully avoiding their claws to get at the juicy meat inside the carapace. In Senegal, the Callithrix monkey even varies its diet with mangrove leaves and propagules.

Mudskippers

Just as mangroves originated on land and have adapted to the vagaries of tidal fluctuation, a fish that once lived in the sea has colonized this capricious environment. But in the process of adapting to its new home it has virtually lost its original identity. Although it is still a fish, it is scared of the water. It can be seen easily only at low tide on the mudflats. It is called the mudskipper.

Mudskippers are characteristic inhabitants of mangroves, skipping across the surface of the mud with the help of their tail, and using their pectoral fins as arm-like crutches. In many species, the pelvic fins are fused into a sucker so they can cling on to aerial roots. As the tide rises, many of them escape the dangers of predators lurking underwater by hanging on to trees and roots, slowly edging upwards as the tide rises more. They have become truly amphibious and spend much of their time in the air – which they can breathe.

For a fish to develop thus demands some serious incentives. Mudskippers are, by virtue of their terrestrial abilities, able to capitalize on a food source in the mangrove forests that few other creatures can exploit. They feed on the myriad tiny creatures on the mud floor (which emerge at low tide to feast on the food particles in the mud) as well as on the rich insect life in the forest. Even their bulging eyes are better adapted for land vision and precise hunting action. But, having become specialized out of water, they are no longer competent in it. With the rising tide they seek shelter, unable to out-swim even the most lethargic aquatic hunter. When they have to cross a stretch of water they do so in a rapid skipping action, flitting across the surface tension at high speed, their eyes always at surface level, on the lookout for trouble. But out of the water does not mean out of trouble – which can come in the form of hungry herons!

 PROPAGATING PROPAGULES

Mangroves are flowering trees and, not surprisingly, all disperse their off-spring by water. A unique feature of the majority of mangrove species is that what leaves the tree is not a seed or a fruit that still needs to germinate, as in most flowering plants, but an unusually developed propagating seedling called a propagule. Propagules are in effect already mini-trees that have spent several months growing on the parent tree. Once they part from it, they cannot resist desiccation like seeds of normal trees do, but they are poised for growth whenever the opportunity offers.

The long, pointed propagules of Rhizophora (left) can plummet like darts into the mud below and establish themselves immediately, but more likely they will float in seawater until finally they lose some of their buoyancy and shift to a vertical position. Then, with the ebb and flow of the tides, the tip will drag over the mud surface and, little by little, take hold, leaving the propagule standing when the tide recedes, ready to set root.

This production of a mini-tree is rare among higher plants and is most probably an adaptation to the tropical tidal marine environment.

THE RED SEA

The continental plates that once formed Gondwana continue to move apart today. This means that, in some places, seas are being closed in. By definition, then, somewhere on Earth a new sea must be opening up. The Red Sea is just such a place.

Over the last 70 million years the African and Arabian plateaux have repeatedly shifted in relation to each other, sometimes connecting the Red Sea to the Indian Ocean, sometimes to the Mediterranean Sea. As little as 300,000 years ago, its tenuous link to the Indian Ocean was re-established.

Today, the Red Sea is barely 300 km (186 miles) across, but is still widening at a rate of 2.5 cm (1 inch) a year. In other words, 200 million years from now it could be as wide as the Atlantic is today!

Coral heaven

The Red Sea is surrounded by deserts and high plateaux. Air movements are dominated by the monsoon winds and are generally either northerly or southerly. Average temperatures for the hottest months are 30–35°C (86–95°F) and rainfall is everywhere deficient. With hardly any river input, evaporation is intense – in the region of 2 m (6½ feet) a year – and the salinity very high. ▷▷

1. Black-spotted sweetlips are nocturnal hunters who spend the day resting in large groups in the lee of the current.

⭐ The Red Sea is the warmest and saltiest body of water on Earth with a connection to an open ocean.

1

Previous page: Beneath the tropical ocean's surface lie some of its most colourful natural treasures. Antheas fish occur in many coral seas but in the Red Sea they have thrived and developed into a new endemic species.

1. The tiniest creatures in the ocean support some of the most immense. Whale sharks, the largest fish in the world, feed on the dense soup of zooplankton in Africa's coastal waters.

With such a water deficit the Red Sea relies almost exclusively on the Indian Ocean as a reservoir, which refills this infant sea over the shallow submarine sill at Bab el Mendeb, between Djibouti and Yemen. The strait is only 100 m (330 feet) deep and 30 km (18 miles) wide, so the currents there are furious and constant, feeding the masses of multicoloured soft corals that proliferate around the Seven Brother Islands just outside the inlet. These, in turn, attract hundreds of different fish species, notably schools of attractive sweetlips and bannerfish.

With such a fierce flow of water a

tenacious grip is needed for any creature to get a hold on the seabed, and one might wonder how an animal such as a coral could ever settle long enough to develop. The answer comes in the coral's method of colonization. It starts life when an established community breeds, releasing eggs and sperm into the ocean. These develop into minute larvae, which travel at the whim of the currents and tides. Those lucky enough to brush against a suitable shallow shoreline swim down and develop into the next stage of their lives, a tiny, soft-bodied creature not unlike an anemone, known as a polyp. The majority of coral polyps immediately set about building an anchor and personal protection by secreting a lime-based shroud around their vulnerable bodies. After building its stone-like mantle, each polyp is able to reproduce without the need for contact with any other. In this way, a rich variety of coral structures begin to shroud the rocky seabed.

Ideal waters

Corals thrive in the ideal conditions provided by the Red Sea. The waters are warm and, with no sediments washing off from the land, are very clear, with a relatively well-protected shallow shoreline. And although the volume of animal life is not immense compared to colder waters, in terms of variety it is unsurpassed, owing to the many different types of habitat provided by a coral reef. Fish whose lives revolve around the reef abound in every colour under the sun. And there is an animal to make the most of every feeding opportunity, from those that eat the coral itself, like parrot fish, to the predatory sharks and barracuda.

In the open water, marine giants feed on some of the smallest creatures in the sea. Squadrons of manta rays cruise sedately in formation, each tucked behind and to the side of the one in front, so the waters can be sieved efficiently as they pass through swarms of plankton, in a display of their 'echelon feeding technique'. These gentle giants look like huge bats as they 'fly' through the dense clouds of minute animals suspended in the upper layers of the sea. The volume of plankton is so great at times that it can support the largest of fish. Whale sharks can measure over 20 m (65 feet) from nose to tail, yet they eat nothing but the tiny animals they filter from these rich waters.

2

2. The planktonic life round Africa's coastline is so rich it can support great shoals of the largest rays in the world. Mantas queue up to sieve the fine animal broth off the coast of Sudan.

⭐ Gently moving, warm, clear water and light are essential for coral reefs, hence they are found no deeper than 30 m (100 feet) and between 30°S and 30°N.

AFRICA'S COLD SHORES

Warm tropical seas may conjure up an image of natural bounty, but the truth is that these warm waters, though rich in variety, are relatively poor as far as the quantity of wildlife is concerned. Coral reefs may appear to be a kaleidoscopic wonder, but in reality they are no more than fragile crusts along the tropical coasts.

To find oceanic life in bumper quantities, one has to travel to more temperate waters which, in Africa, are found in two key places. One is at the southern tip of the continent, where the wind-driven upwelling of the Benguela Current brings with it a profusion of life fed from the colder and deeper parts of the ocean. The other is off the coast of northwest Africa, the continent's second area of cold upwelling and of fantastic biological productivity. The coastline of Mauritania, specifically the Banc d'Arguin National Park, is home to a huge number of sea birds, joined in the winter by northern migrants in a gigantic avian ballet.

1

THE SOUTHERN TIP OF AFRICA

In Africa, cold temperate waters are nowhere more abundant than at the continent's southern tip. Here, the Benguela Current sweeps against the rugged coastline of the south and western shores, bringing with it the most astounding volume of living things. The gaudy colours and delicate structures characteristic of warmer waters have given way to vast shoals of fish, crustaceans, molluscs and other invertebrates. In turn, these support some of the most charismatic of all creatures to be found in or around African waters.

Kelp shores

Where the coral reef is now absent, another garden springs up. As much a life support system as the coral and mangroves further north, kelp forests provide for myriad creatures. The kelp's structure enables it to withstand the hostile waters in this part of the world. In fact, without the constant and often dramatic wave action, and effect of the currents along the southwestern shores, the kelp would soon be starved of the nutrients stirred up by the perpetual battering of the shoreline. In turn, the kelp nourishes the sea. Great rafts of algae are washed ashore or carried out to sea on the currents, and give rise to a vast resource.

A true kelp aficionado can be seen at night or in the early morning wherever rafts of algae have been washed onto a sandy shore. Individually no larger than a toenail, beach hoppers swarm in their millions to devour the kelp as soon as it is stranded. In the dark, these tiny beasts can move around in relative safety, and do so in a fairly sedate and controlled fashion. But as the light of day reveals their

1. Table Mountain on the southern Cape. This is the point where the Atlantic meets the Indian Ocean, a wall of change impassable to many of the marine inhabitants in both seas.

★ One family of white pelicans consumes between 450 and 500 kg (1000–1125 lbs) of fish during the breeding season.

hordes, they become vulnerable to attack from any number of hungry birds. This is when they live up to their common name, as, once exposed or disturbed, they leap into the air. So vast are their numbers that the result is a confusing shower of tiny bugs, hastily springing their way to the open sand above the tide mark, where they dig down to spend the day out of sight.

Many millions are consumed by a variety of birds, from egrets, for whom they are a fiddly but welcome change from fish, to sacred ibis, which cheat, and feast on the tiny arthropods by digging them out of their shallow burrows with their long de-curved beaks.

Rocky shores

On rocky shores another tiny beast lies in wait for wrecks of kelp. Sea slaters generally occur in lower concentrations than their leaping

cousins but, from time to time, they mass and congregate to move upshore and avoid being swamped by a particularly high tide. The resulting migrations over the rocks at dawn can give the impression that the whole surface of a rock has come alive and is drifting in the direction of the stranded kelp.

The abundance of life along temperate shores also attracts some unlikely visitors. Baboons are hardly creatures of the sea, but a few troops of chacma baboons have developed specialized skills and an intimate knowledge of their coastal kingdoms. At low tides they move down to the foreshore to feast on the exposed limpets. They have developed a remarkable technique to lever the armoured molluscs from the rocks: after prising them away with their molar teeth they use their incisors and fingers to pluck the protein-filled muscle from the shell. Even more remarkably, a few have

1

2

3

1. Kelp forests typify the temperate waters of the south, and provide some of the richest marine habitats of Africa's shores.

2. Great swarms of tiny beach hoppers depend on wrecks of kelp for a living. They are so numerous they can clear a ton of kelp in just 10 days.

3. The ultimate opportunists, some baboon families have learned that the lowest tides bring the richest pickings. Here a shark egg provides welcome protein for this chacma baboon.

learned to exploit the lowest of the spring tides, when they go in search of a prize that may be won on only a few days each month. As the waters drop to their lowest ebb, the baboons race to the shore and start to comb through the finer seaweed with their fingers. Their reward for braving the splash-zone is shark eggs. It is here that several species of shark come to deposit their leathery purses, each containing one precious egg, tangled amongst the weed. These represent a rare and welcome protein pack for the baboons, who in the dry season find only poor food on land.

Visitors from the cold meet Africa

There is no shortage of protein further out to sea, where enormous shoals of fish draw some surprising visitors to the continent's shores – the African penguin and the Cape fur seal. Both are prepared to suffer the intense heat of the Namibian coastal desert, where they come ashore to breed, so they may exploit the rich waters offshore. Inevitably there are losses to both penguin and seal populations as a result of heat exhaustion, but other, more discriminating threats lie in wait. Although young seal pups are well protected

by their mothers and other adult seals, skilled and opportunistic predators infiltrate these breeding rookeries.

Seals have traditionally given birth to their pups on islands because these have no land predators. However, in colonizing mainland Africa, fur seals have come nose to nose with predators for which evolution has not prepared them. Hunters from the desert have locked onto this predictable yearly bonanza of food. Brown hyenas, arriving from the desert during the pupping season, have no trouble catching the helpless pups. As the hyena approaches the colony, adults, although they would be able to chase and scare the hyena off with their dog-like teeth, instead back off in fright at the sight of this unknown killer. And the hyena walks off unhindered with another pup. This happens on a daily basis on the Namibian coast. Black-backed jackals also come to feed on the afterbirth and attempt to walk away with pups nearly the same size as themselves! It is another example of strangers on the shores making the most of what this coastline has to offer.

Shark attack

Out at sea the seals may be secure from such depredations and have some respite from the heat, but even here they are not safe. It is here that one of the planet's most successful and efficient hunters patrols the shores. Colonies of seals around the southern tip of Africa are shadowed by the formidable great white shark. These primeval killers have developed hunting techniques that utilize the water conditions to the full. A few hundred metres offshore from the seal colonies, sharks cruise the waters at depth, their enormous frames shrouded by the murky waters. When they sense a seal passing overhead they launch a vertical attack, reaching speeds so great that when they hit their target they clear the water's surface – more than one tonne (2200 lbs) of them!

Whales and dolphins

Even the true goliaths of the ocean are catered for here. Many species of whale feed around these southern seas; some, including the southern right whale, find sufficient food to spend at least half the year cruising the coastal waters in sheltered bays, to the delight of the human spectators. They calve here during October/November on a three-year cycle and mother and calf can sometimes be seen relaxing in shallow water, right next to the shore, their dorsal fins surfacing as a mesemerizing beacon. Even their diminutive cousins, the dolphins, proliferate. And quite apart from satisfied appetites, their sense of fun and curiosity is provided for by the ocean. Strong currents are often met by fierce surface winds, giving rise to some of the best breakers in the world. These great waves batter the shoreline in violent explosions of foam, but for all their

1

fury, are treated as a playground by schools of bottlenose dolphins, which surf repeatedly towards shore before leaping out of the back of the wave in tumbling, aerial acrobatics.

Fishing birds: Cape Gannet

If one creature clearly illustrates the ocean riches in southern Africa, it is the gannet. No bird is better adapted to a life exploiting offshore fish shoals. Unlike the albatross and petrels of the south, gannets cannot make vast pilgrimages in search of fish to support their chicks and so can only flourish where the nearby waters are sufficiently rich.

Colonies of tens of thousands of pairs cram into tiny offshore islands to prepare their single chicks for a life at sea. And, in their turn, the chicks provide an unusual resource. As the chicks make their maiden flights they almost invariably flop exhausted onto the ocean's surface. And lurking beneath the surface are fur seals. Though predominantly fish and squid feeders, a handful of seals have discovered this brief window of opportunity and specialize in snatching the young gannets from the surface to augment their fish diet. It is a surprising and grizzly adaptation, but further illustration of the wealth of wild dramas played out daily in these temperate waters.

1. Black-backed jackals squabble over a dead fur seal pup. The coastlines of Africa can offer fine rewards for those adaptable enough to utilize them, predators and scavengers alike.

2. The numbers of Cape Gannets depend on the ready availability of fish, especially during the nesting season when adults are tied to the vicinity of the breeding islands to raise their single chick. **2**

1

NORTHWEST AFRICA (MAURITANIA, BANC D'ARGUIN)

On the shoreline of northern Mauritania, the contrast with the interior is overwhelming. Millions of birds, like shimmering clouds, follow the rhythm of the tide, and spread over green-coloured mudflats as far as the eye can see. This is the land of never-ending shallow waters teeming with life, against the backdrop of the immense Sahara Desert. It looks as if a painter's palette of natural colour has been cast over the landscape – yellow, blue-green, and a dash of pink flamingos. This is the Banc d'Arguin National Park in northern Mauritania.

Africa's other Atlantic desert shore

The Banc d'Arguin is a mirror image of the shores of Namibia, exactly the same distance from the Equator, but on its northern side. Like the Namibian coast it is influenced by a cold upwelling, promoted in this case by the Northern Canaries Current, which brings scarcely any rain (▷ p. 13). The result is an arid coast with vast fields of sand dunes, deposited by winds blowing from the Sahara. Though it is bordered by desert, the marine productivity of this shoreline attracts millions of animals, from the sea and the land.

    The most visible expression of this fantastic biodiversity is birds, and for them it is an ideal environment. A large offshore sandbank (from which the Park gets its name) protects the inner shore from the strong Atlantic waves and provides thousands of acres of shallow feeding grounds. Sea birds, cormorants, white pelicans, spoonbills and grey herons, as well as six species of tern, come to breed in their thousands on the many sandbanks, where there are few land predators, allowing them to raise their chicks

close to the bountiful seas. Mauritania is also on one of the major migration routes of wading birds, which arrive from as far away as Siberia just at the time of year when the upwelling is firmly established. Every year, about 2 million birds fly in to this coast to feed and to spend the winter in its warm climate. In spring they return home to breed. Their numbers make this the most important wintering location for waders in Africa.

The local fish-eating birds do not suffer from this invasion because few of the migrants eat fish and they do not breed here. What attracts the waders are the vast expanses of mudflats and sea grass that become exposed at low tide. There, a cornucopia of invertebrates (little worms, crustaceans and molluscs) are made available to the birds' prying beaks twice a day. This is the time when the water turns green with eel grass against a stunning sand dune backdrop.

When it flows back in and covers the sea grass beds with blue, the birds concentrate in enormous cloud-like flocks to roost until the next opportunity to feed at low tide.

Fishy waters

The fish live by the opposite timetable, spreading wide over the sea grass to feed at high tide, then concentrating in channels between the mudflats at low tide. For the fish hunters, the time of the mullet migration is a bonanza. Mullets are sea grass eaters and spend their time feeding until the females are ready to lay their eggs and migrate south. This is a time of plenty for bottlenosed dolphins and fishermen alike, and the presence of the Imraguen fishing community is believed to be largely due to these fish, which live in shoals of thousands.

Green turtles also come to feed on the eel grass, grazing at high tide in the shallows and

swimming offshore as the water retreats. From time to time, the local population is augmented by turtles which may have come from as far away as Florida on the other side of the Atlantic, but most of them nest further south on the many island beaches of Guinea Bissau.

Here in Mauritania, where the land meets the sea there are few mammals to take advantage of the rich pickings to be had, many species having been exterminated over the years by over-hunting. One exception is the golden jackal, ubiquitous across the plains and lowlands of Africa, which scavenges and hunts along the beaches. Dead fish, crabs and other marine creatures provide it with a good source of protein. In addition, the jackals hunt birds, usually those that are exhausted or unwary after a long migration. Sometimes, for an easy meal, a few jackals brave a shallow swim to reach islands where terns and other birds are raising their chicks.

CAPE FUR SEALS – ANIMALS OUT OF PLACE?

At first it is the smell that hits you, then the noise. What lies ahead of you is one of the most striking natural scenes on the African coast. There can be few phenomena of greater paradox than thousands of seals, a fish-eating mammal wrapped in blubber to survive cold polar seas, at the edge of the oldest and most arid landscape in Africa – the Namib Desert. The two images simply do not match. And yet, this is where the greatest population of African fur seals now survives. Having battled through the ages against the depredations of humans, they now battle against a new foe – the sun.

2

1. When conditions become too hot, the most experienced mothers move their young from the top of the hill to the cooling sea spray by the shore.

2 The bond between mother and pup is established in the first few hours after birth. It is essential if they are to retain contact in the heaving colony.

3. Nearly two million fur seals live around the coasts, a measure of the fish stocks that persist despite over-fishing and local culling campaigns on the seals.

Killer sun

Cape fur seals are carnivores whose diet is made up predominantly of fish and squid. They can dive up to 200 m (650 feet) but mostly hunt at about 50 m (165 feet) both during the day and night. It is because the Benguela

1

Current is cold and sustains vast shoals of fish, that fur seals have been able to flourish as far north as Namibia. Originally they were sub-Antarctic animals, their pups born with black fur, allowing them to hide amongst the black volcanic rocks of the southern islands and absorb what little heat is provided by the weak Antarctic sun. Another polar relic is that they are all born around the summer solstice, which in the southern hemisphere is 22 December.

But for the massive colonies now established on the African mainland, the black fur of newborn pups can be a killer. In the first few weeks of life, many die of overheating if the cool, strong southerly winds slow down. For adults the sun is not such a problem as they can swim in the cold sea. They can also thermo-regulate with their fins, which are full of blood vessels like an elephant's ears. All

they need to do is hold their wet fins above the water in the strong wind.

Before the arrival of humans, Cape fur seals were limited to offshore islands, where the air is generally cooled by the influence of the surrounding sea. The lions and hyenas patrolling the mainland had prevented colonization by the seals. When European ships first sailed past the tip of Africa, the fur seals were hunted to the brink of extinction for their fur and oil from their fat reserves. As their numbers recovered, the fur seals had nowhere else to go but the mainland, where by then humans had drastically reduced the number of land predators (the islands were claimed largely for sea birds and their lucrative guano production). Seals moved in en masse and there were enough pups born to sustain the reduced predation pressure.

3

A one-week affair

Seals must come ashore to breed, both to mate and give birth. In the breeding season, males and females return to traditional beaches and form vast colonies, during which time very few get the chance to feed. To avoid starvation the whole process of birth and conception is conducted in a matter of weeks, a strategy that is made possible by delayed implantation, the process by which the fertilized egg is put 'on ice' for several months, before development of the embryo begins.

This frees adult seals to feed out at sea for the rest of the year. Both males and females need this. Males lose a lot of weight during breeding because they do not feed at all while guarding a territory, and females can go for only short feeding trips until the pups learn to swim at six weeks.

Seal mothers are fiercely protective of their young. Mother and young recognize each other by scent and call, which helps them to be reunited in the densely packed breeding colonies. These become a seething mass of bodies in a never-ending cacophony of calls. Cows leave their pups between suckling. It is when mothers are not experienced and fail to leave their pup within reach of the sea's cooling spray or available shade that there are many losses to heat exhaustion in the first two weeks of life.

A really endearing sight at breeding colonies is to see the previous year's pup refusing to leave its mother even though her next pup is already born – she suckles it while trying to chase away her yearling.

Another major step for a young seal is the realization of underwater vision. A pup will watch others and tentatively dip its head into a rock pool, taking it out almost immediately, until it discovers that it can actually see much better underwater – an essential skill for its life as a hunter of fish and squid!

◆ TOPIC LINKS

1.1 Island Africa
p.15 Africa's own currents
p.17 Atlantic shores

1.3 Africa's cold shores
p.37 Visitors from the cold meet Africa

MOUNTAINS

THE HIGH LIFE

Africa's mountains present tough physical challenges to wildlife. At altitude the air is starved of oxygen and moisture, solar radiation is intense, and nightly temperatures can plunge well below freezing. Even on the Equator snow sometimes falls. Yet, high on Africa's lofty peaks, animals and plants have found bizarre and intriguing ways to survive. Like castaways stranded on oceanic islands, many of these wildlife pioneers have found themselves marooned in an alien world washed by clouds – their lives governed by climate. Travelling down Africa's tallest mountains is like going from the Arctic to the Equator. One passes from snow-capped peaks to alpine desert and moorland, through heathland and cloud forest before reaching the grasslands below. The scale and nature of these zones depend on the mountain's size, age, height and position on the continent, but each presents wildlife with very different opportunities and obstacles.

Previous page: Kilimanjaro's northern glaciers form a majestic backdrop to Kenya's Amboseli National Park.

COPING WITH EXTREMES

Towering a massive 5896 m (19,344 feet) into the sky, Kilimanjaro is the tallest mountain in Africa. Magnificent glaciers – relics of the last ice age – majestically crown its smouldering summit and dry, cloudless winds whip the peaks, drawing all moisture from the land and shedding it as snow. Kilimanjaro's summit is one of the most hostile places in Africa, and nothing can live here permanently.

At less than a million years old, Kilimanjaro is younger even than humankind – but already wildlife has managed to get to grips with its lower, more forgiving, slopes. Between 3700 and 4500 m (12,100–14,700 feet) a belt of unusual moorland exists, home to a fascinating community of sub-alpine plants.

The giant senecio, which stands up to 10 m (33 feet) tall but grows little more than 2 cm (less than 1 inch) per year and flowers every 10–20 years, probably evolved from smaller senecios living at lower altitudes. Like the feathers of a bird, the leaves are layered in rosettes, which helps to insulate them from frost, and each is covered with a layer of fine hairs to deflect solar radiation. When these leaves die they remain on the plant, lagging the stem. The buds also produce a thick slime that acts as an antifreeze.

A similarly extraordinary plant on Kilimanjaro's alpine moorland is the cabbage

1. A carpet of cabbage groundsels unfurl with the morning sun at the head of Mount Kenya's Telekeii Valley. The silvery hairs on the undersides of the leaves also help to deflect solar radiation.

⭐ The fossil record shows that six species of gelada became extinct in the last 3 million years. One of these was thought to be larger than a gorilla.

groundsel, whose leaves fold into a tight fist every night for insulation and unfurl each morning to greet the sun. After a number of years, the plant throws up a tall flower spike, which attracts scarlet-tufted malachite sunbirds for pollination.

One of the greatest hazards for plants in the alpine zone is the nightly churning of the soil by needles of ice, a process known as solifluction. This makes it very hard for seeds to germinate, but grasses manage to obtain a foothold next to stable rocks and boulders. These grasses form a thick mat of dead and decaying leaves around their base, which helps to insulate the roots and prevent frost heaving in the near vicinity of the tussock. Some mosses have done away with roots altogether. Rolling on top of the churning soil, they are moulded into small, green balls.

Keeping warm

Just as plants have evolved ingenious ways of keeping warm, the animals that inhabit the alpine moorlands of Africa's tallest mountains are equally well protected. On Mount Kenya, highland rock hyraxes are much hairier than their close relatives on the plains below. In the chill of the early morning they often huddle together, sunbathing on exposed rocks to warm up before feeding. Keeping warm and conserving energy at these altitudes is critical.

Gelada baboons, which survive on the highest ground in Ethiopia's Simien Mountains, are coated with thick manes of fur and have evolved an extraordinary lifestyle that minimizes wastage of energy. Geladas travel a long way each day to get the calories they need from grass and to save ▷▷

1. Weighing in at 200 kg (440 lbs) or more, male mountain gorillas are the largest living primates in the world. Their thick, black fur helps them cope with the cold at altitudes of up to 4100 m (13,450 feet).

2. (opposite) Like female gelada baboons, males display a small patch of bare skin on their chests, used for sexual and social communication. It has earned them the name 'bleeding heart monkeys'.

THE ORIGINS OF AFRICA'S MOUNTAINS

Africa does not have mountain ranges comparable with the Himalayas in Asia or the Andes in South America, but the mountains and high plateaus of the continent are no less fascinating and all have very different origins. The tallest are young and volcanic, but the more ancient weathered peaks were formed by the buckling and cracking of the Earth's crust over considerable periods of time.

Birth of a continent

More than 200 million years ago, long before the break-up of Gondwana, folding occurred in the southwest corner of what was to become Africa, creating the Cape Folded mountains and the Drakensbergs. Much later, beginning some 65 million years ago, in the same event that formed the Alps, basement rock also became folded in the extreme northwest, resulting in the Atlas Mountains of Morocco and Algeria. This compression caused extensive faulting in the Sahara, where lava escaped to create three further mountain ranges – the Hoggar, Tibesti and Aïr.

When South America pulled away from Africa about 150 million years ago, the rifting caused volcanic activity in West Africa, building the Cameroon Highlands, which today include Mounts Cameroon, Malabo (on the island of Bioko), Kupe and Manenguba. There is also a smaller area of volcanic highlands in the west of the Guinea forest block spanning Guinea, Liberia and Côte d'Ivoire. The West African rift has been active for tens of millions of years, and is still very much alive. As recently as 2000, Mount Cameroon erupted.

Roof of Africa

The largest area of mountainous land in Africa lies on the east of the continent. The Ethiopian Highlands are the most extensive and are appropriately known as the 'roof of Africa'. These highlands consist of a vast basaltic dome, over 2000 m (6500 feet) high and 1000 km (620 miles) across, made up of different layers of lava that have seeped out over 70 million years. Volcanic activity ceased some 4–5 million years ago when glaciers dominated the high ground. Eventually, the dome was split by the formation of the Eastern or Great Rift Valley.

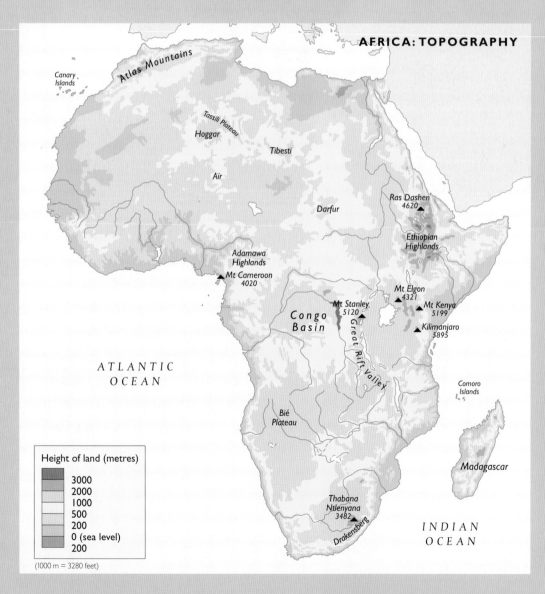

AFRICA: TOPOGRAPHY

Canary Islands
Atlas Mountains
Tassili Plateau
Hoggar
Tibesti
Aïr
Darfur
Ras Dashen 4620
Ethiopian Highlands
Adamawa Highlands
Mt Cameroon 4020
Mt Elgon 4321
Mt Stanley 5120
Congo Basin
Great Rift Valley
Mt Kenya 5199
Kilimanjaro 5895
Comoro Islands
ATLANTIC OCEAN
Bié Plateau
Madagascar
Thabana Ntlenyana 3482
Drakensberg
INDIAN OCEAN

Height of land (metres)
3000
2000
1000
500
200
0 (sea level)
200

(1000 m = 3280 feet)

1

The Great Rift Valley

This vast scar, running for over 6000 km (3700 miles) from the Lebanon to Mozambique, was formed by uplift and splitting of the brittle crust. Along its margins lava has spewed out, creating Africa's tallest and most romantic peaks. The most recent upheavals occurred 22, 6 and 2.5 million years ago, forming Kilimanjaro, Mounts Kenya, Meru and Elgon and the Aberdares. At 5896 m (19,300 feet), Kilimanjaro is the highest mountain in Africa and is actually a cluster of three peaks. Kibo is the tallest and is flanked on the west by Shira (3962 m/13,000 feet) and on the east by Mawenzi (5149 m/16,900 feet). Kibo's most extensive eruption may have occurred as little as 36,000 years ago, and its crater still smoulders.

A western arm of the Great Rift system extends from Malawi to the northeast of the Democratic Republic of Congo, and includes the spectacular Virunga volcanoes. Two of the peaks, Nyamlagira and Nyiragongo, have been active during the last two decades. In contrast, the nearby Ruwenzoris or 'Mountains of the Moon' are not volcanic but formed from a block of ancient crystalline rock that has recently been pushed up between the two branches of the rift. Other non-volcanic mountains also occur to the east of the Western Rift in the form of the Eastern Arc Mountains, which are believed to have originated 100 million years ago. Although none of these mountain blocks are large, many are home to a unique collection of animals and plants.

1. The impressive eastern wall of the Great Rift Valley at Maralal in northern Kenya. This vast scar, visible from space, is one of a number of giant, jagged trenches averaging 40 km (25 miles) in length.

⬦ TOPIC LINKS

2.2 Ancient Peaks
p.59 Crumpled giants
p.62 Thrust skywards
p.63 Ancient volcanoes

2.3 Great Rift Giants
p.69 The fires within

3.1 Africa's Fresh Water
p.83 The water

6.3 Serengeti Grasslands
p.219 The raw materials

energy they often feed sitting down, shuffling along from patch to patch on their bottoms. Genitals are usually used by primates as sexual indicators, but because they spend so long sitting down, female geladas have developed a patch of bare skin on their chests which swells and turns pink when they are sexually receptive. Because of the cold and their poor diet, geladas walk a fine energy tightrope and their lives demand an orderly society. Fights cost a lot of energy, so most squabbles are resolved by other means, such as fluffing their massive manes and lip-flipping.

Because of their isolation from other environments, mountains are places where evolution often springs surprises. In the Ethiopian Highlands, Kilimanjaro, Mount Kenya and the nearby Aberdares range, servals and leopards occur in two colour patterns – spotted and black. The rare black coat pattern, known as melanism, is caused by a recessive gene which – on cold mountains – presumably gives these creatures a thermal advantage as it absorbs heat more readily. Given the absence of large predators on mountains, there is also less need to be camouflaged with spots. Melanism is also found in other upland creatures. Bushbuck, which occur in a wide variety of colours, tend to be darker on tall mountains, and augur buzzards – normally black and white – are sometimes predominantly black. In the Harenna forest of Bale, Ethiopia, a very dark subspecies of bushbuck can be found, known as Menelik's bushbuck. Reports of other melanistic mountain animals include bushbabies, genets and mongooses.

1. The spectacular peaks of Ethiopia's Simien mountains, home to gelada baboons, walia ibex, lammergeyers and a small number of Ethiopian wolves.

2. The endangered bongo antelope.

ISLAND CASTAWAYS

During the last 15 million years – but particularly the last million – the climate of Africa has repeatedly swung between wet and dry, and warm and cool. During colder times vast glaciers once capped the Ethiopian Highlands, and at other times rainforest stretched right across equatorial Africa from Guinea to Mount Kenya. In the course of all this climatic change, animals and plants have become left behind on mountains from surrounding environments, only to find themselves trapped as the climate changed once again. In this sense they are like island castaways, marooned in a sea of cloud.

Among the cool montane forests of Mount Kenya and the Aberdares, giant forest hogs, bongo antelope, Hartlaub's turacos, blue monkeys and pied colobus inhabit a world

2

 GOOD FRIENDS

Scarlet-tufted malachite sunbirds (left) live at greater altitude than any other sunbird in Africa, only inhabiting the alpine zones of East African mountains above 3000 m (9800 feet). On Mount Kenya they rely almost exclusively on the energy-rich nectar from the flowers of the giant lobelia, and in turn the plant depends on them for pollination. Males vigorously defend territories containing stands of lobelias from rivals, and males with the biggest and brightest red chest patches and the longest tails usually dominate the best sites. Presumably these are symbols of the males' fitness, for they serve no obvious practical function.

The flowering spikes of each lobelia contain up to 2000 flowers buried within the leaf bracts. The larger male flowers are situated nearer the top of the plant and contain twice as much sugar as the older female flowers lower down. The male flowers are most frequently visited by sunbirds and benefit greatly from this export of pollen, but female flowers probably only need to be visited occasionally for fertilization to take place. This tightly evolved relationship between bird and plant is undoubtedly the only reason both species have been able to conquer such high altitudes.

1. With its enormous 3-m (10-feet) wingspan and characteristic diamond-shaped tail, the lammergeyer, or bearded vulture, uses updrafts to soar over Africa's peaks in search of bones from animal carcasses.

2. A family of elephants travel among lobelias in the montane forest of the Virunga volcanoes, Rwanda. They are among the most resourceful and wide-ranging of all African mammals, occurring in desert margins, wetlands and savannahs.

far removed from their origins in the warm lowland rainforests hundreds of kilometres to the west. An extreme example of an animal in isolation is the Ethiopian wolf, which lives on the bleak moorlands of the Simien and Bale Mountains National Parks in Ethiopia. Directly descended from the European wolf, Ethiopian wolves probably occupied parts of Africa during recent ice ages, when tundra and glaciers linked Eurasia with north Africa. When the climate warmed they were stranded, unable to penetrate further south into Africa owing to the unsuitable habitat and competition from wild dogs, hyenas and lions.

Today, it is not just climate change that prevents the migration of mountain species to new habitats. With their rich soils and consistent rainfall, the lower slopes of mountains are excellent for agriculture and, throughout Africa, mountain wildlife faces this new human barrier. Perhaps the most graphic example of this is the mountain gorilla, which inhabits the upland forests and moorlands in the Virunga region of Rwanda and the Democratic Republic of Congo, and the Bwindo forest in Uganda. Less than 500 individuals remain in just a few hundred square kilometres, surrounded by land that contains over 300 people per square km (770 per sq mile) – the most densely populated area in sub-Saharan Africa.

▷ MOUNTAIN GORILLAS

Gorillas are our closest living relatives, and today they occur in two very isolated regions – lowland gorillas in Cameroon and Gabon with a scattering in the Lake Kivu region, and mountain gorillas on the volcanic slopes of the Virungas. It is not yet known when the divergence of these subspecies occurred, but the larger and hairier mountain gorillas are the only human-like primates which have so far managed to take advantage of opportunities at altitude in Africa.

Mountain gorillas thrive on unstable conditions – landslides, volcanic disturbance, the bulldozing of trees by elephants, fires and tree-felling are all important in helping to generate the vast quantities of low-level herbs that they require. Galium vines, bamboo and wild celery form the bulk of their diet, though mountain gorillas will sometimes stray high into the moorland to feed on giant lobelias.

Air travel

Reaching new mountains presents great obstacles for those travelling on foot, but birds can make the break with ease. An accidental landfall from much further afield is the only explanation for the existence of the blue-winged sheldgoose in Ethiopia. Sheldgeese evolved in the alpine and temperate grasslands of South America, where they still occur today. During the ice ages they

Wear and tear

Because Africa's tallest mountains are volcanic in origin, they are inherently unstable entities. Their soft pumice ash and brittle lava are rapidly eroded by wind, ice, rain and solar blasting. Kilimanjaro is less than a million years old, but is already on the way down. Mount Kenya, at 3 million years old, was once much taller than Kilimanjaro, but is now 700 m (2300 feet) lower. The nearby Aberdares range is even older, and all that remains of its once-lofty peaks are a few weathered lava stumps, known as 'The Dragon's Teeth', poking out of a windswept moorland. All these mountains will eventually die, their ashes cast across the hot African plains. But this steady wearing down of mountains is both organic and inorganic. Animals play their part too.

Volcanic mountains are generally mineral-rich, but in some locations, due to leaching by rainfall, the vegetation lacks minerals essential for browsers, such as calcium and potassium, so some animals have to supplement their diet by mining. At exposed rock faces and salt licks on the slopes of Mount Kenya and the Aberdares, elephants consume clods of earth that they excavate with their tusks. Once opened up by elephants, other animals such as buffalo, giant forest hogs and bushbuck visit the sites too in order to lick the exposed soil. In the Virungas, mountain gorillas are also known to scrape at rock with their fingers. Perhaps the most fascinating example comes from Mount Elgon, where there is a series of old lava tunnels and caves that are visited at night by elephants and other browsers quarrying for minerals. These caverns, which have been further opened up by the excavations of countless generations of animals, are scoured with a myriad of tooth and tusk marks.

2

2.2 ANCIENT PEAKS

The most awe-inspiring mountains in Africa are the young, majestic volcanoes of the Great Rift Valley, but the continent also hosts other, more ancient highlands that are no less fascinating. Formed by the buckling and upthrusting of the Earth's crust, or the gentle outpouring of lava over millions of years, these mountains are often built on very solid foundations, which means they are less prone to rapid erosion. Their great age gives animals and plants plenty of time to adapt to them, and it is no coincidence that Africa's oldest peaks are often home to a bewildering variety of unique species.

Ancient mountains are found in every corner of Africa. The Atlas Mountains and Ethiopian Highlands crown the north, the Cape Folded Belt and Drakensbergs the south. In the west are the highlands of Cameroon and Guinea, and further east, the Eastern Arc. All of these peaks are very different in character, origin and climate.

1. The majestic Drakensberg mountains of South Africa and Lesotho are among the oldest mountains in Africa, formed soon after Africa emerged from the supercontinent Gondwana.

CRUMPLED GIANTS

Some of the oldest mountain ranges in Africa are found at the tip and the tail of the continent – the Atlas in the north and the Cape Folded Belt in the south. Both arose when the Earth's crust became crushed and folded by massive subterranean forces.

The tallest of these ranges, reaching 4165 m (13,665 feet) high, are the snow-capped Atlas Mountains in Morocco, Algeria and Tunisia which were raised during the same process that created the European Alps. Lions, red deer and Barbary sheep were once widespread in these north African highlands, but increasing human pressure for hunting and the grazing of livestock has strongly altered the wildlife of the Atlas. Despite this, the magnificent cedar, holm oak and aleppo pine forests that cloak the slopes of the Atlas are still home to creatures like red foxes, jackals, wild boar, golden eagles and the rare Cuvier's gazelle, the only true mountain-dwelling antelope in Africa. They are also the last natural outpost for the Barbary macaque, the only African primate living north of the Sahara and a long-term inhabitant of the area, whose fossilized remains, up to 4 million years old, appear in Algeria.

Far more ancient than the Atlas Mountains, the Cape Folded Belt in South Africa was formed by the folding and faulting of rocks about 250 million years ago, soon after the ancient supercontinent, Gondwana, began to break up. These modest peaks, which reach no higher than 2325 m (7600 feet), are the oldest in Africa and run to the north and east of Cape Town. They include the famous flat-topped Table Mountain, which looms impressively over the city.

For much of its history, the Cape Folded Belt has been nurtured by a relatively stable climate of hot, dry summers and cool, wet winters and this has resulted in the evolution of many unique animals and plants in the region, especially heathland or 'fynbos' plants such as species of Erica (heathers), Restio and Protea, which thrive on the region's acidic soils. Close relatives of these flowering plants – and other fynbos species – are found as far afield as Australia and South America, reflecting their common origins in this region of Gondwana before the southern continents pulled away.

Mountain fynbos

The world's vegetation can be divided into six major groups, known as plant kingdoms. The Cape Floral Kingdom (or Cape fynbos) is the smallest of these, covering only 0.04 per cent of the world's land surface, but has 8580 species of flowering plants, most of which are found nowhere else – probably the richest known flora in the world. Although fynbos occurs among the lowlands and coastal areas of south-western Africa, it is most spectacular in the Cape Mountains.

The most showy and varied of all fynbos plants are the proteas. Their stunning blooms, rich in nectar, are particularly attractive to Cape sugarbirds, which may visit 300 flower heads a day. Their long, curved bills collect pollen as they feed, and their sharp claws allow them to grip branches and flower-heads even in strong winds. Proteas are also visited by sunbirds, but their shorter bills mean they have to probe the sides of flowers to gather nectar. In this way they steal nectar without providing the valuable service of pollination.

Protea flower-heads harbour fascinating communities of insects. Cape scarab beetles feed on the flowers and pollinate the plants. The beetles often carry large numbers of hitch-hiking mites, which themselves transport pollen to new plants. Some proteas have evolved radical tactics to attract pollinators. *Protea acaulos* has dull blooms that smell of yeast and lie close to the ground. Although unattractive to birds, rodents such as striped mice and Namaqua rock mice find proteas irresistible. The flowers provide nectar at times of year when other foods that the mice eat are scarce.

1. Cape sugarbirds are important pollinators for many kinds of Protea flowers, named after the sea god Proteus, who could assume many different forms.

Mountain fynbos is rich in flowering plants and their pollinators, but few browsing mammals occur here as most vegetation is leathery and low in calories. However, a few specialist feeders like the grysbok and klipspringer manage to get by on post-fire flushes of sprouting grasses and other palatable herbs. The chacma baboons of the Cape Mountains – the southernmost primates in the world – spend considerably more time foraging than their relatives in the savannahs, but they are skilled botanists, capable of distinguishing the poisonous from the delectable from among thousands of plant species.

The Dragon Mountains

At about the same time that the Cape Folded Belt emerged, so too did a chain of even taller folded mountains spanning Lesotho and South Africa, known as the Drakensbergs, or 'Dragon Mountains' to the Afrikaans. The Zulus called them 'uKhalamba' – 'the barrier of upright spears'. Towering up to 3482 m (11,420 feet), they are the tallest mountains in Southern Africa – spectacular, soaring pinnacles of sedimentary and volcanic rock, cut by deep gorges and pitted with numerous caves.

Although the Drakensbergs lack the huge diversity of the plants of the Cape Folded Belt, some 1800 different species occur here, with 300 being endemic to the region. Grassland dominates the peaks, but heathland and pockets of forest also occur here. Nomadic browsers like eland – once the favoured food of San bushmen (▷ p. 142), a race who finally abandoned the region about 100 years ago – wander these highlands.

The Drakensbergs mark the southernmost limits of the range of the lammergeyer or bearded vulture (▷ p. 54). About 120 pairs soar the updrafts, looking for the carcasses of eland, mountain reedbuck, black wildebeest, klipspringer, blesbok and anything else they can find. Serval and caracal cats are also common in the upland grasslands, where they hunt for small birds and rodents. Perhaps the most fascinating of these smaller creatures is the ice rat, which copes with the cold by huddling in family groups in complex underground tunnels and sunbathing on exposed rocks. The rats also have relatively short tails, which may have evolved as a means of avoiding heat loss.

 THE POWER OF FIRE

Regular summer fires are an important part of mountain fynbos ecology. Sparked by rockfalls, lightning and controlled human burning, fires help to maintain a healthy diversity of plants, many of which have developed strategies to thrive after intense burning. Their underground storage organs – bulbs and corms – often lie unharmed in the soil as the fire sweeps the surface, and many bulbous plants actually require fire to initiate flowering and sprouting. Some plants, including more than 100 species of Protea, produce seeds in thick, fireproof capsules. Though the parent plants die, the capsules split to release vast quantities of tufted seeds to the wind. The burned landscape offers them rich nutrients, fewer rodent predators and less competition from adult plants for space to germinate.

Another strategy used by about 1200 fynbos plant species is seed dispersal by ants. These plants produce seeds with oily, fleshy coatings which release chemicals that attract ants. The ants carry them into their underground nests, where they eat the coatings but set aside the seeds. Below the soil surface the seeds are safe from hungry birds and rodents, and protected from fire. Some insects' eggs, such as stick insects', mimic the appearance of seeds, and they too are taken underground by ants.

THRUST SKYWARDS

Some of Africa's oldest mountains were formed by the breaking and upthrusting of the Earth's crust, often between great rifts or 'faults'. The most intriguing of these are the Eastern Arc Mountains of southern Kenya and Tanzania.

The Eastern Arc is a chain of small forested mountains composed of ancient crystalline rock, which arose around 100 million years ago – about the time that Madagascar split from the African continent. Rising gently from the East African plains to heights of about 2000 m (6500 feet), they are the first high ground encountered by moisture-bearing winds from the Indian Ocean, and receive annual rainfall as high as 3000 mm (118 inches). During warmer, wetter periods in their history, these forest 'islands' were undoubtedly linked to the West African forest block but, after millions of years of isolation, many unique animals and plants have evolved. In fact, the wildlife of the many Eastern Arc Mountains is so diverse and intriguing that they are sometimes referred to as 'Africa's Galápagos'.

About 25 per cent of the 2000 plant species that grow in the Eastern Arc forests are found nowhere else in Africa. The most famous of these is the African violet, prized by gardeners all over the world. Although there are now about 40,000 cultivated varieties, most derive from just two wild species, many of which are found on just a single mountain peak in the Eastern Arc. A quarter of the world's wild coffee species also occur only in these mountain forests.

As well as plants, the Eastern Arc forests are filled with many unique animals. Six species of chameleon occur here, some resembling brown leaves, some lichens and others miniature rhinoceros. On the forest floor the elusive Abbot's duiker feeds on fallen fruits, and in forest streams Sanje mangabeys hunt for crabs. Even the precipitous rock-faces of waterfalls are inhabited by the rare Usambara torrent frog.

 AFRICA'S SNOW MONKEYS

Like Ethiopia's gelada baboons, the Barbary macaques (left) of the Atlas mountains are well adapted to cope with the bitter weather on mountains. They too have thick coats and no tails. This helps to prevent frostbite and reduce heat loss, but they also have a broad diet which helps them cope with the different food available at different times of year. In winter, snowfalls up to 3 m (10 feet) deep sometimes prevent Barbary macaques feeding on the ground, so at this time of year they seek out cedar leaves which are rich in sugary antifreeze, as well as feeding on bark and lichen. When spring comes, the cedar trees pump unpalatable turpentines into their leaves for protection, and so the macaques switch their attention to deciduous leaves and the daffodils and new herbs that carpet the forest floor.

Barbary macaques, like geladas, have a relatively poor diet and live on a tight energy budget, so disputes are avoided by complex social interactions. Females mate with most adult males and because any male may be a father they all take care of infants as if they were their own. Infants are also used to help dispel tensions in the troop. A male will take an infant and approach another male; both then touch and chatter their teeth submissively whilst both holding the infant, or passing it between them.

1

ANCIENT VOLCANOES

Most of Africa's volcanic mountains exploded into existence very recently, but across Africa there are places where gentle and continuous outpourings of lava have built great monuments of rock. The most extensive ancient volcanic mountains are the Ethiopian Highlands, encompassing half of all Africa's land over 2000 m (6500 feet) high, which are aptly known as the 'roof of Africa'. These peaks have been steadily raised over 75 million years until volcanic activity stopped about 4 million years ago.

The Ethiopian Highlands consist of a vast uplifted dome, 400 km (250 miles) wide, which was recently fractured during the formation of the Great Rift Valley. The northern section of the range encompasses the stunning Simien Mountains – a string of jagged, weathered pinnacles and deep valleys – which reach an altitude of 4620 m (15,158 feet) at Ras Dejen. To the south are the Bale Highlands, a windswept moorland plateau, where lava once escaped through many fissures spread over a wide area. Both of these regions are home to fascinating collections of mountain wildlife.

With their sheer slopes and deep valleys, the Simien pinnacles are a precarious place ▷▷

1. A gelada baboon troop, grazing in the Simien mountains. Troops can sometimes number more than 200 individuals.

THE ETHIOPIAN WOLF

Less than a million years ago, when sea levels were lower and Africa and the Middle East were connected, ancestors of the world's rarest and most endangered member of the dog family made their way from Asia to Africa – Ethiopian wolves. Today, only about 400 individuals remain in the harsh high-altitude moorlands of Ethiopia, between 3000 and 3700 metres (9840–12,140 feet) above sea level.

WOLF DISTRIBUTION

SUDAN · Simien Mts
L. Tana
Mount Guna ▲
DJIBOUTI
Menz Highlands
ETHIOPIA · Ankober
Addis Ababa ■
Arsi Mts
Somkaro Mts · Bale Mts
Rift Valley

█ Current mountainous distribution of Ethiopian wolf

1. Ethiopian wolves, sometimes misnamed as Simien foxes or jackals, have a slender build that is ideal for rat-catching.

2. Ethiopian wolves ceremoniously greet one another each morning prior to separating for the day's hunting.

The rat-catcher

Unlike its European wolf ancestors, which chase down large prey in packs, the long-legged and graceful Ethiopian wolf is a specialist rat-catcher. It normally hunts alone, stalking, ambushing and digging out rodents from their burrows. The wolf's sensitive ears, slender muzzle and sharp and outwardly-pointing front teeth (incisors) are all important adaptations for detecting and snatching fleet-footed rats from their burrows. Grass and root rats, along with the prized giant molerats (▷ p. 66), constitute most of the wolf's diet, but it will sometimes

1

take hares, goslings and eggs, rock hyraxes and even mountain nyala calves.

Pack life

Ethiopian wolves live in tight social groups, which share and defend exclusive territories of up to 13 sq km (5 sq miles). Packs normally contain up to 13 adults, of which there may be three to eight related males, one to three adult females and a number of yearlings and pups. The pack gathers for social greetings and border patrols at dawn, noon and evening, scent marking and calling at territory boundaries – before breaking up to hunt alone. They also rest together through the frosty nights, curled up in the open with their noses tucked under their tails. The pack only uses a den during the breeding season. Up to six pups are born to a dominant pair, and when they have been weaned they are watched over by a male babysitter while the parents and the rest of the pack are away hunting.

The future

These charismatic mountain hunters are protected in some parts of their Ethiopian range, such as the Bale Mountains and Simien National Parks, but their survival is still under serious threat. Apart from road kills and direct persecution, the greatest problem for the wolves is the presence of domestic dogs, which people use to protect their cattle from spotted hyenas. Many of these dogs are semi-wild and compete for the wolves' food by foraging for rodents. Worse still, they sometimes mate with female wolves and produce fertile offspring – a very real long-term threat as the pure wolf strain could become 'genetically extinct'. The worst and most immediate threat from dogs, however, is disease in the forms of rabies and canine distemper. Between 1990 and 1992 a rabies epidemic in the Bale Mountains reduced the wolf population by nearly two-thirds and a future major epidemic could cause irreversible damage.

Luckily, an internationally concerted effort by scientists and a conservation programme within Ethiopia, together with the cooperation of the local Oromo people, may save the wolf. Thousands of domestic dogs have been inoculated against disease or sterilized, and community education in schools and settlements, regarding responsible dog ownership, is underway. Only through such concerted national and international effort will these magnificent creatures avoid extinction.

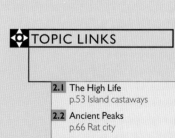

TOPIC LINKS

2.1 The High Life
p.53 Island castaways

2.2 Ancient Peaks
p.66 Rat city

to live. Yet, up here, Walia ibex – close relatives of domestic goats, which probably once crossed to Africa via Arabia – manage to scramble across precipitous rock faces on rubbery hooves to nibble on grass and herbs. Male Walia ibex have the longest and most heavily reinforced horns of all goats, and they use these to crushing effect to defend hilltop territories from rivals. Contestants vie for an elevated position from which to launch themselves at opponents but – with valleys plunging over 1500 m (4900 feet) – these sparring contests can often be fatal. Walia ibex share the majestic peaks of the Simiens with troops of gelada baboons (▷ pp. 48–51), which can also navigate the death-defying crags with ease. Unlike the ibex, geladas probably came here from the hot African plains below, forced into isolation by heavy predator pressure and competition with other primates, including humans.

 RAT CITY

The Bale highlands, like the Simien Mountains, are covered in great swathes of grassland – a perfect habitat for rodents which thrive on grass seeds. In every square mile there are over 100,000 grass rats, root rats and, most impressive of all, giant molerats the size of large guinea pigs, which weigh in at about 1 kg (2.2 lbs). Giant molerats have been instrumental in helping to create the mountain soils, constantly ploughing up soil, excrement and unused plant material from their burrows. But they are also the favoured prey of Ethiopian wolves, which hunt them by stalking and ambush. Because of this, giant molerats are very wary creatures, travelling no further than 30 cm (12 inches) from their nest entrance. Although they have eyes set in the tops of their heads they are quite short-sighted, and so have built up an intriguing relationship with small birds called hill chats. The hill chat takes advantage of any insects attracted to the rotting compost of plant material expelled by the molerat, and in turn, the molerat is warned of danger by the movements and cries of the bird – using them as an early warning system.

Mountains of extremes

Some of the most unusual ancient volcanoes in Africa can be found right in the middle of the Sahara Desert. The Hoggar, Tibesti and Aïr Mountains of Algeria, Tchad and Niger arose from ancient volcanic activity associated with the formation of the Alps. Despite the burning bleakness of the surrounding desert, these rocky islands manage to trap just enough rainfall to sustain trees and shrubs of Mediterranean origin, such as wild olives, myrtles and cypresses. Relic communities of savannah animals such as olive baboons, patas monkeys and rock hyraxes manage to survive among some of these highland enclaves, as does the highly endangered Barbary sheep, which has been hunted close

to extinction across most of its former north African range.

Rising majestically from the rainforests of West Africa are the wettest mountains on the continent – the highlands of Cameroon and Guinea – which receive as much as 10,000 mm (400 inches) of rain a year. Like the Sahara mountains, these peaks were formed from ancient volcanic activity, in this case associated with the birth of the Atlantic Ocean, as South America pulled away from Africa. Even today, some of the volcanoes are still active, and only last year Mount Cameroon erupted. Despite this, their great age and stable climate have created lush, montane forest brimming with unusual animal and plant life, including many endemic species of primates, birds and reptiles.

When he rounded the Cape in 1495, Vasco da Gama named South Africa 'Terra de Fume' because he saw the smoke of so many fires.

1. Female Walia ibex negotiating rocky crags in Ethiopia's Simien Highlands.

2. The Hoggar Mountains in Algeria.

2

2.3 GREAT RIFT GIANTS

Stretching for more than 6000 km (3700 miles) and clearly visible from space, Africa's Great Rift Valley stretches all the way from the Lebanon to Mozambique. This vast scar in the landscape of Africa has been formed by violent subterranean forces that are tearing the Earth's crust apart, causing huge blocks of land to sink between parallel fissures and forcing up molten lava in volcanic eruptions.

Some 30 active and semi-active volcanoes today line the Great Rift, including the tallest snow-capped peaks on the continent, such as Kilimanjaro and Mount Kenya. But for every young, soaring cone there are countless broken-down stubs – remnants of ancient giants whose soft pumice ash and brittle lava have long since disintegrated under the onslaught of sun and ice, rain and wind.

THE FIRES WITHIN

Deep inside the Earth, continent-splitting forces are at work along Africa's Great Rift Valley. Internal heat creates powerful currents which stir solid rock like stiff treacle. These currents push up and fan outwards beneath the Earth's crust, stretching it like opposing conveyor belts. In the process, a layer of molten rock or 'magma' builds up – when the stretching reaches an intolerable level, the Earth's crust fractures and magma rushes out, emerging as the molten lava of an erupting volcano.

Along the Great Rift Valley there are many signs of subterranean turmoil, from smouldering craters in the Danakil Depression to spectacular steam fountains on the fringes of Lake Bogoria in Kenya. Nyamlagira and Nyiragongo, two of the Virunga peaks, have both been very active in recent decades, and even today there are places in the Virunga range where carbon dioxide leaks from their slopes, collecting in depressions and forming fatal traps to any wildlife that should wander through. In other places along the Rift, new mountains are bursting towards the African sky, such as Ol Doinyo Lengai in northern Tanzania – the Maasai 'Mountain of God'. This conical mountain, which belches steam from fumeroles in its crater, last erupted in 1966 and threatens to do so again. But wildlife has been quick to establish itself on its volatile slopes. Baboons, klipspringers and eland crop the tough herbs and grasses already established on the thick layer of ash.

So violent are some eruptions that mountains can literally 'blow their top off'. A classic example of this is Ngorongoro, the largest caldera in East Africa and the sixth largest in the world. Its cone may once have been as high as 4500 m (14,700 feet), but a great explosion 2–3 million years ago ripped the top of it apart, the resulting debris being absorbed by the underlying magma.

1. The Virunga range of mountains includes some of the most active volcanoes in Africa today.

2. The smouldering crater of Ol Doinyo Lengai volcano in Tanzania – a new mountain in the making.

CROWNING THE CONTINENT

Kilimanjaro (5896 m/19,344 feet) and Mount Kenya (5199 m/17,057 feet) are Africa's tallest mountains. Both rise majestically out of the equatorial plains, their snow-capped summits glinting under a hot, tropical sky. Although nothing can live permanently on their peaks, there has been a remarkable sighting of a pack of wild dogs on the Kilimanjaro glaciers and there is also evidence that leopards may occasionally cross the peaks. Being such a young, tall and dry mountain, Kilimanjaro is relatively impoverished in wildlife terms, but it is home to a few unique plant species, such as the Kilimanjaro balsam, the cabbage groundsel (▷ pp. 47–8) and a pale blue gentian.

There is only one mammal endemic to Kilimanjaro – a high-altitude shrew.

Mount Kenya is three times older than Kilimanjaro and is thought to have once been much higher – maybe reaching 6500 m (21,300 feet). Its greater age, combined with its damper soils, make it a more suitable habitat for wildlife than Kilimanjaro. One of Mount Kenya's most impressive residents is the McKinders eagle owl, which can often be seen roosting among stands of giant senecios, where it is extremely well camouflaged. From this vantage point it swoops on unsuspecting rodents such as striped mice. Another rare and unusual inhabitant of the moorland is the Mount Kenya viper, which emerges on sunny days to bask on rocks, its black skin helping to absorb heat.

Unlike Kilimanjaro, which lacks surface water, Mount Kenya is cut by myriad streams and upland lakes or 'tarns'. These lakes are so cold and lacking in nutrients that few plants can survive in them, but in some places bottom-dwelling algae can form spectacular circular growth patterns known as 'fairy rings'.

Streams flowing off Mount Kenya and the nearby Aberdares range flow into rivers and, in places, form amazing waterfalls. These torrents provide security for colonies of slender-billed chestnut winged starlings, which nest on rocky ledges behind the tumbling water. Each morning, amid a cacophony of calls, the birds bathe and preen on the lip of the falls, before setting off to forage for insects in the moorland.

⭐ The Kikuyu people believe Mount Kenya, which they call 'Kere Nyaga', meaning 'Mountain of Brightness', to be a holy mountain, home to their god Ngai and his wife Mumbi.

1

1. Even though Mount Kenya sits on the Equator, each morning its bleak moorland resembles a winter wonderland.

2. (opposite) Magnificent glaciers crown the summit of Kilimanjaro. Some scientists predict that, with global warming, they may disappear in the next 15 years.

Life in the clouds

Being at cloud level, the lower flanks of Africa's tallest mountains receive the most rainfall. A broad tideline of cool, wet montane forest, dominated by impressive Podocarpus and juniper trees draped in lichens, ferns, bryophytes and orchids, thrives on their flanks. This forest is alive with strange noises – at night the unearthly screams of tree hyraxes pierce the forest, to be replaced by a deafening chorus of roaring at dawn as troops of pied colobus advertise their strength to neighbours.

These forests are alive with many unusual creatures, some rarely seen – such as the crested or maned rat. This large, slow-moving nocturnal rodent with woolly black and white fur has little need to conceal itself – when alarmed it hisses and growls and opens its fur to reveal a gland on its flank that may be poisonous. Chameleons, which are a favourite prey for birds like hornbills, take the opposite strategy, and conceal themselves in the foliage. On Mount Kenya and the Aberdares, the bizarre three-horned Jackson's chameleon uses its dinosaur-like protuberances to battle with rivals for treetop territory. Chameleons thrive in these forests on the many insects attracted to an abundance of flowers, such as the bright orange blossoms of Leonotis.

As well as accommodating many unique species, the cloud forest is also visited by wanderers from the hot plains below. Elephants routinely migrate between Amboseli National Park in Kenya and the forested slopes of Kilimanjaro in Tanzania in search of good browse. Warthogs – generalist grazers most abundant in savannahs – can be found up to 3000 m (10,000 feet) up Kilimanjaro, where they share the forest with bushpigs. Hunting, habitat loss and change, and predation by lions have all taken their toll on montane browsers – giant forest hogs, black rhino, bongo (Aberdares only) and Abbot's duiker (Kilimanjaro only) are all now extremely rare in the highlands of East Africa.

Kilimanjaro and Mount Kenya owe their existence to the formation of the Great Rift Valley, but there is another Great Rift mountain range that stands over 5000 m (16,400 feet) high with quite different characteristics – the Ruwenzoris or 'Mountains of the Moon'. ▷▷

1. A number of spectacular waterfalls cascade off the moorland of the Aberdares range in Kenya.

2. Giant forest hogs regularly visit clearings in the Mount Kenya and Aberdares forest to excavate minerals from the soil with their lower incisors.

3

3. A pair of male Jackson's chameleons fight for territory in the montane forest of Kenya's Aberdares range.

Overleaf: Kibo is the tallest and youngest of Kilimanjaro's three peaks.

 GIANT FOREST HOGS

Giant forest hogs (opposite) occur across equatorial central and West Africa in lowland rainforest, but in East Africa they are restricted to just a few forested regions where there is reasonable humidity and plenty of shade. Broken montane forest provides ideal conditions, as forest hogs like to lie up in dense thickets during the day and visit clearings at dawn and dusk to feed on grasses and sedges.

Sounders consist of up to five sows with their offspring of up to three litters, accompanied by a boar. When two sounders meet they will often mingle, but the boars are intolerant of each other and if neither backs down they may engage in a bout of head-butting. Backing off up to 30 m (100 feet) they charge at each other with heads lowered – smacking into each other with a sharp pistol-like crack, produced by the escape of compressed air from their heavily reinforced crania. Repeated charges may continue for up to 30 minutes, the rivals jaw-champing, spitting and squirting urine.

Giant forest hogs often visit bare-earth clearings in the forest to excavate soil with their lower incisors, providing them with valuable minerals.

'Mountains of the Moon'

As early as 500 BC, the Greek dramatist and poet, Aeschylus, wrote of 'Egypt nurtured by the snows', but it was Claudius Ptolemy, the distinguished astronomer and geographer, who first coined the phrase *Lunae montes* or 'Mountains of the Moon', and recognized the range as the primary source of the Nile. Indeed, to the local Bakonjo and Baamba people, Ruwenzori means 'Hill of Rain' – a fitting description for the wettest mountain range in Africa, where rain falls almost every day.

Although thrust upwards as recently as 2 million years ago between the faulted arms of the Western and Eastern Rift, the foundation rocks are ancient – as much as 1800 million years old. At 5109 m (16,762 feet) tall, the snow-capped summit of Mount Stanley is the highest of more than 20 peaks in the Ruwenzori range.

Nurtured by the heavy rains, magnificent stands of giant lobelias, senecios and tree-heathers cloak the Ruwenzori moorlands – the most impressive afro-alpine flora in all of Africa. Among tumbled rocks, colonies of Ruwenzori tree hyraxes emerge to feed on grasses, sedges and senecios – quite different habits to their solitary, nocturnal relatives on other mountains. The forest streams of the Ruwenzoris hide other surprises. Here, rare and primitive otter shrews use their whiskered, hydrofoil noses to snuffle out worms, insects and small crabs in forest streams. The dreamy, lichen-clad forests are also home to endemic turacos and horseshoe bats, as well as a local race of pied colobus.

▷ KILIMANJARO – THREE MOUNTAINS IN ONE

Kilimanjaro is not a single volcano, but a composite of three. The Shira plateau, on the west of the mountain, is the remains of a volcano that died half a million years ago; taller Mawenzi in the east is the jagged skeleton of a second giant; while in between, Kibo overshadows both beneath its huge, icy dome.

The Chagga people of Tanzania, who live in the foothills of Kilimanjaro, have a very interesting legend regarding the geology of the mountain. They say that one day Kibo was approached by Mawenzi, who said 'Good day, friend, the fire in my hearth has gone out'. Mawenzi, having accepted a gift of fire and bananas, carried them off, only to return, saying his fire had gone out again. After two more gifts of fire and bananas, Kibo finally lost patience and so beat up Mawenzi to such an extent that his battered profile still bears the scars of Kibo's pestle.

Kibo's last major eruption was 36,000 years ago, but it is just possible that this Chagga folklore recounts a lesser, but much more recent, event. Today, Kibo's crater still smokes, and there is every possibility Kilimanjaro may one day erupt again.

1

1. The afro-alpine flora of the Ruwenzoris is the richest of any mountain range in Africa.

THE PIED COLOBUS OF TROPICAL AFRICA

African monkeys are divided into two groups: the colobids or 'thumbless' monkeys with long limbs, large bodies and small heads, and the 'cheek-pouch' monkeys, which include the colourful guenons and stocky baboons. Colobids are found throughout Africa's tropical forests and, unlike the omnivorous cheek-pouch monkeys, are specialist vegetarians, able to digest tough and sometimes noxious plant matter. Like ruminants they have large, chambered stomachs which are able to break down cellulose through fermentation and also detoxify the compounds that protect leaves and seeds. Their long tails and thumbless front limbs are also adaptations for a life spent predominantly in the forest canopy.

The pied colobus of East and North Africa
With their striking black and white coloration and furry capes, pied colobus are the most impressive of all colobids. Five different species occur across tropical Africa, but the mountains of East and North Africa are populated by only two – the highland guereza colobus on Kilimanjaro, Mount Meru, Mount Kenya, the Aberdares and the Ethiopian Highlands, and the Angola pied colobus in the Ruwenzoris and Eastern Arc Mountains. Of the pair, the highland guereza colobus is more adapted to cold forests, its fur longer and thicker than all other pied colobus. Most distinctive are its bushy white tail and flowing mantle.

1. Living in cool montane forests, the highland guereza colobus is the most heavily furred of the five species of pied colobus. 1

Guereza colobus – Africa's mountain monkey
Because it can get by on a diet of coarse and mature leaves, the guereza colobus can live in extremely small territories and densities as high as 500 individuals per square kilometre in prime habitat. Troops, which normally number six to ten individuals, are very cohesive and highly territorial. Prior to sunrise, dominant males roar from treetops to proclaim their territory to neighbours – a dramatic morning roll call that gradually builds around the mountain as successive males join in.

Each troop divides its day between sleeping, sunning and feeding in the trees, using

regular treetop pathways and sometimes leaping in spectacular fashion between trees. These leaps may involve drops of up to 15 m (50 feet), using the rebound of branches to gain extra momentum and distance for the following jump. Just occasionally – where there is broken cover – the troop will visit the ground, running with awkward bounds. However, most time is spent just sitting peacefully – feeding, digesting, nursing infants and grooming. A colobus eats 2–3 kg (4½–6½ lbs) of leaves and other plants a day – equivalent to up to a third of its body weight. Leaves are mainly gathered by gripping them between flexed fingers, but round fruits like figs are usually taken directly by the mouth. When resting, their most typical posture is squatting on a branch, leaning forward with their elbows on their knees, sometimes with their chin resting on their chest – giving pied colobus the appearance of tired old men. On particularly cold mornings all members of the troop will sometimes huddle together on a single branch.

Each troop usually has three or four adult females and they give birth at roughly 20-month intervals, often during the rainy season. Infants are born pure white and only assume the pied colours of the adults at 14–17 weeks. However, in certain localities, some infants never become pied. On Mount Kenya, a small and highly localized population of pure albinos exists. After 5 weeks of being carried by their mothers they begin to move about alone, and are looked after by all members of the troop. At this precocious age they are most at risk of falling from the canopy or predation by crowned eagles. When on the ground they are also susceptible to predation by leopards.

Guerezas are abundant in most parts of their lowland range and in protected upland reserves, although they are declining elsewhere. In Ethiopia continuous habitat loss and hunting over centuries for their magnificent pelts has reduced a formerly very extensive range to a wide scatter of relic populations.

2. The Angola pied colobus of the Ruwenzoris and Eastern Arc is distinguished by its flamboyant white epaulettes.

3

LAKES AND RIVERS

AFRICA'S FRESH WATER

An astronaut spinning high over Africa would have the privileged view of jewel-bright lakes, strewn in a relatively orderly fashion over the surface of the continent. Some lakes would be shining a dull jade green and others spangled silver in the sun. There are also emerald and turquoise waters and the surreal ruby-red waters of Lake Natron in Tanzania.

Some rivers meander in long, lazy loops, while others cut straight across the continent to the sea. There is the Nile, the longest river in the world, and many other mighty rivers such as the Zambezi and the Congo. Tiny, ice-cold mountain springs tumble down precipitous slopes. And at Victoria Falls, the sheer volume of water thundering over the precipice makes the ground shake.

'Water has some kind of powerful mystery about it. Still waters, moving waters, dark waters; the words themselves have a mysterious, dying fall', wrote the novelist H.E. Bates.

Previous page: Elephants drinking at Chobe River in Botswana can, in the dry season, gather in herds of thousands – the largest elephant concentrations on earth.

1. After passing through a mountain, a molecule of rainwater in a river contains many more chemical substances than it did when it left the ocean.

THE RAIN-MAKERS

Added to the poetic magic of water is the simple fact that, without it, there would be no life as we know it today; and there would be almost no water in Africa's rivers and lakes without Africa's mountains. But first the wind has to blow. The major planetary winds are caused partly by the spin of the Earth on its axis. As these winds blow over the Earth's surface, they pick up water by evaporation from the oceans. When they pass over the land, their flow is interrupted by the chains of mountains that lie in their path.

Forced upwards in order to flow over the tops of the peaks, most of the wind's moisture condenses and falls as rain, hail or snow. Slopes which lie directly in the path of rain-bearing winds catch most of the water, whilst the mountain peaks and lands that lie on the leeward side are deprived of rain.

And so the marriage of wind and mountain gives birth to water. Africa has a multitude of rivers and all of them rise somewhere in the huge plateau and mountain areas. The character of each depends very much on which mountain is the partner in the marriage. Rainwater contains substances that react with the chemicals in the rocks and earth on which the rain falls, to produce salts.

The water

Some mountains were created from alkaline or 'basic' lava. The water that runs from these is mildly alkaline and when it accumulates in lakes, the alkalinity becomes more concentrated due to evaporation. Some of these lakes have no outlets at all, and in these the water collects and concentrates into a spectacular soup of alkalinity. The Usambaras and other mountains are composed of granites and sandstones, which filter out the most minute of particles. The water that emerges is sparklingly clear, but is no longer as fertile and so supports far less life.

Water also affects mountains. After heavy storms, rainwater pours down slopes, carrying soil and stones. It joins other small trickles and finds the path of least resistance. The rush of water gathers power and momentum. Carrying branches and bushes, the torrent begins to cut into the sides of the gully. With a dull, rumbling roar, stones and boulders are gouged out and rolled along the bottom of the stream bed. This is erosion in action.

When rivers run into lakes, the soil and debris are dumped on the bottom. As the torrent's fierce power and velocity are swallowed up by the still water, the heaviest objects are dropped first, followed by the smaller soil particles until the finest of silt particles are deposited. And when the silt is so powdery fine that it is held in suspension, it turns lakes into vibrant colours.

1

THE WATER SUPPLIERS

Environmental change is the principal player in the story of life on this planet, but the same water has been re-used all through the Earth's history. It has gone through different stages – frozen, melted, evaporated, condensed and moved from place to place – but essentially it is the same.

There are some startling statistics. Of the 1.4 billion cubic km (326 million cubic miles) of water on the planet, 97 per cent is held in the oceans, which shows just how vital they are to the wellbeing of our world. Just over 2 per cent is locked up in icecaps and glaciers, whilst lakes hold a tiny 0.017 per cent and rivers an almost imperceptible 0.0001 per cent.

The rivers and lakes in Africa receive this water in three main ways. The most important, called 'run-off', is caused when the land becomes so saturated that it cannot absorb any more water, and shallow sheets of water cascade down even the slightest of slopes. The second is from a vital under-ground reservoir known as 'groundwater'. Only a tiny fraction of the rain that falls on the ground is held by plants in the upper layer of soil. The rest drains down until it reaches watertight bedrock, where it slowly accumulates. This underground reservoir is huge and inestimably valuable, representing some 37 per cent of the total contained in lakes and rivers. Here, water inches along at a snail's pace, following the contours of the bedrock. It can travel several hundreds of miles and be thousands of years old before it reappears on the Earth's surface as springs, wells or geysers.

The third source of water for lakes and rivers is provided by rain. For most rivers this is negligible but for Lake Victoria, the second largest lake in the world, its immense surface area soaks up about 70 per cent of the lake's total supply from the heavens above.

1. Streams tumble down from Mount Kenya and one lake is still coloured green with silt particles brought down by glaciers thousands of years ago.

2. The Okavango delta as seen from the air is a kaleidoscope of jewel-bright greens and blues: a lush haven for wildlife.

ROCK PRATINCOLES

Rock pratincoles (left) are smart little birds, both in appearance and behaviour, and are only found on the larger rivers south of the Sahara.

In the nesting season, pairs cement existing bonds through a variety of ritual displays, before choosing a nesting site – and only rocks surrounded by fast-flowing water will do. No nest is made, but the eggs are beautifully camouflaged with a variety of dull, mottled greys latticed with snaky black lines.

Here the risk of predation from land animals is minimal but this luxury is achieved at the expense of enormous heat stress to the parents, since surface rock temperatures can soar to well over 50°C (122°F). Shading the eggs is a punishing business, and the parents take regular turns so that the other can cool off. Observers have only recently noted that, at the same time as drinking, parents dip their brood feathers in the water, which helps to cool the eggs by latent evaporation. When the young are born, they seek shade in tiny crevices and overhangs.

Pushing the limits of life in this way pays, since competition for nesting sites and predation is decreased to almost nothing. On the other hand, the eggs and chicks are both vulnerable to sudden flash floods.

AN EVOLUTIONARY PERSPECTIVE

The different processes of solution, erosion and deposition associated with lakes and rivers are all relatively slow but continuous. In time these processes start to affect both mountains and lakes. Water wears down mountains and, given enough time, rivers can kill lakes. After thousands of years of supplying water, silt-laden rivers eventually turn the tables and smother the life out of lakes by filling them with so much sediment that they can no longer hold any water. The opposite can also happen. Lakes that are full to the brim are quick to invade the surrounding land. Since 1961, Lake Naivasha in Kenya has risen many feet, hungrily swallowing hectares of pasture and turning them into lily lagoons, where millions of fish and birds now thrive.

The vagaries of climate change in Africa can be quite local and very specific. In just 10 or 20 years, lakes can change radically in size and in the numbers and types of species that they support. On a longer timescale the changes are even greater. About 3 or 4 million years ago, Lake Naivasha was some 36 m (120 feet) higher than it is now. A river flowed out of the lake and emptied into a flat swamp between Suswa and Longonot, then drained through the Kedong Gorge and finally filled another lake at Olorgesaile. Remains of our distant ancestors have been found here, together with their tools and the bones of animals which show that these swampy lakes were home to a variety of fish, giant hippos and other animals now lost to a bygone age.

So, like other ecosystems, lakes are subject to a finite life. They are born, thrive for a while, and then start to die. Hanging on to life, they linger on as swamps until finally they give up the ghost. As the last few drops of water trickle away, grass begins to sprout and soon the site of the former lake is taken over by grassland.

Waterfalls

The landscape dictates the course a river takes and, combined with the relentless power of moving water, can create spectacles that are truly breathtaking. A visitor to the Victoria Falls on the Zambia/Zimbabwe border in 1876 wrote: 'No human being can describe the infinite; and what I saw was a part of infinity made visible and framed in beauty.' The falls are indeed unimaginably beautiful and the scene is ever-changing with endless moments of majesty, movement and magic.

So much water pours over in the wet ▷▷

BLACK EAGLES

Black eagles, also known in East Africa as Verreaux's eagles, are big birds and powerful fliers. Often found in mountainous areas, they soar high on the thermals that rise from steep-sided gorges and ridges.

Black eagles often nest in the gorge at the bottom of Victoria Falls, where pairs swoop and somersault in breathlessly spectacular displays. They do not migrate and their numbers are limited by the abundance of their favourite prey, hyrax, and the availability of cliff nesting sites.

This may well be the world's most intensively studied eagle and there are some interesting nuggets of information. With a clutch of between one and three eggs, the female spends some 80 per cent of a 24-hour period incubating them, with the male sharing the duty during the daytime.

Chicks hatch at about 2 months and the emergence of one chick was timed at 69 hours. With hatching taking place at intervals of 3 days, sibling rivalry is intense and, as in other eagle species, the elder chick normally kills or dominates the younger. During incubation, the male catches all the food for the pair until the female resumes hunting shortly after the eggs hatch. Some 115 hyrax are needed to feed the female and the babies before the young fledge at 100–125 days.

1. (opposite) A black eagle perches, majestic, before the spectacular Victoria Falls.

AFRICA'S UNPREDICTABLE WATERS

With the exception of the dark, damp rainforest zone, Africa today is generally an arid country. However, the continent has hundreds of thousands of rivers, a multitude of lakes and a range of wetlands – ice-cold mountain tarns, ponds, marshes, bogs, steaming-hot soda lakes and pans, and vast, fertile floodplains. Over millions of years this water has shaped the continent and the wildlife that it supports. Today, key words that sum up the essence of many of Africa's rivers and wetlands are seasonality and drought-stricken. This has resulted in many adaptations that enable animals to thrive in a world of watery unpredictability.

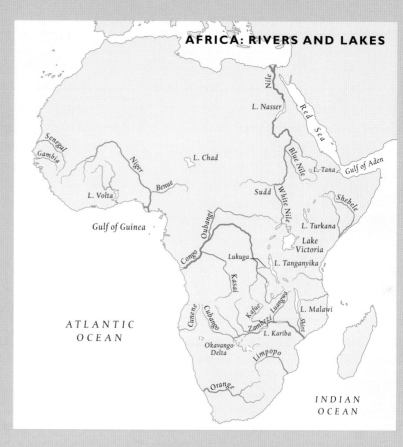

AFRICA: RIVERS AND LAKES

A living fossil

There are three species of African lungfish, all of which can cope with long periods of drought. As the water evaporates into mud, they excavate burrows and begin to secrete a mucous cocoon that protects them against moisture loss. Having primitive lungs, they can breathe through a small slit at the top of the cocoon and are able to lie dormant for months, or even a couple of years, until the rains come again. This period of bare existence, known as 'aestivation', is an indication that the African lungfish has a history of great antiquity.

Lungfish fossils have been found that are, give or take the odd year, a mind-blowing 350 million years old. Lungfish are also found in Australia and South America and, since they have never become marine animals, this shows that they evolved well before the break-up of the mother of all continents – Gondwana.

The opportunists

The most ephemeral, transient and magical of all African ponds must be those made when elephant footprints fill with rainwater and the tiniest of pools are born. Some fish species have such refined lifecycles that they can make the most of even this happy accident. These tiny fish are known as rivulins, some species of which can survive for five years without any water at all. Unlike lungfish, it aestivates not as an adult but as an egg, which lies in a state of suspension until development is triggered by

rain. Within days the egg hatches and, since the fish is so small, it can grow, mature and spawn in as little as four weeks. And so the most is made of any opportunity, however short or small.

Some fish in Lake Tanganyika use empty snail shells as refuges or breeding sites. There are about 20 or even 25 species that employ a whole range of subtly different behaviours, including those that employ rascally deeds such as stealing not just shells but also females from other nests.

The secrets of Africa's wetlands

On a larger scale, the lakes and rivers of Africa are also the setting for any number of virtuoso visual spectacles. There are the breeding colonies of lesser flamingos, rarely seen but

one of the world's greatest ornithological marvels, and concentrations of rosy-breasted bee-eaters, with tens of thousands of birds nesting on sandbars in the great West African rivers.

Mammals, such as elephant and buffalo, also build up into spectacular concentrations around water and there are the vast herds of aquatic antelope too, the lechwe, and the far more secretive and less numerous sitatunga. Then there are the rarer and more elusive characters. Some are a little eccentric to our eyes, like the extraordinary-looking shoebill stork. Others have highly unusual calls, like the Pel's fishing owl, whose unearthly wails were once unforgettably described as similar to 'a man who has lost his soul falling down a bottomless pit'.

Water may once have played a huge and vital role in our own development as a species. Today, however, it is certain that we have a significant effect on it. Wetlands are among the continent's most threatened ecosystems, with water resources under increasing pressure from urban and industrial use and with the demand for agricultural land eating into floodplains and tidal wetlands.

1. Pel's fishing owl is a large owl confined to riverine habitats where it roosts by day and feeds on surface fish and other aquatic

1 animals at night.

◆ TOPIC LINKS

3.3 Special Feature: Saga of the Flamebirds
p.114 The breeding sites

4.1 Under the Glare
p.120 Hot Spot: Water storage
p.121 Capturing water

season that mist hangs in the air and drips from every branch and leaf. These conditions are perfect for a rich array of moisture-loving plants. Some of the 400 or so species identified here are found nowhere else, and others are more normally associated with the humid temperatures of rainforests. Below the falls, Taita falcons, bateleur and black eagles soar on the thermals in the gorge.

The waterfall was created thousands of years ago when the Zambezi River found a vertical crack in the region's rocks at right angles to its course. Working its way through, the river gradually deepened and widened the crack. Today, the waters plummet some 100 m (330 feet) and the width of the falls is about 2 km (1¹/₄ miles). But the life of the falls is finite and subject to the vagaries of fate. In this area, the basalt through which the Zambezi runs is characterized by very marked joints or cracks, which may have developed as the molten lava cooled. The water, which can flow at an amazing 7.7 million litres (2 million gallons) a second, constantly cuts back the lip of the falls. Each time the lip meets a new crack, another slot-like chasm is formed.

The present falls are actually the eighth to have formed over the last half million years or so. Already the river has started to gouge out a new crack, which goes by the somewhat sinister name of the Devil's Cataract. One day, the waters will pour into this crack and when that happens, the present falls will be left high and dry.

1

THE AQUATIC APE THEORY

A startling idea on our origins is derided, hotly debated and goes right against the establishment view outlined in the final chapter of this book. It is the 'aquatic ape' theory.

DNA research shows that the split between our distant ancestors and the other great apes happened some 5 million years ago. So far the earliest evidence for bipedal locomotion are fossilized footprints 3.6 million years old and supporters of the aquatic ape theory say that the revolutionary upright stance results from the Red Sea inundating the Rift Valley with water about 6 million years ago, i.e., prior to the evolution of the bipedal ape. They suggest that, at that time, one very ape-like primate that was still walking on all fours on the ground or swinging through the trees may have become isolated on forested islands. To survive, members of this species began to wade or even swim across channels from island to island in order to find food.

Although the waters created an obstacle for the apes, they also provided abundant shellfish and fish, new opportunities for nourishment. Those that could use tools, for example, to crack open shellfish would have flourished. Walking upright facilitates wading, and as more time was spent in the water, the ability to stand up on two back legs was enhanced. In time, the result was a hominid.

The evidence

There is in fact no evidence in the fossil record to support the 'aquatic ape' hypothesis, but its supporters claim that it neatly explains various puzzling anomalies that have so far bedeviled anthropologists. These anomalies are that, unlike any of the other great apes, our species is largely naked, we have a downward-pointing nose with a lowered larynx, and we give birth to babies who are able to float, swim and instinctively hold their breath under water. As supporters of the 'aquatic ape' hypothesis consequently point out, fat is a far better insulator in water than hair; a downward-pointing nose reduces the entry of water when swimming; and breath control is essential in a semi-aquatic lifestyle.

Ultimately, new finds may discredit some of these arguments but, for the moment, this theory provides a stimulating challenge to more conventional theories of human evolution.

 KINGFISHERS

The sudden, swift flight along waterways, the quick dive in a shimmer of brilliant metallic blue, the skilful snatch of a fish – all these really do seem to sum up the king of all fishers. But, strangely enough, two-thirds of the world's species of kingfisher do not catch fish at all. They are catchers of insects. In fact, the streamlined plunges into water probably evolved originally as an efficient way of plucking prey from the ground.

Related to hornbills and bee-eaters, kingfishers are found in many of Africa's habitats, ranging from dry woodlands to watery inlets and magnificent lakes. Malachite kingfishers (right), which are found close to water and do catch fish, have such colourful feathers that they seem almost unreal.

The biggest species in Africa is aptly named the giant kingfisher. With a total length of 40 cm (16 inches) and a weight of 400 g (1 lb), it is indeed huge compared with the smallest. Found in central Africa, the black-fronted pygmy kingfisher is only 10 cm (4 inches) in length and weighs no more than 10 g (a third of an ounce).

Only one species of kingfisher is able to hover. The pied kingfisher's aerial skills give it a major advantage over other species, as it does not rely on a perch but can give hunt wherever the fish are most plentiful.

1. Does the key to the most significant development in our evolutionary past lie in a watery world?

AFRICA'S RIVERS

The sun, burning high overhead, illuminates a desolate landscape on the floor of Africa's Rift Valley. All around, sheets of lava, frozen by time, radiate heat. Mirages float on the skyline, and a hot, dry wind whistles over the rocks. But the lassitude and monotony brought on by this immense heat is broken by a glorious gurgling of water.

There are literally thousands of rivers and streams in Africa in every kind of habitat: they can be found trickling through deserts, bisecting the great savannah plains and meandering through forests choked with trees.

There are the great living rivers and their vast alluvial basins: the Nile, the Congo, the Niger, and the Zambezi. But there are many more rivers that have been choked by sand and are effectively dead. However, the tracery of their flowing pathways can still be seen from the air, etched deep into the surface of the land.

Previous page: A Nile crocodile snatches an unsuspecting wildebeest from the banks of the Mara River in Kenya.

1. The Murchison Falls in Uganda tumble down in a torrent of white-water and spray.

THE NATURE OF RIVERS

The largest living rivers in Africa cluster into three major groupings. Lake Victoria empties into the Nile which is also associated with the Chad and Niger River systems, forming by far the biggest river network of them all. The second is the Congo which, with its great biological diversity, receives its waters from Lake Tanganyika. And the third is the Zambezi, which is associated with Lake Malawi. The ages of these three lakes are very different, which affects the river fauna, while the very nature of river water creates a particularly dynamic environment for living organisms.

Heraclitus, a Greek writer who lived just over 2500 years ago, came up with a neat turn of phrase when he wrote, 'You cannot step twice in the same river for fresh waters are ever flowing upon you'. He was right, of course, for river water is constantly on the move. Supplies of oxygen, carbon dioxide and nutrients are quickly replenished in rivers, and in response some aquatic organisms have speeded up their metabolism. For example, mayfly nymphs in rivers consume more oxygen than similar species in lakes, and one species of algae not only respires more rapidly but can also absorb phosphorus ten times faster than other species. But there are plenty of larger animals that have also adapted to living in a torrent.

Life in fast water

All African rivers originate in the plateau and mountain areas of the continent and flow down towards the sea. During its long journey, a river undergoes a range of changes. Near its source, the river is often fast and shallow unless it is in flood. It rushes along the bottom of a very narrow, deep valley which, every second, is deepened by the debris-laden waters pound-

1

ing into the river's bed. The waters churn down the hillside in a flurry of potholes, spattering waterfalls and rapids. Running water creates a wide variety of biological niches and each is home to specially adapted flora and fauna. The different speeds of running water also provide a host of environments for insects, fish and birds.

Insects reach their maximum variety of species in water that flows. Stone flies are dependent on cold, swift-flowing water that is well oxygenated. The female drops an abundance of eggs into the water, where they are dispersed by the current before falling to the bottom. The eggs are covered with adhesive hairs that help them to stick to the stream bed until they hatch. At this stage, the emerging larvae are called 'nymphs'. Their behaviour, however, belies such a romantic label for they are voracious predators.

Another fast-water specialist is the slender-billed chestnut-winged starling. These glossy birds live high on Kenya's mountains, feeding on snails extracted from giant lobelias. On Mount Kenya, the steps created by old lava flows have resulted in a large number of vertical waterfalls. Over time, the water has gouged out caves behind the curtains of water and these make great nesting areas for the starlings.

Sedate middle age

As the river continues, the waters become wider and deeper, and the river valley flat and broad. As temperatures rise, the sandbanks become full to bursting with basking crocodiles and hippos snoozing in the sun. Herons stand motionless in the shallows while the strident calls of fish eagles echo from bank to bank.

So many tributaries have joined the river that the volume of water is much increased. Now the river looks sedate and gentle, almost as if it has abandoned the youthful swirls and bubbles and settled into sedate middle age, but, despite appearances, the water velocity actually *increases* downstream. Rivers lose up to 97 per cent of their energy to friction – with air, the stream bed, and within the turbulent water itself. Here, where barely a ripple breaks the surface, erosion has smoothed the stream bed, so friction against the bed and bank is considerably lessened.

The river now carries millions of tonnes of fine sediment in suspension. As the river nears the sea, there is almost no gradient left in the land. Now the waters seem really sluggish and around 75 per cent of the sediment is dropped before the river reaches the sea.

Over time, rivers and streams lower continents by taking materials from one place and depositing them in another. And in doing so, they create some very different habitats.

 FOREST OF HORNS

A forest of horns dark against a sky slashed with red and orange is one of the unforgettable dusk-time sights of the Kafue flats on the flood-plains of Zambia.

Restricted to well-watered areas, red lechwe feed on the abundant and nutritious grasses that grow in flooded water meadows bordering Africa's major rivers. Comfortable feeding up to their shoulders in water, the herds generally follow the shoreline across the floodplain as it advances and recedes during the year. They are relatively mobile and highly gregarious animals, travelling as much as 80 km (50 miles) a year in search of food. When threatened, they seek safety in deeper water and can often be seen bounding through the shallows (right).

Feeding on green pastures most of the year, reaching and utilizing areas that other herbivores cannot, red lechwe numbers can build up to around 1000 animals per sq km (2590 per sq mile). At the beginning of the twentieth century, the Kafue population may well have been in the order of half a million animals. However, a combination of pressure from hunting and alteration of the natural flooding cycle by the construction of a hydroelectric dam has reduced the numbers to some 50,000.

1. Blue wildebeest trek towards the Okavango River, attracted by the annual floodwaters that have spread across the dry floodplains.

RIVERINE HABITATS

Floodplains are created when the river regularly bursts its banks to flood over a wide, flat belt of land. The waters, thick with mineral-rich alluvial soils, create an excellent environment in which vegetation can flourish. The periodic inundation keeps woodland encroachment at bay and enables grasslands to thrive.

At the entrance to the sea, the speed of the river is abruptly checked. The remaining load of silt and mud is dumped and, if there are no strong sea currents or if the amount of material is so heavy that it resists dispersion, it gradually builds up to block the river. Then the river either divides and flows around the barrier, or breaks through, creating a delta. In this way, the wilderness wetlands of Africa were formed.

Deltas can also be created when the river's flow is stopped by lakes or, in the case of one of Africa's most famous deltas – the Okavango – by coming up against the harsh, unyielding sands of a desert.

About 4 or 5 million years ago, the Okavango River system flowed through the Kalahari and spilled into the Atlantic Ocean. Then geological instability shifted the river's flow to the east, where it eventually entered the Indian Ocean. After yet more geological change, the river system as it is today winds its way for 1000 km (620 miles) across northern Botswana, but never reaches the sea. Instead, there are 1800 sq km (700 sq miles) of lush delta before the river filters into the insatiable, arid sands of the Kalahari, which means that really this is not a delta at all and should more correctly be labelled an 'alluvial fan'.

The wildlife of the Okavango Delta

The low-lying wetlands that make up the Okavango Delta are crammed with forested islands, dense papyrus swamps and innumerable waterways. It is a world dominated by hues of emerald greens and sapphire blues, where elephant, buffalo, wildebeest, hartebeest and zebra roam, pursued by predators like wild dogs, lion, cheetah and leopard. Hyenas and jackals are common. Crocodiles haunt the water channels and the air is rich with the calls of a plethora of bird species.

Three species of semi-aquatic antelope – the waterbuck, the red lechwe and the sitatunga – can be found here. The sitatunga is elusive and shy. The only large mammal able to inhabit and feed on papryus reedbeds, the sitatunga is probably the antelope best

⭐ The largest Nile crocodile on record was shot in 1952 on the Semliki River in Uganda. It was 6 m (19½ feet) long and weighed over a tonne (2200 lbs).

adapted to life in the water. Its hooves, at about 18 cm (7 inches), are nearly twice as long as those of other similarly sized antelopes and distribute the animal's weight, which in the case of the males can be over 100 kg (220 lbs). In water, the hooves splay outwards, enabling the sitatunga to move easily through mud and over floating vegetation.

The Luangwa River

The Luangwa River in Zambia is one of Africa's great seasonal rivers. During the wet season the river rises and floods the surrounding short-grass plains. In the dry season, from April to November, the river shrinks until, by October, only a bright thread of water gently meanders its way through vast banks of sand.

Many animals have adapted to these dramatic seasonal changes. In the South Luangwa National Park, huge herds of hippos crowd the banks, piled together, fast asleep in the noon-day sun. Their numbers are matched by Nile crocodiles, lying as motionless as pieces of driftwood, until one golden-flecked eye opens with a particularly intense gaze.

The Luangwa River has a distinctive shape, snaking across the landscape in large, lazy loops with a large number of 'oxbow lakes'. These are formed when the river forges a straight new channel and cuts off a length of curved section, which is then divorced from the main river. The highly characteristic meanders are created as the river traverses a gentle slope covered with fine-grained, easily eroded alluvium. When the waters are high and enter a curve, centrifugal force hurls the

1

1. Nile crocodiles are magnificent, living relicts from the age of the dinosaurs.

2. Thornicroft's giraffe is a unique subspecies found only in Zambia's Luangwa Valley.

3. Long-tailed starlings are found in low-lying areas 800 m (2600 feet) below sea level.

faster-moving water near the surface against the outside bank of the bend. In just one wet season the river can eat several metres into the bank, uprooting trees that for many years have provided perches for kingfishers, darters, storks and cormorants.

Zambia and Tanzania are the only countries that have substantial numbers of puku, a short, stocky antelope restricted to short-grass floodplains of rivers and other water bodies. South Luangwa National Park is also home to two unique subspecies of large mammal – Thornicroft's giraffe and Cookson's wildebeest. These two distinctive races have arisen due to members of each species being isolated from others of their kind. This has probably occurred due to gradual changes in the climate turning several hundreds of kilometres of land surrounding the Luangwa Valley into unsuitable habitat. Isolated from other members of their respective species, these two subspecies now look quite different.

Continued isolation and further evolution may mean that one day these subspecies will become separate species.

Birds of Luangwa Valley

In July and August, as the Luangwa River dwindles to just a small trickle confined to the river channel, pools of water are left in shallow depressions. Full to the brim with fish, these lagoons are also home to herds of hippos. Early evenings are idyllic. (A filigree of sharp black reflections made by the trailing branches from surrounding trees contrasts sharply with the lagoon waters, coloured a rich gold by the sinking sun.) The wind drops and fish begin to rise to the warm surface. Suddenly, the quick pop-pop sound of gulping, leaping fish breaks the still air. This is the time when skimmers begin to fly.

As their name suggests, these birds skim back and forth across the lagoons on a regular beat, leaving an arrow-straight black trail in

the water behind them. A perfect mirror reflection reproduces their every move. Their fishing technique is a study in simplicity. They fly low with their beaks open and held at just the right angle to break the surface of the water and scoop up unwary fish.

Over the next few weeks, the waters sink lower and lower and parties of fish-eating birds begin to build. There are yellow-billed and saddle-billed storks, flocks of pelicans and groups of darters, taking advantage of waters boiling with catfish. Then, one day, there are no birds at all, just mud beginning to crack and peel in the hot sun.

Even later in the dry season, billows of red-billed quelea drift across the skyline in spectacular roosting displays. Each dark, undulating cloud is composed of thousands of tiny birds and, after a day's foraging on seeds, they feel safe roosting amongst the reeds. But the most wonderful bird spectacle must be the bustling nesting sites of the carmine bee-eaters.

⭐ In the dry season, about once every 3 days, 45,000 elephants visit the Chobe River in Botswana – the densest gathering of elephants on Earth.

1. Family groups of little bee-eaters are common and widespread, with pairs often nesting in river banks.

Carmine bee-eaters

The lives of carmine bee-eaters are almost as regular as clockwork, with the birds nesting in the second week of September and returning to the same place year after year. At this time of year large areas of sandy bank are exposed on the Luangwa River. Like other bee-eaters, carmines industriously excavate a new hole every season and it may well be that both males and females have to perform a certain amount of digging before they are ready to enter the next phase of reproduction.

Using beaks and feet they tunnel quite a long way in, although there are some false starts and tunnels are abandoned if they meet an obstruction or soil of the wrong consistency. Since they are colonial nesters, thousands of holes can be created over a few years. The bank is soon peppered with holes, some of which are in use and some not. In time, all this underground activity weakens the bank itself; some observers have seen whole colonies wiped out as the bank collapses with a huge splash into the river.

There is no doubt at all that carmines are beautiful. Their feathers are a shocking Schiaparelli pink mixed with a heavenly azure blue, and the foraging birds provide an iridescent shot of colour in the sky as dozens of them sail high above, taut wings stretched in effortless glides. There are 24 species of

bee-eater and by far the most important part of their diet is bees and social wasps. It is thought that carmines are the only birds able to de-sting bees without breaking their flight, although they are more often seen on a perch, hitting and rubbing the bees before swallowing them. There are exceptions to every rule and carmine bee-eaters do not just eat bees, they also go fishing.

Opportunists

Bee-eaters, therefore, are opportunists. Scientists examining the pellets of blue-breasted bee-eaters from the Kenyan shore of Lake Victoria have discovered the remains of tiny fish, so carmines are not alone in their catholic habits. Elsewhere in Nigeria, a single genius was seen in action. Out of a whole colony of red-throated bee-eaters, one bird had learned that it was easier to provide its nestlings with stolen food. Instead of flying to foraging grounds, it lay in wait for others to come back laden with trophies. Selecting any of them, apart from its own mate, it gave chase, hassling the bird until it dropped its prey.

Insects, fish and animals exploit the opportunities offered by running water in lots of ways. And the scarcely moving, multi-coloured waters of African lakes have a different spectrum of strange and spectacular forms of life.

1

HIPPOS

On a hot African afternoon, hippos can be seen wallowing comfortably in the mud, blowing water loudly through their noses, while egrets and jacanas wander unconcerned over their massive, barrel-shaped bodies, picking off delicious morsels. The name 'hippopotamus' comes from two Greek words meaning 'river' and 'horse'. Fossil remains show that hippos used to inhabit Britain and Europe but today they are found only in Africa where there are two species, the common and the pygmy hippo. **2**

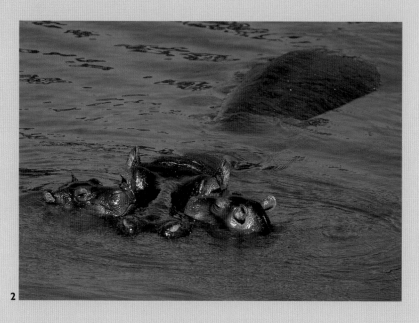

1. Hippopotami evolved from a pig-like ancestor some 40 million years ago, and cannot now survive long outside of water.

2. Hippos have a number of ingenious solutions to their amphibious existence, including the ability of young to suckle underwater.

Hippo distribution

Discovered by the Western world only recently – towards the end of the nineteenth century – very little is known about the habits of the pygmy hippo (▷ p. 162) in the wild. Living in West African forests, it is less aquatic than its relative and feeds mainly on leaves and fruits. Largely nocturnal, it spends most of the day lying in wallows, swamps or possibly hidden away underground in burrows in the river banks. One endearing folk story relates that these hippos carry diamonds in their mouths to help light their way in the dark forest night.

The common hippopotamus once inhabited virtually every river system in Africa and was venerated as a god by the ancient Egyptians. However, over the centuries, their numbers have declined steadily. Records show that the last hippos in the Nile Valley were shot during the mid-1800s. They are now confined to rivers and lakes in mainland Africa south of the Sahara.

Hippo facts

Common hippos can weigh up to 3200 kg (7050 lbs), making them, along with elephants and rhinos, one of the few megaherbivores left in the world today. They are large, conspicuous and noisy animals, whose impact on their environment is considerable. However, since individuals can be hard to follow, much of their social life is still shrouded in mystery.

Big bull males hold territories consisting of small, linear strips of shoreline and bank, which they defend against other aggressive bulls. Non-territorial males group together and, so long as they are submissive to the territorial bulls, are allowed free access. Females live within a territory but there may be no social bonds, except for those between mothers and their calves.

However, new research by William Barklow has revealed that their communication system is unique and sophisticated: 'Hippos may well transmit sounds in stereo to

both air and water and can receive sounds in stereo, with their jaws serving as the under-water channel and their ears the surface channel.' Pitch and harmonics are so varied that the variety of sound is capable of communicating subtle information. Such vocal complexity is also found in some other mammal species, all of which have sophisti-cated social systems, so the hippos' social structure may be more complex than previ-ously thought.

Primarily grass eaters, they can wander up to 11 km (7 miles) inland to graze, following well-worn trails and resting in temporary wallows. Hippos pluck grass with their lips and are expert at cropping low-creeping species. Usually returning to the water before dawn, hippos spend the day digesting, saving energy and defecating in liberal amounts. Defecating with such gay abandon means hippos are immensely beneficial to the aquatic food chain since they help to speed up the vital replenishment of nutrients.

Hippos are also important builders of the landscape. They habitually follow the same trails which, in marshy conditions, serve an important function as drainage channels. On dry land, hippo trails leading away from rivers can quickly form deep gullies. The topsoil washed down these gullies into a lake or river eventually forms an alluvial fan. In particular, hippos have a significant effect on the compli-cated system of channels and water courses in the Okavango Delta.

Hippo surprises

Despite their avuncular appearance, hippos have carnivorous tendencies – recent reports tell of hippos killing and feeding on a male impala and there is even a case of cannibalism. In complete contrast, a hippo

3

was observed apparently saving an impala that had been chased into the water by wild dogs, by guiding the exhausted animal back to dry land.

The last surprise in the hippo tale dates to 1989. It was the first continent-wide estimate of the total population and the result was a count of only 170,000 animals. This was so much lower than many people had expected that hippos were given some measure of legal protection under the CITES convention.

3. Daytime watery refuges tend to be overcrowded and the heavily developed canines and incisors take the brunt of fighting.

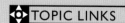

TOPIC LINKS

3.1 Africa's Fresh Water
p.87 An evolutionary perspective

There is one lake in Africa where, in the half light of dawn, steam wraps the shore in mystery. There is a cacophony of noise from hundreds of thousands of birds that are largely unseen. Occasionally, pale shapes appear, then vanish once more, swallowed up by the clouds of dense, white mist.

Every few seconds there is a rumbling roar and the ground shakes as a geyser jets water high into the pale turquoise sky. A million water drops fall into a small rivulet that gurgles over threads of bright copper and emerald-green algae. This is Lake Bogoria in Kenya and it is one of the best feeding grounds for lesser flamingos.

But Lake Bogoria is only one of many lakes in Africa. This continent contains lakes of an almost infinite variety, from freshwater lakes to caustic lakes of soda. There are tiny lakes that are like oases in this dry continent and lakes so huge that they are more like inland seas.

Previous page: Elephants are the largest land animals alive today but it is hard to appreciate just how big they are until other animals nearby give you a sense of scale.

THE BIGGEST AND THE DEEPEST

Lake Victoria is as big as Ireland. It is the biggest lake in Africa, and in terms of surface area it is the second largest in the world. Its waters are fresh but relatively shallow with 180 m (600 feet) or so being its greatest depth. The middle of the lake receives some 200 to 250 cm (80–100 inches) of rain every year – far more than anywhere on the shoreline – and the lake is quick to rise dramatically, inundating the surrounding land. Lake Victoria is also full of fish.

At the beginning of the century there were over 300 different kinds of fish here, most of them unique to the lake. Then, 30 years ago, people introduced one more – the Nile perch.

Fossil records show that the Nile perch once flourished here but died out for some unknown reason. In its absence other species thrived, but with the reintroduction about half of the native kinds disappeared, for the Nile perch is huge – and it eats fish. The waters of Lake Victoria have always been productive and, today, Nile perch is a major part of the catch. Individual weights of 40 kg (88 lbs) are commonplace but the record stands at 200 kg (440 lbs), a truly enormous fish that did not get away.

The waters are also the source of an extraordinary phenomenon. Some of the first white explorers that travelled into the heart of Africa told tales of lakes that smoked, as if on fire. At times, billows of smoke do apparently rise and drift across Lake Victoria but, in fact,

In prehistoric times, the Makgadikgadi pans were part of the largest lake Africa has ever seen. Covering 250,000 sq km (96,500 sq miles), it was far larger than the present-day Lake Victoria.

1. At Lake Nakuru in Kenya, on an average day, 300,000 lesser flamingos remove about 180 tonnes (162 tons) of blue-green algae.

these choking clouds are swarms composed of uncountable billions of lakeflies.

Like Lake Victoria, Lake Tanganyika just misses out on a world record, losing to Lake Baikal in Siberia. With a maximum depth of 1470 m (4820 feet), Lake Tanganyika is the second deepest lake in the world. However, recent measurements show that a layer of sediment, several hundred metres thick, lies on the bottom of the lake, which could mean that the real depth is considerably greater.

The waters are among the clearest of any lake in the world and, oddly, the temperature is relatively stable, with a drop of only 3°C (6°F) between the top and the bottom. The waters of Lake Tanganyika are warm all year round and it is one of only three lakes in the world, all of them African, that contain 'fossil' water. Fossil or 'relict' waters are of great interest to scientists since, as the writer Anthony Smith says, 'they are time capsules from previous ages and can therefore provide undisturbed information about the past'. In Lake Tanganyika, these waters are the result of huge volumes of dead water which are never circulated by currents, a

situation unlikely to occur in similar lakes in more temperate regions, which experience great variations in temperature.

The waters are 'dead' because they are rich in hydrogen sulphide and so deficient in oxygen that no life can survive in them. At the northern end of the lake, the depth of water suitable for life is a mere 45 m (147 feet), while at the southern end it is more like 200 m (656 feet). But this is still incredibly shallow compared with the world's oceans, which contain life to depths of 11,000 m (36,000 feet).

Although it offers only a small window of opportunity for life, the fish of Lake Tanganyika have taken full advantage of it and have evolved into some of the most weird and wonderful fish found anywhere in the world.

The cichlid story

Lake Tanganyika is the grandfather of the great African lakes. It is about 3 to 6 million years old, whereas Lake Malawi, which is similar in size and configuration, is only about 2 million years old and much shallower.

Lake Victoria is even younger still. However, all of these three lakes have one thing in common – they are populated by cichlid fish.

'You may note that the waters are Nature's storehouse in which she locks up her wonders,' wrote Isaak Walton in *The Compleat Angler*, and cichlids are certainly amazing fish. The zoologist, Jonathan Kingdon, says that the separate and independent development of cichlid fish in each of the three great lake systems rivals even the fauna of the Galápagos as an example of evolution. From different sets of ancestors, the cichlids have radiated into a similar range of types, despite major physical differences between the three lakes. Cichlids are different to other fish species in several ways. Their skulls and body proportions change easily, and even more importantly, they invest in relatively small numbers of carefully tended eggs instead of spawning a superabundance of eggs whose survival is left to chance.

Today, many cichlid species in these lakes go by the descriptive name of 'mouthbrooders'. After spawning, they take the eggs

★ Many cichlid fish have mouths that are so capacious they can easily accommodate some 1000 eggs. After hatching, the fry are also brooded in the mouth.

1. An arena of cichlid nests. Measuring about 60 cm (24 inches) in diameter, the crater-like nests are excavated from the sand by the male fish.

2. Lake Tanganyika and the Mahale Mountains. Two thirds of the fish in Tanganyika are cichlids (150 species in total).

into their mouths, where they hatch, and only let the fry out when they can fend for themselves. Because they have a much less hazardous start to life than the fry of other fish, a higher proportion survives to adulthood. There is also a rapid turnover of generations since cichlids mature and breed quickly. So, in the evolutionary race to colonize Africa's lakes, the fish that reproduce more slowly and less successfully have been left out of the picture, while the cichlids have romped ahead.

One day in the distant future the clear and sparkling waters of Lake Tanganyika will change, for the Ruizisi River and others that flow into the lake are bringing in silt and rocks. Slowly but surely, the lake is filling up with sediment and one day, who knows, perhaps millions of flamingos will have taken the place of the cichlids.

2

 ## WEIRD AND WONDERFUL CICHLID

In Lakes Victoria, Tanganyika and Malawi there is a vast array of weird and wonderful cichlid fish; some are vegetarians, some are carnivorous. And a few of these have peculiar adaptations. Cichlids (right) with the sinister name of the 'kiss of death' fish suck the eggs and fry out of their mouth-brooding cousins. Others tackle the matter head-on. Known as 'rammers', these cichlids have powerful weapons. Upturned jaws are used to hit other females, forcing them to expel their eggs or fry.

Some cichlids have taken ambushing tactics to the extreme. One hogs the limelight as a highly successful actor. Falling out of the shoal, it effectively buries itself in the sand and plays dead. Other cichlids curiously swim over to scavenge from the lifeless corpse, only to fall victim to a fish that is still very much alive.

Another species would not be out of place in *Alice in Wonderland*. Called the 'upside-down' fish, it is light-coloured above and darker underneath and makes a living by hunting mbuna — small cichlids that hide amongst rocks. When the mbuna rush to their refuge, the upside-down fish turns upside-down, and becomes invisible. Out come the mbuna and, somewhat inevitably, the upside-down fish gobbles them all up.

1

LAKES OF SODA

To our eyes, flamingos are the epitome of delicate beauty but in reality they are tough birds that flourish on soda lakes, the waters of which would burn our skin within minutes.

Although soda lakes are found throughout Africa, most lie on the eastern side of the continent, in the Great Rift Valley. Soda waters are created when springs or rivers become saturated with soluble mineral salts from volcanic rocks. The waters become alkaline, giving them a bitter taste and caustic properties. The character of a soda lake depends on just how alkaline the water supply is and whether or not the lake has an outlet. Lake Natron in Tanzania is one of the most extreme examples. In a typical year it receives a scant 400 mm (16 inches) of rain, but over the same period 3300 mm (130 inches) of water evaporate. In the searing heat, the salts crystallize, cracking the surface of the lake into great irregularly-shaped plates of soda, coloured blood-red by the presence of a unique form of bacteria which can cope with life in a furnace.

In contrast, the waters of Lake Turkana in northern Kenya are only very slightly alkaline, but its appearance is equally surreal. The lake has jade-green waters and, at the southern end, the skyline is interrupted by one jet-black volcanic cone, and another almost pure white. Along the shores are frozen layers of ancient, purple lava. The alkaline water that runs off these volcanic rocks is diluted by a vast wash of fresh water – almost one-sixth of its supply – from the Ethiopian River Omo.

Lake Turkana was once connected to the Nile River system and, today, as well as Nile perch, several thousand Nile crocodiles live and breed here, making Lake Turkana one of their last strongholds. Crocodiles are living history, relict creatures from an era known as the age of the reptiles, 150 million years ago.

2

1. In a very dry season, the waters can evaporate entirely from a soda lake and the surface is firm enough to support the weight of a wandering waterbuck.

2. When they hit the water from a high dive, African fish eagles close their eyes to protect them from the impact, opening them when they emerge.

FISH EATERS

The climate was so warm and damp 150 million years ago that swamps full of soft vegetation flourished. Then the world became cooler and drier, and plants became tougher to cope with the new conditions. One reason that so many of the herbivorous reptiles became extinct during this period was that their jaws and teeth could not cope with these changes in vegetation.

Reptiles are expert snappers but they cannot grind or shear. Even today, as the zoologist Harvey Croze points out, the crocodile's trap-like jaws are designed purely to open and shut. A crocodile deals with a big fish by snapping its mouth firmly shut over its victim's body. Holding it fast, the crocodile then spins its own body around by powerful corkscrew thrusts of its tail; chunks of flesh are torn, twisted off and swallowed whole.

Crocodiles can be notoriously hard to spot but the most conspicuous predators in any lake must be the fish-eating birds. Their beaks are generally similar – robust, sharp and rapier-slim. But their fishing techniques are totally dissimilar. One of the most important fish eaters in the African lakes is the pelican. Both the white- and the pink-backed species use their huge beaks as nets with which to scoop up their prey. White pelicans form groups that serenely sail the waters in a tight line formation. Then, acting in unison to a signal undetectable to humans, the line closes into a horseshoe shape and the birds dip their heads into the water. Lucky individuals catch one or two fish, their heads reappear, the line re-forms and the birds swim on.

In contrast to the easy, elegant harmony between pelicans, fish eagles rely on enormous strength and split-second timing. Like other eagles, the fish eagle hunts by stooping. As it strikes and grasps the fish below water, it is at full stall. From this position of no return, it has to take off with a heavy fish before it sinks. This display of pure bravado has earned fish eagles the luxury of hunting a relatively abundant food source and, in some areas, pairs are able to nest every 183 m (600 feet) or so.

The specialists

In shallow waters are found the masters of stealth – herons. From the huge and aptly named goliath heron to the tiny rufous-bellied heron, they fish with almost mesmeric stillness. They can stand in the reeds for minutes on end with beak poised to strike. One species has a devilish trick to play. The black heron flings open its wings into an umbrella of feathers, casting a deep shadow on the surrounding water. With deft moves of its feet, it stirs up the mud. Disturbed fish are encouraged to seek safety in this dark shelter, only to find they have unwittingly come within easy striking distance. However, herons are supreme generalists and some forage on dry land, catching anything from lizards and snakes to mice or frogs.

One of the world's rarest fishing specialists is found only in Africa – the bizarre-looking whale-headed or shoebill stork, both names reflecting its striking appearance. It is a unique bird but shares several characteristics with other species of stork as well as having some affinities with herons. Pewter-grey all over, shoebills tower a metre (over 3 feet) tall and have massive bills. The bill is a particularly effective spear when combined with the bird's weight as they thrust downwards from their great height. Their favourite catch is lungfish but they will also catch snakes, turtles and, occasionally, large frogs. Shoebills prefer to ambush these animals as they travel along pool edges or channels. Here the water is sluggish and the birds remain motionless for extremely long periods, waiting for the right moment to strike. Their range is very restricted since these conditions are only found within major swamps on slow-moving river systems.

Shoebill storks are far more than the eccentric characters they first appear to be. Their bodies are intricate and wonderful pieces of design by evolution which has honed them perfectly to fit neatly in a very particular niche. They are true specialists; the result of isolation, time and a changing environment acting together as the agents of evolution.

Africa's lakes and rivers are full of specialists. At perhaps the most extreme end of this spectrum, is a fish known as *Tilapia grahami*. It is the only fish species that can cope with hot, alkaline waters. Lake Natron in Tanzania is a soda lake that is dramatically volatile, subject to sudden, severe flooding and years of great drought. High up on the shores is a warren of tiny pools which are occasionally inundated with lake water. As the waters recede, small numbers of these fish have been left stranded. Today, many of these pools contain sub-species, all differing from each other in small details of colouration, all living in their own miniature worlds.

But specialists such as these are also the most vulnerable of all species. If their environment suddenly vanishes, so do they. Only now can we fully appreciate this because we are lucky enough to live in a time with an unprecedented accumulation of knowledge. Slowly, dedicated amateur naturalists and professional scientists are unravelling the workings of the world around us. We can begin to appreciate the complexities of life, both past and present, and that helps put our own position into perspective, for our species is just one within a brilliant kaleidoscope of organisms and species that make up life on Earth today. And some of the most extraordinary live in areas where water is in very short supply indeed – the deserts of Africa.

▷ THE LAKEFLY SWARMS

At certain times of the year, Lake Victoria and other lakes witness a phenomenon that begins near the time of a new moon.

First midge eggs hatch into almost transparent larvae or 'chironomids', which drift with the plankton. Soon they develop tiny buoyancy chambers that enable them to dive and ascend. During the night, they feed on detritus in the upper layers of water, but at dawn the larvae retreat to the bottom to feed and hide in the mud.

Two moons later, the larvae are ready to hatch into adult flies and to mate. But to maximize their chances, they must all hatch together. Far out in the lake, larvae begin to hatch and then, in a way still not fully understood, each homes in on its nearest neighbour. The swarm is born. On any one day there may be hundreds of swarms that join together to create massive, living clouds 300 m (1000 feet) high and 1.5 km (1 mile) long.

1. (opposite) Shoebill storks live a mainly solitary existence. Their huge toes enable them to move easily over floating vegetation.

SAGA OF THE FLAMEBIRDS

Even using the best superlatives and the most poetic turns of phrase, it is impossible for an observer to conjure up the visual majesty and sublime beauty of flamingos as these unusual birds feed on one of their favourite lakes. And, at night, as the flock takes wing with wild calls and undulates in long skeins against the full moon, mysteriously passing overhead on the way to unknown destinations, they truly seem to inhabit a world apart.

1

The romance and reality of the specialists

Romantically known as 'flamebirds', both lesser and greater flamingos are found in Africa, but it is the lesser flamingos that gather in huge numbers, creating one of the miracles of nature. As the zoologist and writer, Harvey Croze points out, 'specialization usually produces a marvel of design and architecture'.

Lesser flamingos feed on blue-green algae called Spirulina, which thrives on a combination of strong sunlight, high temperatures and the carbonate- and phosphate-rich waters of shallow soda lakes. The algae colour the waters a dark, opaque green and although enough sunlight for photosynthesis can only penetrate the top 25 cm (10 inches) or so, winds ruffle the surface, stirring up the water, allowing Spirulina to colonize virtually all the lake.

When the Spirulina is in bloom, the weight of the algae reaches something in the order of 200,000 tonnes (180,000 tons) in 29 sq km (15 sq miles). That is equivalent to the productivity of over 260 sq km (100 sq miles) of good grassland. But since only lesser flamingos can make the best of this harvest, their numbers can build to astonishing proportions. Ornithologists have calculated that flocks may sometimes number 2 million birds – by far the biggest gatherings of any inland waterbird in the world.

Flamingos 'graze' the top inch of the water, using a pumping mechanism to suck water in and over fine hairs inside their mandibles, filtering out the rich algae. Carotenoid pigments in the algae colour their feathers an exquisite range of pinks and reds. But their dainty, fragile appearance contrasts starkly with the world beneath their feet, for the lava rocks just below the water's surface are knife-sharp, and the water both bitter and harshly caustic. To add to their problems, Spirulina is a productive but highly unpredictable food source. After blooming for weeks, it can die out almost overnight. So flamingos must be long-distance nomads, able to fly many kilometres between soda lakes in search of algal blooms.

The breeding sites

Specialization brings advantages but it also has its bad points. And it is, perhaps, at their breeding sites that these birds are most vulnerable. The whole African population of 4 or 5 million birds depends on just two main breeding sites: Lake Natron in Tanzania and the Makgadikgadi pans in Botswana.

Lake Natron must be one of the world's harshest nurseries. Here, daytime temperatures are so high that the air is like the heat from an oven. The temperature of the mud on the surface has been measured at 60–65°C (140–150°F). However, Lake Natron is ideal for flamingos. The lake is big and shallow enough for the birds to build huge nesting colonies right in the middle. Painstakingly gathering small globules of mud in their beaks, they build cone-shaped nests to elevate the eggs and chicks a few vital inches out of the boiling hot soda mud. Here they are safe – the miles of sinking mud separating the colonies from the shore and deterring even the most foolhardy of land-based predators.

2

But both Lake Natron and Makgadikgadi are as unpredictable as the flamingos' food supply. Sudden rains can flood the colonies, killing thousands of chicks, or a run of dry years may mean no nesting at all. A successful breeding year for even a tenth of the world's flamingo population can be a rare event.

A fitting tribute to lesser flamingos comes from Leslie Brown, a spirited and dedicated naturalist who, after years of perseverance,

was the first person to find the breeding site on Lake Natron in 1954:

'I did not dream that they would give me the adventures I have had, that I would more nearly come to a sticky end in their pursuit than at any other time in my life, that they would force me to learn to fly myself, or that I would behold beauty transcending all my wildest imaginings. But they gave me all these things, and all I ever asked of them as well.'

1. Individuals move from the harsh alkaline lake waters to the fresher spring waters to bathe and drink.

2. Lesser flamingos are highly social birds that gather in huge numbers along the edges of soda lakes to preen and rest.

 **TOPIC LINKS**

3.3 Africa's Lakes
p.110 Lakes of soda

| 4 | |

DESERTS

UNDER THE GLARE

Because of its sheer size and position on the Earth's surface, Africa is a relatively dry continent. Apart from the Equator, mountain ranges and coastal strips – which benefit from the rain coming off the surrounding oceans – the rest of the continent receives very little moisture indeed, and in the harshest places rain may not fall for years at a time. The driest and largest desert in the world is the Sahara, which covers one-fifth of the African continent, and the most ancient is the Namib, at 80 million years old. Along with these famous deserts, drylands cover virtually the entire Horn of Africa, and most of the southwest, including the Kalahari and the Karoo.

Deserts pose the toughest challenges to African wildlife. Freezing cold nights follow burning hot days, the solar radiation is intense, moisture is scant and unpredictable, and food and shelter are in short supply. Yet, despite this adversity, animals and plants have found ingenious ways to survive.

Previous page: The majestic dunes of the Namib desert.

1. *Welwitschia mirabilis* – one of the toughest plants in the Namib desert. Individuals may live for over 1000 years.

WATER – THE CURRENCY OF LIFE

Life on Earth evolved in water, and today no animal or plant can live without it. In deserts, water is the currency of life. It is scarce, difficult to obtain regularly, and disappears rapidly. The health and success of animals and plants depend on them maintaining a healthy water balance, matching fluid lost with fluid gained. Water can be lost in a variety of ways – by evaporation across the body surface or leaves, by breathing, sweating, excreting, lactating and laying eggs. Being unable to escape the heat, desert plants have evolved some of the most ingenious ways to reduce water loss.

Plant design

By minimizing the surface area they present to the sun and wind, and maximizing their capacity for storing water, desert plants can dramatically reduce their water loss. The most practical designs for this are the spherical and barrel-shaped stems, branches and leaves which are found among many African desert succulent plants such as euphorbias and stone plants. Stone plants such as Lithops, Fenestraria and Haworthia have just a pair of small barrel-shaped leaves which lie virtually hidden underground – significantly reducing the surface area over which water can be lost. The broad, fleshy leaves of *Massonia depressa* lie flat on the ground, helping it to trap moisture during the night and preventing water loss from the soil and the bulb beneath them.

Some plants take a different approach – acacias have tiny leaves which help to minimize evaporation, and they can even fold up during the middle of the day when solar radiation is greatest. The nara plant of the Namib Desert goes a step further, having lost its leaves altogether – its tough green stems and thorns carrying out all photosynthesis for the plant.

Desert plants can also reduce water loss through the design of their surface layers. Most succulents are covered by a protective coating of fats and oils embedded in wax and some, like Psammaphora (from the Greek 'sand bearing'), even have sticky leaves with which to trap windblown sand. Not only does this further reduce water loss, but it helps camouflage and defend the plant from any browser tempted to take a gritty mouthful. Spines, thorns and close-packed branches are still another way of saving water as they help trap air pockets, which provide an effective barrier against evaporation.

Animal tactics

Unlike plants, desert animals can escape the dry heat by shading, burrowing or emerging only at night or when rain arrives. However,

1. The fog-basking beetle of the Namib climbs to the tops of dunes on foggy mornings to intercept moisture.

2. Male ostriches fighting. Although ostriches are flightless, their sheer size, speed and powerful kicking legs make them a formidable adversary for any desert predator.

evaporation from the surface layers, breathing, sweating and excretion must all be carefully controlled. Like desert plants, the tenebrionid beetles of the Namib have a waterproof cuticle with layers of fats and wax. Near the Atlantic coast, where humidity is highest, these layers are thinner and the beetles appear mostly black, but further inland the humidity is less and the beetles are a blue-black or white colour – reflecting more extensive layers of protective waxy blooms. To further reduce water loss, tenebrionid beetles have given up the power of flight. Their wing cases or 'elytra' are fused down the middle and sides to form a solid case with just a single opening to the outside at the rear, through which they breathe. In terms of saving water, this is much more effective than the usual insect design of a series of small breathing holes or 'spiracles' opening directly to the outside.

Compared with insects, mammals and birds lose large amounts of water through their moist nasal passages. Exhaled air is almost always saturated with moisture from the nose and lungs, but some desert animals – such as rodents and antelope – have relatively large nasal passages for their size. When they inhale the dry desert air, extensive evaporation occurs inside the nasal passages, cooling the nasal surfaces. Then, when they exhale warmer and saturated air back across these surfaces, it is rapidly cooled, so carrying slightly less water vapour than it would at normal body temperature.

Only two African desert animals with short nasal passages have come up with a way of reducing the amount of water vapour in exhaled air – the camel and the ostrich – both of which can live in the harshest places. The exhaled air of the ostrich may be saturated as little 87 per cent and 3–4°C (5–7°F) cooler than

WATER STORAGE

Given the unpredictability and shortages of water in the desert, animals and plants that are able to store it have an obvious advantage. Succulent plants have expandable cells in their stems and leaves which fill during wet periods, and as water is gradually used up in the dry months they slowly shrink. Many other desert plants have large underground water-storage organs – the tubers of the gemsbok cucumber can hold about half a litre (about 1 pint) of water each. These are highly sought after by creatures like gemsbok, porcupines and brown hyenas. Damara molerats (▷ p. 127), which live permanently underground in the Kalahari, rely exclusively on bulbs, corms and tubers like the gemsbok cucumber for water as they cannot drink – their lips are unusually situated behind their front teeth so they do not swallow sand when they are burrowing.

But water-storing plants can also exploit the seemingly destructive attentions of animals. In the Namib Desert the moisture-laden fruits of nara plants are in demand by creatures like elephants, cape foxes and gemsbok. In return for the food and water they temptingly offer, the nara plants benefit by having their seeds carried in the animals' stomachs to new destinations.

2

its body temperature. The bird's long neck and trachea and its wide and complex nasal passages are clearly important designs for cooling the exhaled air, but it is still a mystery why it is not fully saturated.

Capturing water

In balancing water loss, animals and plants need to find ways to replenish their fluid levels. Because desert rains are unpredictable, few mammals rely on regular drinking, but elephants, black rhinos, spotted hyenas and chacma baboons must ensure their home ranges include some form of permanent water. However, most desert herbivores, such as springbok and addax, get nearly all the water they need directly from plants. In fact, the addax is so efficient at absorbing water

that its moisture-laden rumen has long been prized by nomadic Saharan hunters.

Like mammals, many desert birds can survive without regular drinking but some, like the Namaqua sandgrouse, cannot. Air-dried seeds, which have a very low water content, are their main diet, and so Namaqua sandgrouse must drink regularly. During the breeding season, the male sandgrouse soak their belly feathers in the water and carry this precious cargo back to the nest, where the chicks can strip the liquid off with their beaks – a remarkable adaptation for desert life.

Most desert plants depend on absorbing water through their roots, and are commonly found along drainage lines, among rock fissures or on the tops of dunes – wherever there is an increased likelihood of trapping soil moisture or dew. *Stipagrostis* grasses in the

Namib Desert have thin, blade-like leaves which can channel dew droplets either inwards to their core roots or outwards to their tips, creating strategically positioned drips to roots spread just beneath the sand. Amazingly, some desert lichens have done away with roots altogether, and spend most of their lives in a dried-out state. At the slightest hint of rain or fog they can unfurl and photosynthesize before the sun returns them to a desiccated state once again.

One of the most remarkable methods of water gathering is practised by tenebrionid beetles in the Namib. One species, *Onymacris unguicularis*, staggers to the tops of dunes in the early morning to fog-bask. It stands head-down facing the incoming fog, which condenses on its body and runs down to its mouth.

SUMMER EVERY DAY, WINTER EVERY NIGHT

With so little water vapour in the air to impede the sun's penetrative rays, and so few plants on the ground to absorb its energy, deserts receive more solar radiation than anywhere on Earth. The bombardment of radiation by day, and its rapid escape at night, result in extremes of temperature – ground temperatures in the Kalahari Desert in Southern Africa can climb to 75°C (167°F) by day and plunge well below freezing at night. How do animals and plants cope with this stress?

Internal control: mammals and birds

Being warm-blooded, mammals and birds control their own body temperatures, and must maintain them between strict operational limits – approximately 34–38°C (93–100°F) for mammals and 39–42°C (102–8°F) for birds. Although this gives them the freedom to be active day or night, and through summer or winter, it also means they must be very careful not to overheat radically or cool off.

Fur and feathers both trap layers of air and this helps impede the flow of temperature to and from the body. Small desert antelope like springbok carefully use their fur to control their body temperature. When the air temperature exceeds 30°C (86°F) they often orientate themselves in line with the sun's direction, so minimizing the amount of solar radiation striking them. They will also sometimes raise a layer of white pronk hairs on their lower back which, together with their white belly fur, helps them to reflect 75 per cent of solar radiation. However, because their fur is thin, springbok suffer terribly on cold nights, shivering to keep warm.

Being highly social, meerkats huddle together in their burrows at night to keep warm and, come dawn, emerge to bask in the warming sun. When the temperature gets too hot they either move into the shade of a bush, or scrape away the surface layers of soil and lie on their bellies on the cooler ground beneath. The ground squirrel uses very similar tactics to the meerkat, but benefits further in having a long, bushy tail, under which it can shade itself during the hottest times of day.

Just as mammals use their fur to control their temperature, desert birds use their feathers. Ostriches use their large wings as umbrellas to shade their bodies and naked thighs, drooping the tips and at the same time

 THERMAL SHELTERS

One way in which desert animals can control their body temperature is to build their own thermal shelters. The sociable weaver birds of Southern Africa build huge communal nests, which can be up to 6 m (20 feet) long and 2 m (6½ feet) high, in the branches of camelthorn and kokerboom trees, on telegraph poles and even on windmill platforms – wherever there is a raised sturdy structure. These nests (right), built out of grass over years, can weigh more than a tonne and contain up to 50 individual compartments, each with an entrance on the underside.

During winter, the air temperature in Southern Africa's deserts often drops to 0°C (32°F), yet air pockets trapped in the thatch can keep the nest temperature as much as 20°C (36°F) warmer than the outside temperature. Most of this warmth is generated by the weavers themselves, which huddle together in the compartments. In summer, the situation is reversed: the nest acts as a valuable shade umbrella, maintaining temperatures below those outside. To further dispel heat from the nest the weavers spread themselves singly around the compartments. An important consequence of having a buffered nest temperature is that sociable weavers can breed at any time of year, providing enough food is available.

1 & 2. The Namaqua chameleon uses its skin pigmentation to control its body temperature, turning white to offload heat and black to absorb it.

raising the back feathers to allow the breeze to offload excess body heat. On cold nights they sit tightly on the ground, their legs tucked beneath. It is the chicks of desert birds that are most susceptible to overheating. Male and female Sclater's larks take turns to shade their chick by standing over it with wings drooping as the other searches for food. At times, when the chick is left alone it lifts its head and opens its mouth in the direction of the incoming breeze. A bizarre tuft of spiky feathers on its head probably serves to scatter solar radiation!

External control: insects, amphibians and reptiles

Being cold-blooded, insects, amphibians and reptiles are unable to self-regulate their body temperatures. However, by moving between shade and sun they can offload and absorb heat. The disadvantage of being at the mercy of

the weather is that cold-blooded animals cannot be active all the time, but when they are inactive and their temperature drops they can save a lot of energy, which is very valuable in deserts where food and water may be scarce.

Most cold-blooded desert animals are active in the morning and afternoon when the air temperature is most comfortable, but some have special adaptations for keeping active at the very hottest time of day. The Namib ant (*Ocymyrmex robustior*) uses this period to hunt for prey which have become heat-stressed and are easier to capture. It can withstand sand surface temperatures up to 67°C (153°F), but only by thermal respiting – periodically climbing 1–2 cm (½–1 inch) up objects like grass blades or pebbles. This small elevation brings the ant to temperatures as much as 15°C (27°F) less than on the sand itself. Six seconds are all it needs to cool itself by about 6°C (11°F)! The desert beetle (*Stenocara phalangium*) is another extraordinary heat-specialist,

⭐ With a top speed of over 1 metre (3 feet) per second, the tenebrionid beetle *Onymacris plana* has solved the problem of crossing scorching sand by running faster than any other insect on earth.

which keeps above the burning sand on stilts – its legs are the longest of any beetle in the world. It lives on gravelly plains so is unable to burrow beneath the surface to cool off. Like the ant, it takes advantage of small stones to lift itself up to cooler air when the going gets tough.

The shovel-snouted lizard remains buried in the sand at dawn until the sand temperature warms it to an operational temperature. While warming, the lizard pokes just its head out of the sand and this absorbs heat, which is carried to the rest of its body via the blood. When foraging the lizard can tolerate temperatures over 40°C (104°F), but when the sand gets too hot it stiffens its legs, lifting itself as high as possible. Sometimes it will also raise its front and back legs alternately to cool them in an amusing 'thermal dance'!

Rooted to the spot: plants

Unlike the desert animals, plants are unable to move and must take the full force of the desert sun. Although they can tolerate much wider temperature fluctuations than animals, they have evolved some intriguing designs for reducing the impact of the sun's harmful rays. Spines, scales and bumps help to scatter and reflect solar radiation and create pockets of air that buffer temperature extremes. The waxy blooms of desert succulents also increase solar reflectivity, and some plants further protect themselves by retaining a layer of dead leaves to protect the new, tender ones.

Another tactic of many desert plants such as many mesembs and euphorbias is to send their spiky leaves and stems directly upwards, so minimizing the surface area they present to the sun. The 'half-men' plants of northern Namaqualand in Southern Africa provide an example of this. Their stems point upwards and are crowned by a clump of leaves that provide shade for the stem below. Furthermore, all half-men plants lean to the north and this allows their leaves to receive the maximum amount of sunshine during the short winter growing season.

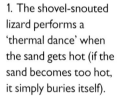

1. The shovel-snouted lizard performs a 'thermal dance' when the sand gets hot (if the sand becomes too hot, it simply buries itself).

2. Most people think of deserts as hot places, but nights can be freezing cold, which is why many nocturnal animals – like the brown hyena – have thick, shaggy coats. The hyena raises this when alarmed.

1

2

1

FINDING FOOD

Once the problems of solar radiation and water shortage have been overcome, desert organisms must also find sufficient food – no easy task in Africa's bleakest environment. For plants that manufacture sugars by photosynthesis, availability of water is the main limiting factor for growth, but desert animals have full control over how, when and where they find and gather food.

Because digestion in ruminants is a slow process (▷ p. 197), many desert herbivores are very fussy about what they eat. The Damara dik-dik, which lives in the Kalahari, is a tiny antelope weighing only 5 kg (11 lbs) and with a high metabolic rate. It cannot afford the long time needed to digest cellulose so it avoids woody shrubs and concentrates its feeding on young shoots, flowers and fruits. In this way, food stays in its stomach for up to only 20 hours – the fastest fermentation among all African ungulates.

Larger ruminants can get by bulk-feeding on poor-quality plants because the energy demands for their size are relatively lower. African elephants need up to 300 kg (660 lbs) of roughage a day, yet they still manage to survive in the hostile deserts of northern Namibia. They manage this by being careful not to heavily damage the limited food that they can find – in fact, it has been shown that the Namib elephants do less damage to trees than floods, drought and fires. However, the secret to the survival of these 80 or so elephants is their ability to travel up to 30 km (19 miles) a day between waterholes and good grazing.

Living off detritus

Among the shifting sands of the Namib Desert few plants other than tough grasses can survive, yet this barren land supports a

2

1. A desert elephant reaching for seed pods in a desert floodplain in Namibia.

2. To avoid swallowing sand while digging underground, Damara molerats have teeth in front of their lips.

whole chain of life built on detritus – wind-blown bits of dead plants and seeds – which accumulate on the slipfaces of dunes. Tenebrionid beetles, fishmoths and termites are among the few insects that have evolved enzymes to digest the cellulose in the detritus, and they in turn support a much wider community of birds, lizards, moles, spiders and reptiles. In fact, so important is detritus in the Namib, that male shovel-snouted lizards compete for dune territories that have the most reliable accumulations of detritus and beetles, the best of which can support three breeding females.

In terms of numbers, termites outweigh all other insect groups in Southern Africa. A single colony of harvester termites may be thousands-strong, and by day and night the workers tirelessly collect strips of grass from desert detritus and parched clumps of grass, which they carry back to their underground nest. There, the grass is stored in vast quanti-ties, but unlike most African termites, which feed on fungus grown in special chambers, harvester termites feed directly on the plants they collect. To do this they have evolved a special collection of cellulose-digesting micro-organisms in their hindguts. By

recycling dead plants so efficiently, harvester termites are undoubtedly the most important decomposers in the deserts of Southern Africa.

Teamwork

Social insects may be the epitome of group success, but many other animals benefit by collaborating in the search for food in deserts, especially as it can often be widely dispersed and short-lived. Brown hyenas live in clans of up to 10 individuals and are nocturnal omni-vores, scavenging anything edible from leftover carcasses and insects to fruits and birds' eggs – in fact, some 58 different types of food have been identified in their droppings. All clan members help to find food and provision the cubs at the den, travelling up to 30 km (19 miles) a night within their home ranges, which can be over 1000 sq km (386 sq miles) in size. Clan members advertise ownership by scent-mark-ing grasses and bushes with a pungent paste and studies have shown that over a year a single clan left approximately 145,000 marks throughout their property! Interestingly, brown hyenas can leave two different types of marking – a white paste, which is long-lasting

and probably serves to warn rival clans to keep out, and a short-lasting black paste, which may inform fellow clan members of the individual's identity. More importantly, it is thought that this chemical message may also tell clan members that the area has already been recently searched for food.

Perhaps the most extraordinary social mammal in Africa is the Damara molerat, which lives in the Kalahari Desert. It is so social that biologists categorize it along with bees, ants and termites as eusocial – with a single queen, soldiers and different types of workers! Damara molerats live exclusively underground and rely on bulbs, corms and tubers, which they find by random burrowing. However, in dry conditions these are widely dispersed and in the southern Kalahari a single molerat would have a less than 10 per cent chance of finding a tuber before dying of starvation. But a colony of 25 molerats all seeking food would have near-certain success. Furthermore, during the winter months, when the soil is damper and therefore easier to burrow through, molerats are most active and hoard bulbs in under-ground larders, as a provision for the leaner months ahead.

THE DESERTS OF AFRICA

Africa is a relatively dry continent, with more than 60 per cent of the continent's surface consisting of low-rainfall or desert areas. African deserts are not just endless expanses of sand dunes – they can be gravel plains, mountain ranges, seasonal pans or even wooded grasslands, depending on their origins, location, age and amount of rain they receive. Deserts are commonly classed in three categories depending on their average annual rainfall: extremely arid deserts (up to 100 mm/ 4 inches), such as the Namib and the Sahara; arid deserts (100–250 mm/4–10 inches), such as the Karoo and the Horn of Africa; and semi-arid deserts (250–500 mm/10–20 inches), such as the Kalahari. In all of these places the rainfall is also highly unpredictable, infrequent and variable from year to year.

1

The Sahara
The Sahara is the largest true desert in the world – its dry heart is about as large as the USA and it covers over 20 per cent of Africa. It is so vast that moisture-laden clouds may not penetrate the interior for years on end. It is the eroded remains of extremely ancient mountain ranges and today is a mosaic of sand dunes, gravel plains, dry riverbeds and rocky highlands. Over its history the Sahara's climate has changed radically, pulsing wet and dry. At times it has been inundated by the oceans and swept by mighty rivers, at other times it has been covered in wooded grass-lands and cut by rivers and vast lakes. But during the last 2.5 million years, a steady period of climate desiccation, combined with the recent impacts of wood-cutting, livestock grazing and marginal land cultivation, have brought the Sahara to its current arid state.

The Horn of Africa
The other great dry region of Africa north of the equator is the Horn of Africa, which includes all of Somalia, eastern Ethiopia, Eritrea, Djibouti and parts of northern Kenya. This region is a very ancient and relatively stable corner of Africa with a rich variety of dry-adapted animals and plants. Although consistently drier than the Sahara, it too has witnessed numerous climate shifts and become increasingly arid in the last 6000 years, with the keeping of domestic livestock further aggravating the situation. However, the presence of species such as the oryx and Kirk's dik-dik in the Horn as well as in Southern Africa suggests that these two regions were once linked by desert.

Deserts of Southern Africa
The deserts of Southern Africa are among the

most ancient and persistently dry regions in the world. They can be broadly divided into three key regions. The Arid Savannah is an area of semi-arid deserts, typified by the Kalahari, which are dominated by grasses and woody trees or shrubs and subject to short, intense summer storms. The Karoo Desert is a vast arid (and often mountainous) region of dwarf shrubs and can be further subdivided into the Succulent Karoo, which is a low winter rainfall area and the Nama Karoo, a region of slightly higher summer rainfall. The third region is the True Desert – extremely arid and typified by the Namib – a sea of sand and gravel plains with meagre rainfall but life-supporting coastal fogs. Annuals are the dominant plants here.

Though it is true that deserts generally support less life than most other environments, long periods of a relatively stable climate have allowed the deserts of Southern Africa to evolve and nurture the richest diversity of life of all the deserts in the world.

2

1. Male gemsbok frequently spar for females, or in defending waterholes from rivals.

2. The Namib Desert. The term 'desert' derives from the Latin *desertus*, meaning 'abandoned'.

◈ TOPIC LINKS

THE GREAT SAHARA

The Sahara is the world's greatest desert, stretching across northern Africa from the Atlantic Ocean to the Red Sea – 9 million sq km (3.5 million sq miles) of dunes, mountains and rocky plains. At its bleak heart, where rain may not fall for years on end, the landscape is almost lunar – scoured and sculpted by wind over millions of years. However, even in these seemingly 'dead spots' the land is not completely lifeless – tiny particles of vegetation carried by wind from the farthest margins of the desert support fragile communities of animals and people, with scattered oases providing life-giving water.

The Sahara has not always been so. Throughout its history it has witnessed great shifts in climate – at times it has been flooded by the ocean and swept by mighty rivers. Even relatively recently, parts of it were covered in forest and grassland, and inhabited by hippos, giraffes and elephant, as beautifully illustrated in the magnificent rock art that adorns the region.

WORLD OF CHANGE

The birth of the Sahara was not a sudden or catastrophic event, but proceeded by fits and starts. Today's desert is the result of thousands of millions of years of geological and climatic change – a period in which mountains rose and fell, the oceans flooded the land and retreated, windblown sands filled ancient lakes and river courses, and savannah turned to desert.

The steady drying out of the Sahara can be broadly attributed to a few key events over the last 100 million years, the most notable being the slow, northerly drift of Africa across the globe, which brought the Sahara region from wet equatorial to dry tropical latitudes. Furthermore, the closing of the Mediterranean basin meant that Saharan Africa effectively became the western limb of a vast desert stretching all the way across Arabia to the Himalayas, bringing it under the influence of an easterly jet stream of dry, subsiding air – and further from oceanic moisture-bearing clouds. Glaciation in Antarctica and the development of the cold coastal Benguela Current in the Atlantic further contributed to the Sahara's increasing aridity.

Today, air currents circulating over this vast, arid body of land prevent little moisture from gathering. In winter, clouds from the Mediterranean region push south to the desert's northern fringes and in spring tropical clouds from West Africa move north, spreading over the southern Sahara – but rarely do these meet in the interior. Some places are denied rain for 10 years at a time.

In more recent times, particularly over the last 2.5 million years, shifting climatic patterns have brought wet and dry cycles to the Sahara. The last dry period ended about 12,000 years ago following the last ice age, and for the next 6000 years the Sahara

became a fertile land of lakes and rivers, at times heavily vegetated with savannah. Since then, however, under both human and climatic influences, the desert has progressively dried once again.

The once-green Sahara

The changes that swept the Sahara are today exquisitely preserved among Stone Age rock art and human artefacts. Within the last 10,000 years the Sahara has been home not only to elephants and rhinos, but buffalo, giraffe, reedbuck, roan, greater kudu and hippopotamus. Stunning rock paintings by the people of Tassili document the rise and fall of their culture. About 7000 years ago they were hunters who pursued giraffe, antelopes and other savannah animals.

1. The shimmer of a Tuareg camel caravan crossing the western Tenere desert, Sahara.

1. A lion depicted in rock art from the northwestern Sahara.

2. The desert monitor is the largest lizard in the Sahara.

Then they took to the breeding of cattle and their 5000-year-old murals depict immense herds. During this 'golden age' of the Sahara, these cattle-herders also hunted gazelles, giraffe and mouflon (also known as Barbary sheep) with bows and arrows and dogs to track and bring down prey. Finally, from about 1500 years ago their pictures show the appearance of horses and chariots – and then, much later, camels imported from Arabia – reflecting a much harsher climate. Soon after this their culture was obliterated by military conquest.

Although much of the original savannah wildlife of the Sahara has either been steadily eradicated by climate change and human pressure – or retreated towards the edges of the expanding desert – some fascinating creatures still survive in remote enclaves where there is sufficient moisture and adequate human protection.

Islands of life

Mountains and rocky areas make up a large proportion of the Sahara's total surface area. The larger massifs, like the Hoggar, Air and Tibesti, all harbour considerable water resources in the form of springs and rain-fed pools and these are an important resource for many Saharan mammals like the mouflon, especially during the hottest months. Mouflon, like the sheep and goats to which they are distantly related, can feed on a wide variety of plants, and among their favourites are the thorn trees, *Acacia ehrenbergiana* and *A. tortilis*. When these trees are in fruit, mouflon will sometimes ram the trunks with their skulls to dislodge the energy-rich pods. Long prized by hunters for their skin (for tents) and meat, mouflon are extremely wary and seldom leave their mountain strongholds, except during the wet season when they come

down to remote valleys to rut. Here, they have few natural predators except the occasional cheetah or leopard.

These rocky enclaves, where typically Mediterranean trees like myrtles, olives and cypresses can still be found, are also home to isolated populations of anubis baboons, patas monkeys, rock and bush hyraxes and warthogs. As recently as 1932 there were even lions in the Aïr Mountains. Among the Ennedi Mountains in Tchad, isolated pools of fresh water, which were once linked to the Nile, even contain a relic population of just four crocodiles, surrounded by a desert expanse! Though savannah species have steadily retreated to these moister islands in the face of increasing aridity, out on the parched plains where the vegetation became dominated by quick-growing annuals, a small number of well-adapted herbivores took advantage of a vast and expanding habitat.

EXPERTS IN SURVIVAL

Just as the mouflon reigns supreme in the mountains, the desert sands are the realm of the addax. Despite a dumpy appearance, its short legs, level back and broad hooves are ideal for long-distance trekking across sand in search of food – and it can penetrate more deeply into the Sahara than any other herbivore, even the camel. Once common across the Sahara, hunting has reduced the addax's range to small pockets of remote desert in Niger, Mali and Chad, where it subsists on coarse grasses, acacia and herbs such as Indigofera – from which it can extract just about all the moisture it needs.

A close relative of the addax, but one that inhabits the semi-desert fringes of the Sahara, is the scimitar-horned oryx. Though now nearly extinct in its natural habitat (except for about 1000 individuals in Chad and Niger), only a few centuries ago the population inhabiting the sub-Saharan

grasslands must have been enormous – rather like the Serengeti wildebeest or the North American plains bison. Traditionally hunted by Tuareg people for their meat and tough hides – used for battle shields and even shoeing horses – it was the motor vehicle, which allowed hunters to pursue herds to the remotest places, as well as intense competition with domestic livestock, that spelled the oryx's downfall.

The gazelles have been the most successful of all the Saharan ungulates. Of the five species found within the limits of the Sahara, the Dorcas gazelle is the most widespread. Mainly active at night, they rely on a protein-rich diet of herbs, succulents and shoots of shrubs from which they can extract adequate moisture. Gazelles are brilliantly designed to cope with desert life. During the day they can withstand abnormally high temperatures, up to 46°C (115°F) and, like the gemsbok of Southern Africa, blood entering the gazelle brain is cooled by about 3°C (6°F) through a

★ A Saharan desert snail which had been glued to a display card in the British Museum for four years revived after being put in water.

2

complex system of blood vessels around the nose. Though sweating also helps cool the animal it is costly in terms of water and so gazelles have a high 'switch-on' temperature at which sweating begins. They can also tolerate a high degree of dehydration when deprived of water – sustaining and recuperating a 20 per cent loss in body weight.

Life in the sand

Although relatively few large mammals can survive in the hostile open expanses of the Sahara, a diverse community of small mammals, reptiles and amphibians uses the sand and rocky shelters to escape the heat and conserve water. Gerbils and jerboas live in burrows in the vast open plains and dunes. Jerboas are strictly nocturnal and during the day they rest in burrows up to 2 m (6½ feet)

deep, where they are protected by relatively constant humidity and temperature. Not only do their burrows stay warmer than the outside air temperature at night and cooler by day, but their increased humidity helps reduce evaporative water loss. At night, jerboas emerge to feed on seeds, stems and roots of desert grasses from which they extract water. They also produce very concentrated urine, which helps to conserve fluid. Their large black eyes and elongated hind legs help them detect and escape from predators such as fennec foxes, which use their oversized ears to locate the faint rustlings of prey.

Fennec foxes occur in the most arid regions of the Sahara and can get by without drinking anything at all – they receive all the water they need through their diet of small mammals, lizards and insects. Because of their water-rich diet they can afford to offload

heat by panting and sweating when heat-stressed. Their large ears also act as radiators, dispersing body heat through myriad fine blood vessels near the skin surface.

Because amphibians depend on water for their early stages of development only a few species can survive in the Sahara, as standing water is confined to a relatively small number of oases and mountainous areas. In sharp contrast, there are nearly 100 species of reptile in the Sahara, including skinks, geckos, chameleons, agama lizards, monitors and snakes. Most small lizards feed on insects, but the large desert monitor may travel several kilometres a day from its burrow to raid the nests of birds and excavate the burrows of rodents. The Tuareg and Arabs sometimes carry the head of a monitor as a kind of talisman against the potentially lethal bite of vipers. ▷▷

 THE TRANS-SAHARAN MIGRATION

Every year in spring and autumn, hundreds of millions of birds migrate across the Sahara between their summer breeding grounds in Europe and Siberia and their winter feeding grounds in tropical Africa – a journey of up to 9000 km (5600 miles) for birds that may weigh as little as 100 g (4 ounces)! This remarkable event is full of hazards, particularly heat stress and dehydration, but hot winds, lack of food and predation by raptors such as sparrowhawks and falcons also account for the high mortality levels.

Most migrants travel at night at heights of 1500–2500 m (4900–8200 feet). Not only does this reduce predator attention and temperature stress, but the thinner air at altitude means that their flight speed can be increased by as much as 20 per cent. Most small birds have flight speeds of about 40 km (25 miles) per hour, whereas larger birds like waders and ducks can travel at about 80 km (50 miles) per hour. For many birds, in favourable conditions the desert crossing might take them 30–40 hours. However, a great many – perhaps half of all those setting out – die on this perilous journey, and can be found emaciated and dehydrated in places like desert oases or mountain ranges where they have sought relief.

1. (opposite) The sand cat feeds on a wide range of prey including insects, birds, rodents and even venomous snakes, such as this sand viper.

THE ARABIAN CAMEL

The Arabian camel or dromedary, with its characteristic single hump (as opposed to the 'Bactrian camel' of Asia, which has two humps), was domesticated and imported to North Africa from Arabia in about 400 BC, replacing the horse as the main means of travel. Although not a true African mammal, it is the most important domesticated animal in the harshest regions of the Sahara today.

Ships of the desert

Known as 'ships of the desert' because of the way they rock from side to side as they walk, Arabian camels are the most brilliantly designed animals for desert life. Their feet are broad and so spread the animal's weight over a large area, making it easier to walk on soft sand. Their long eyelashes protect the eyes from wind-blown sand and their nostrils can close, which also helps to keep the sand out. Furthermore,

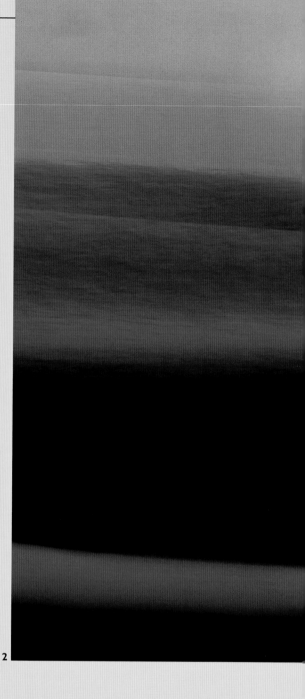

thickened areas of skin on their knees and other parts of the body protect them from the burning hot sand when they sit down.

Getting the hump

Perhaps the camel's most remarkable attribute is its hump. Most people think that it acts as a water store, but in fact it acts as a fat reserve that can help sustain the animal for several months without food. The fatty hump and heavy fur also help to insulate the camel so that it hardly sweats at all. Compare this to a human, who can sweat up to 3 litres (⅔ gallon) in just a single hour of walking in the desert. Furthermore, a special arrangement of blood vessels at the base of the camel's brain keeps it at a safe temperature, while the rest of the body rises to about 46°C (115°F) – a level that would be fatal in most other mammals.

Camels can go 5–7 days with little or no food and water, losing more than a quarter of their body weight without affecting their performance, and can even tolerate a 40 per cent loss in body weight for short periods if seriously dehydrated. This is twice as much as most other animals, but when water becomes available again they can replace this weight

quickly – drinking one third of their body weight in just 10 minutes. When needs must, they can even drink salty or brackish water. Camels store water in a number of muscular pouches in their stomach, and release it as required.

The work-shy workhorse

Arabian camels are not choosy about their diet – their lips are thickened to withstand

the coarsest of plants and they will also eat salty plants rejected by other grazers. Their sturdy build means they can carry a 200-kg (440-lb) load up to 65 km (40 miles) per day, but they are also known for their loathing of work and sometimes spit foul-smelling stomach contents when annoyed!

Camels can live for 40 years but most working camels retire around the age of 25. As well as their great value for transport, virtually every part of their body can be used: tents are made out of camel-hair cloth, the flesh of young camels is said to taste like veal, the skin makes good leather and the dung is burned for warmth on cold desert nights. The milk is much more nutritious than that of the cow, lower in fat and lactose but higher in potassium, iron and vitamin C. With so many attributes it is no wonder the Bedouin refer to the camel as Ata Allah, meaning 'God's gift'.

1. The ancestors of the modern camel first appeared in North America 40 million years ago.

2. Exquisitely designed, Arabian camels are among only a few large mammals able to survive in the Sahara.

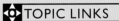
TOPIC LINKS

4.2 The Great Sahara
p.131 The once-green Sahara
p.139 Nomads of the sands

World of the miniature

The greatest diversity of all animal life in the Sahara is displayed by insects, many of which have fascinating ways of finding food. There are as many as 66 different ant species in the desert and though most are carnivorous, some specialize in eating grass seeds, which they harvest and feed to their brood.

Ants themselves are important prey for the larvae of ant-lions, which excavate ambush pits in fine sand. The larva of the ant-lion positions itself at the bottom of the pit and attacks passing insects that slip in. During the day the larva orientates itself within the pit so its body is always in the coolest, shadiest position and can function normally at temperatures as high as 48°C (118°F).

In areas where camels, goats and other domestic animals are common, dung or 'scarab' beetles abound. They break up dung, and roll it into balls, which they push around with their hind legs. When they find a suitable piece of ground, they bury the dung ball in an underground chamber, where they can feed safe from predators and the harsh weather above. In the autumn, a larger ball is stored in a bigger chamber, where an egg is deposited.

However, developing larvae are not entirely safe – scolid wasps excavate them with their short, strong legs, before paralyzing them and laying an egg on them. This hatches into a larva, which eats the beetle grub and then spins a cocoon in its empty skin.

Many Saharan insects have amazing tactics for deterring predators. From glands in their leg joints, blister beetles secrete a yellow toxic substance that can cause skin blisters, and the desert grasshopper can squirt two well-aimed jets of irritating and toxic fluid. The poisonous ingredients of this are obtained directly from its food plant.

 ## LOCUST SWARMS

Swarms of desert locusts (left) have plagued agriculture in North Africa from the earliest recorded times: the eighth plague of Egypt recorded in the book of Exodus (c. 1300 BC) was caused by locusts. In 125 BC Pliny wrote that Saharan locust swarms caused 800,000 people to perish in Cyrenaica and 300,000 in Tunisia. Even with today's careful pest control, the desert locust remains a formidable threat.

Desert locust plagues can invade an area of some 30 million sq km (12 million sq miles) from the Atlantic Ocean to eastern India, and from the southern republics of the former USSR to southern Tanzania. Desert locusts have even been known to reach southwest Europe and have been seen flying at sea as far as 2400 km (1490 miles) from land!

Locusts are opportunists, undertaking their life cycle rapidly as soon as temperature and rainfall conditions are favourable. Spring rains in the northwestern parts of the Sahara usually trigger hatching, and the hoppers form dense bands that devour their own weight in vegetation every day during their development to fledging 30–70 days later. The winged adults generally migrate south to summer rainfall areas – often flying at night – and, providing they find enough green food, soon reach sexual maturity. Female locusts lay their eggs in damp soil and the new hoppers hatch within 12–70 days, depending on the temperature. In average or low rainfall years the locusts remain nomadic in this way, moving between spring and summer pastures, but in the event of widespread rains and continuous breeding, numbers build until they reach plague proportions.

NOMADS OF THE SANDS

'No man can live in the desert and emerge unchanged. He will carry, however faint, the imprint of the desert, the brand which marks the nomad.' (Wilfred Thesinger, *Arabian Sands*.)

At first it seems unbelievable that people can live in the Sahara – a vast, bleak and hostile expanse with little vegetation and only a scattering of springs, oases and rain-fed pools. Yet, there are probably 1.5 million nomadic herdsmen here, of whom the Tuareg – traditionally the fiercest and most warlike nomads – are perhaps the best known.

The Tuareg are fair-skinned Berbers, descended from the original inhabitants of North Africa. They call themselves 'Imohagh' or 'Imajughen', meaning 'noble ones', have their own language and alphabet, and the men wear over their heads a characteristic blue veil, which protects them from the burning sun and blowing sand. Following the Arab invasions in the seventh and eleventh centuries, the Tuareg established themselves as camel traders in the central Sahara. For centuries they controlled the valuable trans-Saharan caravans that took slaves, gold and ivory from West Africa to the Mediterranean, taxing the goods they helped to convey and raiding neighbouring tribes. In modern times their raiding was subdued by the French who ruled Algeria, and since the 1960s it has been increasingly difficult for the Tuareg to maintain their nomadic life. However, despite political change and great periods of drought and famine in past decades, 300,000–400,000 Tuareg still cling to their traditional lifestyle – herding livestock and driving across the desert spectacular camel caravans of rock salt and dates, which they exchange for millet, or they may sell the surplus of their livestock, butter and cheese, depending on the season.

1

2

1. The Tuareg people are among the few Saharan tribes still maintaining a traditional lifestyle.

2. The lethal fat-tailed scorpion can flick venom from its tail and cause temporary blindness.

The fat-tailed scorpion of the north Sahara is one of the most venomous in the world; its sting can kill a human in 4 hours and a dog in 7 minutes.

THE DESERTS OF SOUTHERN AFRICA

Deserts dominate southern Africa. These parched lands are far more ancient than the Sahara, and their great age, influenced by a relatively stable climate, has allowed them to develop the most complex communities of desert plants and animals in the world.

These deserts can be divided into three different regions depending on their rainfall and vegetation. The oldest and driest region is the Namib Desert, which stretches along the coastal plains of Namibia. Further south, the Succulent Karoo is an area famous for its spectacular spring blooms of flowers, and inland is the Nama Karoo, a bleak expanse of plains and mountains and once the home of a rich mix of dinosaurs and mammal-like reptiles. The Arid Savannah, which includes the famous Kalahari National Parks, is dominated by grasses and seasonal pans. It is the wettest desert of them all, and manages to support the greatest concentrations of desert animals on the continent.

AFRICA'S WETTEST DESERT: THE KALAHARI

The Kalahari is a vast region of sandy, porous soils that extends over much of south central Africa – even as far north as the Congo, where ancient desert sands lie beneath lush tropical rainforest. However, it is only in the lower rainfall areas to the south – between Botswana, eastern Namibia and northern South Africa – that the Kalahari sands become true semi-arid desert. Here, where the temperature can fluctuate wildly from −14°C (7°F) at night in winter to 40°C (104°F) by day in summer, there are great, rolling, red dunes, saltpans, dusty plains, ancient riverbeds and a sparse plant life which, for most of the year, lies withered beneath the scorching sun. But, just occasionally during the summer months, the wind picks up and cumulus clouds slowly gather into brief and localized thunderstorms, dropping as much as 250–500 mm (10–20 inches) of rain in a given area over a year. Many small animals and plants must wait patiently until this sudden bounty reaches them, while others can take the initiative and head straight for the greening pastures.

1. Rainfall comes to the Kalahari in brief but intense seasonal storms.

1

Abdim's storks often turn up in enormous flocks within days of a good Kalahari rainstorm to feast on insects, lizards and amphibians that have emerged to breed after rain. They are sometimes joined by herds of hundreds of eland – the greatest nomadic wanderers of southern Africa's deserts – which arrive to crop the fresh growth. Just as the eland seem, mysteriously, to 'know' where the rain is falling, so too do greater and lesser flamingos, which can suddenly turn up in their millions at rain-filled pans like Etosha and Makgadikgadi to breed. Many birds will have travelled here from their feeding grounds on the Atlantic coast of Namibia and South Africa, hundreds of kilometres away. As well as these unpredictable movements of life some animals, such as blue wildebeest

and Burchell's zebra which require good-quality food all year, follow regular migration routes between summer grounds in the south central Kalahari and winter grounds further north. Unfortunately, fences built to prevent the wildebeest spreading disease to cattle now prevent the wildebeest from reaching adequate winter food, and over the last few decades the population has been sadly decimated.

Bushmen of the Kalahari

Up until recently, the great herds that trekked seasonally across the Kalahari expanse were an important source of food for a race of hunter-gatherers called the Kalahari or 'San' Bushmen, nomads who ranged all over Southern Africa

as little as 3000 years ago. Their weapons were simple but effective: wooden bows strung with sinew, and arrows tipped with poison extracted from snakes, scorpions, certain plants and, most often, from the leaf-cutting beetle. As well as game meat, the Bushmen's diet was complemented by some 300 types of plant food, including edible berries, roots and tsamma melons. In times of drought the Bushmen would also store water in eggshells, burying them at strategic points beneath the soil surface for later recovery. The shells were used for ornamentation, and animal skins for clothing. But being highly mobile, their possessions were few: nothing was owned that could not easily be carried. However, when Bushmen inhabited the Drakensbergs of southern Africa (▷ p. 61), they created beautiful stick-animal artwork, which can still be seen in many of the caves in these mountains.

Today, due to political change, competition for land and persecution by early Cape settlers, fewer than 70,000 Bushmen remain. Most have abandoned their nomadic lifestyle and have settled on farms or in areas set aside for them. Only those few people protected in Botswana's Central Kalahari Game Reserve have managed to resist outside pressures and continue to follow the hunter-gatherer lifestyle.

A brief moment of glory

Within hours of a storm passing, the Kalahari takes on a new personality. For many creatures, life becomes frenetic, for there is so little time to emerge, feed and reproduce before the water is gone. Puddles, pools and flooded pans quickly fill with insect larvae, helmeted terrapins, frogs and small crustaceans such as tadpole shrimps. Tadpole shrimps hatch from eggs and begin rapidly devouring detritus,

algae and other shrimps – dead or alive – before mating and laying their eggs, all in less than a week. Once the desert dries out again these eggs can withstand extreme desiccation and scorching temperatures, surviving for years in the sand until the next rains arrive. They are surprisingly mobile too, moving between waterholes stuck to the muddy feet of birds and mammals!

As these seasonal pools dry out, larger animals like bullfrogs take on extra water, which they store in special bladders in their intestines before burrowing deep into the soft mud. Within eight days they can reduce their metabolic rate to one quarter of its normal resting level, leaving only critical organs like the heart and kidneys active. Gradually, a cocoon of shed skin and mucus forms over the frog and forms into a tight, waterproof skin, broken only by two small holes for it to breathe through. In this protected, dormant state the bullfrog can survive months of drought before re-emerging at the next rains.

★ The fossil record shows that tadpole shrimps have remained virtually unchanged for 230–280 million years.

1. Ju/Hoan Bushman making a fire in Namibia.

2. Cheetahs are desert-adapted hunters and the principal predators of adult springbok in the Kalahari.

THE BLEAK INTERIOR: THE NAMA AND SUCCULENT KAROO

Covering approximately 605,000 sq km (234,000 sq miles), the Nama Karoo is the second largest desert region of southern Africa after the Arid Savannah. The landscape is generally flat or gently undulating, dotted with rocky outcrops called 'koppies' and broken by great mountain ranges. This vast area, which covers much of the South African and Namibian interiors, receives slightly less rain than the Kalahari and is dominated by hardy shrubs and grasses. To its south and west and bordering the Atlantic Ocean, lies the Succulent Karoo, named for its astounding richness of small shrubs. Both the Nama and Succulent Karoo are home to a unique collection of desert plants and animals.

Namaqualand – the Garden of Africa

Running along the southwest coast of South Africa and southern Namibia, within the Succulent Karoo region, is a very special area known as Namaqualand. Its cold coastal fogs and small, but predictable, amounts of winter rainfall (20–290 mm/1–11 inches per year) have given rise to a breathtaking variety of plants able to survive the dual challenge of moist winters and dry, very hot summers.

The most distinctive plants of Namaqualand are dwarf shrubs with succulent leaves, branches and stems, of which there are almost 2000 species, such as mesembs or 'vygies' (which include the famous stone plants), crassulas, euphorbias and haworthias. Geophytes – seasonally active plants which store food reserves in underground bulbs, rhizomes and tubers –

are also unusually diverse here, with over 500 species including romuleas, moraeas, lachenalias and exquisite amaryllids. However, it is the annuals – of which there are more than 300 species – that catch the eye during spring, when the desert transforms into a riot of colour.

These dazzling displays are designed to attract the attention of pollinators such as insects and birds. During the cool, wet and windy flowering season only a limited number of days are suitable for insect activity, so competition is fierce. Some plants beat their competitors by producing the showiest blooms possible, while others specialize. The spiky, purple-pink, long-tubed flowers of Lapeirousia, Babiana and Pelargonium are designed specifically to lure long-tongued flies (*Prosoeca* spp.). With tongues (or 'probosci') up to 40 mm (nearly 2 inches) long, they are the only insect

1. Desert tortoises, which are abundant in the Karoo, make the most of the vegetation during the short flowering season.

2. (opposite) The spectacular blooms of Namaqualand annuals are a result of the intense competition between flowering plants for pollinators.

visitors able to reach the precious nectar at the bottom of the long, floral tubes, and in doing so, they collect pollen grains and carry them to other plants. Interestingly, not only do different Prosoeca species have different tongue lengths for different plants, but each plant has subtle differences in where it places the pollen on the fly's body, effectively reducing the possibility of pollen 'contamination' between plants.

Some flowers, especially those that are red tubes held erect on branches, are specifically designed to attract birds that have good vision at the red end of the colour spectrum. Recent research has discovered that the small, twisted flowers of *Microloma sagittatum* attract nectar-feeding lesser double-collared sunbirds. As the sunbird probes the flowers, detachable pollen parcels are clamped firmly to the tip of the bird's tongue!

Throwing caution to the wind

To maximize their chances of reproductive success, desert plants typically produce masses of seeds. Very few of these will survive to find the right place to germinate – most will be eaten by rodents and birds like sandgrouse, or collected by ants such as the harvester ant. For the vast majority of annual plants in the Succulent Karoo, such as daisies, the wind is the most effective way of spreading seeds to new destinations. The seeds are often equipped with a range of lightweight structures, ranging from long, silky hairs to single or multi-veined 'wings', which work like parachutes. They may not actually fall far from the parent plant, but the wind will continue to drag them across the ground. In this way the seed's protective coat gets scoured, and this actually helps germination as oxygen and water can more freely reach the embryo inside.

Some wind-dispersed seeds get a helping hand from birds. Fluffy seeds make a soft lining for the nests of birds like the Cape Penduline tit or the malachite sunbird. They are durable, insulating and water-repelling. But the seeds also benefit as not only are they carried away from their parent plants, but when the nest finally collapses several months after the birds have left, the seeds are in an ideal condition to germinate. Not only are they surrounded in their own organic fertilizer (bird droppings and old nest material) but they usually fall into the shade.

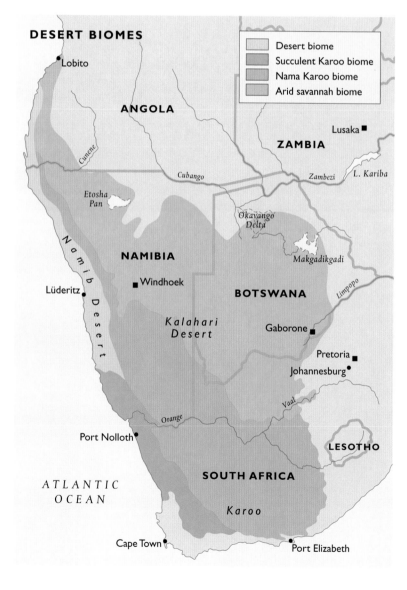

DESERT BIOMES

Lobito

	Desert biome
	Succulent Karoo biome
	Nama Karoo biome
	Arid savannah biome

ANGOLA

Lusaka

ZAMBIA

Cunene

Cubango

Zambezi   L. Kariba

Etosha Pan

Okavango Delta

NAMIBIA

Makgadikgadi

Lüderitz

Windhoek

BOTSWANA

Limpopo

Kalahari Desert

Gaborone

Pretoria

Johannesburg

Vaal

Orange

Port Nolloth

LESOTHO

SOUTH AFRICA

ATLANTIC OCEAN

Karoo

Cape Town

Port Elizabeth

1. The cold Benguela Current, which sweeps the Atlantic shores of the Namib Desert, starves it of rain but also provides it with life-giving fogs.

Overleaf: The hardiest nomad of southern Africa's deserts, a solitary gemsbok wanders in the vast expanse of the Namib.

SEA OF SAND: THE NAMIB

The Namib is Southern Africa's most extreme desert. Receiving little more than 5–85 mm (⅓–3 inches) of rain per year, this strip of dramatic sand dunes, gravel plains and parched riverbeds stretches more than 2000 km (1240 miles) along the coast of southwest Africa – a truly ancient world that has been arid or semi-arid for the best part of 80 million years.

Rainfall is so low in the Namib that it is surprising anything can live there at all, but salvation comes in the form of life-giving fogs, which drift across the landscape from the ocean. These are formed by moist air masses heading inshore from the mid-Atlantic, which are cooled as they cross ▷▷ **1**

 ## THE TREKBOKKEN

At the dawn of the twentieth century, travellers who ventured into the Succulent Karoo during the winter rainfall period may have witnessed more than just carpets of flowers – some recorded fields of springbok antelope further than the eye could see. In 1925, S.C. Cronwright-Schreiner wrote about a trek he witnessed in 1896: 'We eventually computed the number to be not less than five hundred thousand – half a million springboks in sight at one moment … now to obtain some rough idea of the prodigious number of bucks in the whole trek it must be remembered it was computed that they extended twenty-three hours in one direction and two to three in the other – that is, the whole trek occupied a space of country one hundred and thirty-eight by fifteen miles.'

At the hands of European farmers, the springbok herds (right) took massive losses during their treks between the summer rains in the southern Kalahari and Nama Karoo and the winter rains in the Succulent Karoo. Slaughtered for biltong (dried and salted meat) and to protect farmland for sheep, these vast herds were quickly decimated.

No one really knows what once triggered these huge aggregations of springbok, but the most likely reason is the unpredictability of rainfall and browse in the Karoo.

1. The diminutive Grant's golden mole, a nocturnal sand swimmer of the Namib.

2. Black-backed jackals are common in the coastal margins of the Namib, preying on everything from fur seal pups to lizards.

the cold, coastal Benguela Current.

As mentioned in Section 4.1, many animals and plants of the Namib depend on trapping and storing this fog for moisture, and rely on wind-blown detritus (dead plant matter, seeds, etc.) as the basis for a unique food chain. Resources here are so limited that some animals have evolved some extraordinary tactics for both hunting and avoiding predators. Spiders cannot build hanging webs in the Namib because the wind is too strong and they have too few plants to suspend them from, so the spoor spider spins on the sand surface a small, camouflaged disc of silk, which it crawls beneath. Any ant or small insect that walks over it is immediately immobilized by the sticky silk, which acts like velcro, and is pulled under the web by the spider. Some spiders, like the jumping spider, take a more direct approach. Its size and colour pattern perfectly mimic the aggressive Namib dune ants among whose colonies it lives. Presumably it gains immunity from attack by predators that have learned to avoid the evil-tasting dune ants, but it also stealthily hunts the ants. The ants are unable to recognize it as danger, possibly because the spider is also able to mimic their odour by absorbing chemicals from its prey.

Sand travel

Travelling over soft sand is a tiring and energy-consuming business and it is not surprising that many Namib residents are most active in the early morning, when temperatures are bearable and nightly fogs have brought extra moisture to the sand, making it slightly easier

▷ INVENTING THE WHEEL

Some desert animals have evolved extraordinary ways of escaping from their predators. The spider *Carparachne aureoflava* (right) has adopted the wheel. It lives on the steepest slopes of the Namib sand dunes, in burrows about 50 cm (20 inches) long, sealed with a highly camouflaged silk trapdoor. Its chief enemy is the pompilid wasp, which runs across the sand 'tasting' for the spider. Once it locates a burrow, it tries to enter through the trapdoor, but the spider can usually beat it off by flailing its legs or collapsing the end of its burrow. Failing that, the wasp digs a hole from above, excavating a tunnel 15 cm (6 inches) deep in less than 2 hours.

As soon as the burrow is breached, the spider makes a desperate dash for safety, running downhill then flipping onto its side, cartwheeling away at up to 44 turns per second — a very dizzy escape! The spider can cover 10 m (30 feet) in less than 10 seconds, far faster than the wasp, and it jinks as it goes, leaving a complicated scent trail for the wasp to follow on foot. If the spider is lucky enough to find another burrow it can reach safety, but when confronted in the open by the wasp it resorts to a dancing threat display. Though it looks intimidating the wasp is usually not put off and moves in with a paralyzing sting.

to move over. However, most of these creatures also have special designs to help improve locomotion. The shovel-snouted and wedge-snouted lizards have similar modifications on their feet and toes. Their hind legs are long and splayed, and the wedge-snouted lizard can even run extremely fast on two legs across the sand when confronted by a predator. Both types of lizard can also dive under the sand and, using rapid twists of the body, 'swim' to safety. But in the event of a rare rain shower they are extremely vulnerable, as the wet sand prevents them from burrowing to safety. Peringuey's adder, which buries itself in the sand to hunt lizards by ambush, uses another tactic for getting around. It can propel itself forward by 'side-winding' its body on the soft sand.

One of the most extraordinary creatures living in the soft Namib sands is the Grant's golden mole. It is the only truly sand-swimming mammal in the world. Like the lizards it has a tough, wedge-shaped nose, but no eyes. The mole spends the day motionless in the sand, on which it relies to warm its body to a temperature of about 30°C (86°F) by dusk, when it becomes fully active. By night it may walk up to 5 km (3 miles) on the sand surface, looking for food such as termites, pausing every now and then to put its head in the sand to listen for them. Normally, however, it 'swims' just beneath the sand surface, leaving a tell-tale trail along its path. At the end of its foraging period it retires to an appropriate depth of sand which will ensure that, after cooling to whatever temperature the sand drops to at night, it will again be heated to its operational temperature the next day.

★ Namib dune ants get all the food and moisture they need in the form of honeydew, milked from aphids, mealy bugs and scale insects that infest plants in their territory.

2

THE SOCIAL LIVES OF MEERKATS

Of all the members of the African mongoose family, meerkats have evolved the most advanced level of sociality. Living in groups of up to 30 individuals, they are found throughout southern Africa's deserts, wherever the land is dry, open and often stony with sparse bushes and trees. With so few hiding places, meerkats need to be alert, and by living as a group they benefit from a highly organized system of predator detection.

Posting sentries

Jackals, snakes and large birds of prey, especially martial eagles, are the meerkats' main predators. In response to these dangers, meerkats have evolved a system of posting sentries, which means that the rest of the group can forage without wasting valuable time scanning the skies and horizon for danger. Time for them is valuable – summer in the southern Kalahari and Karoo can be so hot that the meerkats only have a few hours in the morning and evening when it is cool enough to be out.

Meerkats feed by digging for insects and their larvae and, while engaged in these activities, they cannot easily spot predators. This job is done by the sentries, whose constant repertoire of calls keeps all members of the group aware of what is going on around them. Different calls prompt different responses. The most dramatic is a shrill, sharp bark which means 'get out, now!', and sends all members diving for the nearest burrow. This is only used when a known, dangerous predator like a martial eagle has been spotted nearby, or is attacking. The sentries also use less dramatic calls which, for example, may carry the message 'aerial predator nearby but no imminent danger: decide what you want to do'. This may simply cause a few members of the group to edge closer to their burrows, and others to sit on their haunches and watch. There is also an alarm call which is used specifically to announce the presence of a jackal nearby.

The sentries are sub-adult males, which take turns to stand guard so that each gets a chance to feed. The safety of the group depends on its size and the number of sentries it can post. If the group gets too small it will not survive for long. This sometimes happens in drought years when sentries are

forced to abandon their duties to spend more time looking for food. When this happens, the group often joins up with troops of ground squirrels and yellow mongooses for the extra pairs of eyes, and they will even share communal warrens. The three species do not compete for food: the squirrels are herbivorous, the mongooses eat mainly termites, rodents and birds and the suricates prefer beetles and scorpions.

Warren life

Meerkats have many warrens within their territories and this ensures they are never far from safety. They regularly move from warren to warren, efficiently quartering their territories in the search for food. During the cool of dawn, meerkats stand outside their burrows facing the sun with their chest fur erect to absorb the warmth of the sun. If an individual happens to cast its shadow on a meerkat standing behind it, the one behind will shuffle to a new position! On very cold days the group will even huddle together for warmth – another benefit of group living. When it comes to rearing young, only one dominant female breeds, but all the sub-adult females are enlisted as babysitters to protect the young from predators like snakes. Even though they and the sentries appear to be putting the interests of the group above their own, all members of the troop have a vested interest in each other's welfare and that of the babies. This is because they are all related, thus sharing each other's genes. Also, by biding their time in a group, the females may get their own chance to breed and the males to win a territory elsewhere. These options are infinitely better than trying to go it alone where the chances of survival are far lower than living in the troop.

2

1. Many eyes see more. By sticking together, meerkats greatly increase their chances of survival.

2. Yellow mongooses sometimes cohabit with meerkats for greater group defense.

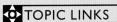 TOPIC LINKS

4.1 Under the Glare
p.122 Internal control: mammals and birds

5

JUNGLES

THE GREEN HEART OF AFRICA

On Africa's Equator, water from warm, tropical oceans is evaporated by the African sun and transformed into vast, boiling, billowing storm clouds. As they rumble and churn they carry their load up to 2000 km (1200 miles) inland and dump it on the continent as tropical rain, buckets of it, in some places as much as 10 m (30 feet) a year. So much water, combined with the heat and light of the tropical sun, creates conditions that could not be more perfect for plants.

From Senegal in the west to Kenya in the east, stretches one of the greatest proliferations of plant life on Earth. This is Africa's lowland tropical rainforest, or jungle – a lush swathe of green at the heart of a brown continent. Since the age of the dinosaurs this part of the African continent has been ruled by plants, not merely conquering but actually becoming the environment itself, a three-dimensional world of trunks and leaves that contains within it over half of Africa's wildlife.

Previous page: Massive trunks and buttresses are the scaffolding of the rainforest, supporting a roof of leaves over 30 metres (100 feet) up in the African sun.

1. The sun rises over the misty canopy of the Taï forest in the Côte d'Ivoire. Half of Africa's wildlife is contained in tropical rainforests.

FIGHT FOR LIGHT

Being terrestrial animals, humans first encounter rainforests at ground level. As a newcomer, stepping into an African rainforest for the first time can be a strange and puzzling experience. Here you are, on the Equator, where the sun shines longer and stronger than anywhere else on Earth and you are in the dark. It is too dark to take a photograph without a flash. You are standing in one of life's great laboratories, where half of all of Africa's species are supposedly housed, but it feels still, quiet and dead. Apart from the myriad ants that, no matter how careful you are, crawl up your trouser leg and bite you, the occasional, beautifully coloured butterfly, doing its best to keep afloat in the wet, heavy air, is just about the only animal you can easily spot. It does not seem to make sense.

But, straining your neck and eyes to look far up above, you half catch a glimpse of the truth. Through small gaps in the canopy, light filters down from the heavens above. A hornbill glides overhead like an archaeopteryx with great swooshes of its wings. African grey parrots squawk and gossip in a fruiting tree. A crash of foliage like the rustle of a big tarpaulin and a chattering troop of guenon monkeys leap to bridge a gap in the forest canopy.

The truth is that the forest is divided. Most of the work of the rainforest and most of the diversity it supports is up there, as much as 40 or 50 m (130–160 feet) away in the vast sea of leaves that is the canopy. It is a world in itself, quite apart from the forest floor underworld. In the canopy, conditions are more like those on a savannah. The sun is scorching hot, there are drying winds and the landscape is alive with the buzz of insects, monkeys' chatter and bird song.

Jungle time

But this is not to say that the forest down below is entirely lifeless – far from it. The life is just difficult to see. One of the reasons the forest seems so still is quite simply a matter of time. Plants live on a completely different time scale to us and so, walking through the rainforest, we do not see the true nature of what is going on. If we could see in plant time, in which perhaps 10 of our years are, for a tree, just a fraction of a second, the rainforest would take on a whole new character. Instead of a stable, still world where movement is confined to the flap of a butterfly's wings or the marching of a column of ants, we would see a heaving, dynamic plant world locked in mortal combat.

In a place where conditions for plants are so perfect, competition is the driving force. That competition is for the one commodity that is limited here – light. Light is the key to the process called photosynthesis, whereby green plants combine water from rain and carbon dioxide from the air to make simple sugars. Light is the life force of the plant world and the source of light is upwards. The higher and faster a tree spreads its leaves, the more light it will get and the better it will grow. As it does so it throws competitors into shade and gains a further advantage.

In plant time we would see saplings straining upwards, trying to escape from the darkness below, pushing out legs and buttresses as they grow to support their increasing bulk. Lianas would spiral upwards and strangler figs grapple with their tree host, throttling the life from its woody soul in a selfish bid for a place in the African sun. The massive hardwood trees of the rainforest, like mahogany, sapele, moabi and okume, all over 50 m (160 feet) tall, are simply the end result of this battle. They are living edifices to the real hard currency of the jungle – light.

CHEMICAL WARFARE

No sooner has a tree started to turn sunlight into food than it comes under attack from animals. For ants and elephants alike, trees hold the key to the energy of the sun. They are the primary producers and, for animals that eat plants, that means food. But plants have not thrived over several thousands of millennia by simply surrendering their hard-won gains – they produce thorns and hairs, spikes, sticky resins and waxy cuticles, all designed to deter herbivores.

And when physical protection is not enough, they turn to chemical warfare. Strychnines, cyanides, pyrethrums and tannins are only a few of the 30,000 compounds manufactured by plants to help protect them from being eaten. And these are just the ones that have been identified – many more are yet to be discovered. If we could see the full extent of the chemical nature of the forest, like seeing in plant time, we would see another world again – a chemical world superimposed on the physical and just as complex. For each plant poison there is an animal that has invented an antidote, and for each antidote there is another counter-attack from a plant. This is another arms race fuelling evolution, like the physical but infinitely more complex, fought this time on chemical terms.

The dynamic forest

In the African forest it is the needs of plants that have made the environment. A three-dimensional chemistry laboratory in countless layers, each with its own unique set of climatic conditions, from damp, cool forest floor to dry, hot canopy. Such sheer diversity of habitat offers an infinite number of niches to be exploited by animals. This breeds diversity.

1. A strangler fig chokes its host tree as it climbs upwards, ensuring its place in the African sun.

2. An African grey parrot, loved by pet owners for its ability to talk and sing, is part of the rich diversity that has evolved in Africa's rainforest.

But it is the fact that the forest is a living environment that gives it a real edge. In a desert, animals battle against the ravages of climate, which though harsh are constant. The sun, the wind, the sand. The forest environment is dynamic – it reacts to those that live in it. As soon as life adapts one way to exploit it, it counteracts in another, it bites back, reinventing itself, creating further challenges for life. This again leads to diversity.

One final factor completes the backdrop to the unique drama that is the African forest. As a habitat in Africa, forest has been around for longer than any other – since the days of the dinosaurs – and so the forces of evolution have had longer to work there than anywhere else. Recently it has been discovered that the exact extent of the forest cover in Africa has altered dramatically over that time, expanding and contracting on a massive scale in phase with alternate periods of global cooling and warming. Change over time is always a recipe for diversity and as the forests expanded and contracted, their characteristics altered in subtle ways, especially at the forest edges, so further fuelling evolution.

These are the peculiar factors that have combined to make the rainforest Africa's primary hotbed of evolution. Although in terms of numbers of species the African forests are less diverse than those of South America or Southeast Asia the legacy of this 'engine of evolution', the particular species that evolved here, is one of, if not the, most important on earth.

1. This tiny Demidoff's bushbaby, with its forward-facing eyes and insect-eating, nocturnal lifestyle, closely resembles early primates.

THE AFRICAN FOREST PHENOMENON

Although rainforest covers only 7 per cent of the land surface of Africa, its legacy to the continent and indeed the world, far outweighs its relative extent today. This is largely because of a small group of animals that appeared in the forests of Africa over 30 million years ago.

With forward-facing eyes for three-dimensional vision, opposable toes for climbing trees, and large brains, they were unmistakably an early form of primate. Early primates were generally small tree-dwelling, insect-eating animals and largely nocturnal, a bit like bush babies today. But these animals were different. They had eyes adapted for daytime living, teeth adapted for a diet of fruit rather than insects, and an enlargement of the parts of the brain that handle vision. These were one of the African forests' finest creations – the anthropoids. They were the ancestors of a group of primates that was eventually to spread to all four corners of the world – the apes and monkeys.

The ancient ape, with its characteristic lack of a tail, was the first great anthropoid success story. With over 60 different species in Africa alone and representatives throughout the Old World as far as China, they ruled the forests of the day. Though less successful, the tailed monkeys were, nevertheless, widespread and, most significantly, found a way across the emerging Atlantic Ocean to colonize South America. Their legacy is the current remarkable diversity of New World monkeys. But, again, it was in Africa's rainforests that the stage was set for the next anthropoid revolution.

Age of the monkey

Around 10 to 15 million years ago the Earth's climate cooled significantly and Africa's rainforest began a cycle of massive contraction. At the time, apes accounted for 80 per cent of Africa's anthropoid primates. Ranging from 3 to 300 kg (6½–660 lbs), there were forms adapted to all manner of forest living. But as the forest contracted and more open woodland appeared, monkeys rapidly gained the advantage. This was probably because they evolved to eat fruits before they were ripe, and as fruits became scarcer in the shrinking forest, the apes were out-competed.

The result was a massive radiation of monkeys, whereas only one lineage of apes survived. Small, lightweight and agile, monkeys rapidly became the dominant primate in the African treetops. The reaction of the apes was to become big, not only in body but also, most significantly, in brain. Today's successful apes, the chimpanzees and gorillas, are not only bigger and stronger than any monkey but a quantum leap smarter. And it was this revolutionary move that eventually gave the apes their trump card.

About 5 million years ago the forest was again retreating. What happened next is one of the most hotly contested topics of modern science. The consensus is that, as the forest habitat became more broken and fruiting trees more dispersed, an ape evolved to move out of the closed forest and live more widely on the emerging broken woodlands and savannahs. Here, it began to walk upright, to use tools and fire and then to dominate the world. *Homo sapiens* had been born. Though the origin of our species, *Homo sapiens*, is most likely to have come about in the African savannah, we are the direct descendants of apes that once dominated the forests. The African lowland rainforest is our ancestral home.

THE FINAL FRONTIER

For people in the Western world, rainforests have always been the stuff of folklore, synonymous with impenetrable darkness and unexplored mystery. In the Africa of fiction lurk undiscovered monsters, cannibals and almost certain death. From Tarzan to *Heart of Darkness*, no other continent's rainforests have inspired this image quite like Africa's. Most likely it is an image born from the fear of the untameable, the inaccessible, the unknown. But these fears are only natural. African peoples are just as fearful of the forest and even those who actually live in them have their legends of monsters. The pygmy people who live throughout the central African rainforest keep alive the legend of a monster called Mokele-Mbembe, a giant lizard with the neck of a giraffe, the legs of an elephant and the head of a snake. They, along with many modern crypto-zoologists, believe it really exists, and perhaps it does. Even today, this is

the final frontier of the African continent and much of it is still unknown. There are vast tracts of the forest that are unexplored and countless new discoveries, as yet unseen, uncollected and unnamed by science.

A threatened landscape

Today there are 2 million sq km (770,000 sq miles) of tropical rainforest remaining in Africa, a fifth of that in the whole world. But, as huge as it seems, the African forest is used to change. This area represents only 7 per cent of the land surface area in Africa and, many times in the past, what is essentially a dry continent has all but claimed this swathe of green. Climate changes in the last 20,000 years have had far more drastic effects on the rainforests of Africa than on those of Southeast Asia and South America. The marching African desert is ever threatening on each side.

Although fluctuations in forest extent with climate change can be drastic, even in ▷▷

2. Chimpanzees and humans are descended from a common ape ancestor that lived in the forests of tropical Africa.

THE PULSING FOREST

The African rainforest needs over 2000 mm (79 inches) of rain a year to thrive. Though continents have broken apart and glided across the planet's surface through the ages, Africa has nearly always had a huge swathe of land on the Equator, where the conditions are just right for rainforest growth. So, for millions of years, the rainforest has been one of Africa's most stable habitats, nurturing in its green fingers the products of a peculiarly African evolution. But this long-term stability has been punctuated by short-term change. Though there has always been rainforest somewhere on Africa's Equator, the extent of it has changed dramatically over time. And the most dramatic changes have been in the relatively recent past.

1

Ice age refuge

In repeated cycles over the long term and particularly in the past 2–3 million years, subtle fluctuations in the orbit of the Earth have resulted in 21 major ice ages. Ice ages are cooler times for the planet, and for Africa cool means dry. With less water evaporating from the tropical oceans, less rain falls on the land. For Africa's rainforest these subtle changes have had very dramatic consequences. Just a small reduction in annual rainfall can have a critical effect on a rainforest and so these cycles of alternate cooling and warming have led directly to corresponding cycles of forest contraction and expansion on a massive scale.

At its greatest recent extent, about 10,000 years ago, the forest stretched in an unbroken belt from the west coast of the continent to the east. But only 18,000 years ago, in the depths of the last major ice age, Africa's forest became drastically reduced and retreated into small pockets, or 'refugia', where conditions have always been warm and wet. Modern-day Sierra Leone and Côte d'Ivoire in West Africa and Gabon and Cameroon in central Africa have always received a liberal drenching because of their proximity to the tropical coast. They still have some of the wettest forests today. Far to the east, it is the highlands of the Albertine Rift, squeezing every last drop of moisture from tropical clouds, that have ensured the survival of a major rainforest refuge at their western edge. And in the centre of Africa, deep in the heart of the vast Congo Basin, lowland rivers and swamps have always ensured warm, moist stability.

In these refugia, forest species of plants and animals have survived that otherwise would have become extinct. In Cameroon

and Equatorial Guinea, the perennial wetness has allowed the evolution of the biggest frog in the world, the Goliath frog, about the size of a human child. In Liberia, the shy pygmy hippo wallows in hidden forest swamps, a 'living fossil' and a reminder of the stability of the forest. For each of these areas there are countless unique species or 'endemics' that can be found nowhere else. Here, in the stability of these forest hideaways, evolution has progressed unhindered for longer than anywhere else on the African continent.

2

Africa's green heart

Ironically, just as important for the creation of Africa's rich diversity of rainforest species is the way in which the forest has changed over the years. With climate change, these wet, stable areas have been repeatedly separated and then joined together again. When previously continuous populations of a species become separated by the retreat of the forest, they start to evolve in isolation, perhaps to feed differently from one another, or to communicate in subtly different ways. When the forest expands and they are joined

together once more, they are no longer the same species. The incredible radiation of both African forest chameleons and guenon monkeys is the result of this process.

And this is not the only effect the changing extent of the forest has had on Africa's wildlife. Through the ages, with repeated expansion and contraction of the forest, countless savannah species have been 'engulfed' and turned into something new. The ancestor of the giraffe, the okapi, was almost certainly an animal of the grasslands that was

engulfed by the forest, and today's majestic herds of savannah elephants once found their refuge in the extensive forests of millennia past. Over consecutive ice ages Africa's rainforest has pulsed like a great, green heart in the centre of the continent, throwing out new species into the mix with every beat. But it is the incredible explosion of apes and monkeys that occurred in Africa's forests over the last few million years that is probably the most significant product of this remarkable 'engine of evolution'.

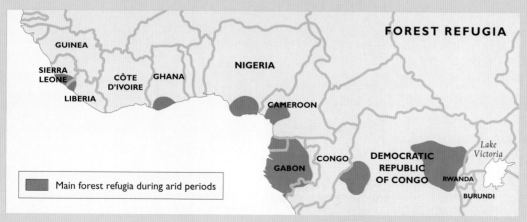

FOREST REFUGIA

GUINEA

SIERRA LEONE
CÔTE D'IVOIRE
GHANA
LIBERIA
NIGERIA
CAMEROON
GABON
CONGO
DEMOCRATIC REPUBLIC OF CONGO
RWANDA
BURUNDI
Lake Victoria

■ Main forest refugia during arid periods

1. The pygmy hippo is found only in West Africa, and even then it is almost impossible to glimpse one. It is very shy and spends most of its time underwater.

2. The Goliath frog; the size of a human baby, it has found refuge in some of the wettest places in Africa.

evolutionary terms, the African flora and fauna have always kept pace. Always, that is, until humans came on the scene. Now it is suspected that our influence even predates us as a species. There is evidence that as long as one and a half million years ago our hominid ancestors were using fire to manage the savannahs. We still do not know just how great an effect early hominids and humans had on the forest, but it may have been considerable. Some scientists believe that the use of fire by early humans was in fact the formative force in holding back the forest and creating the modern African savannahs.

The beginning of the end

Certainly by 4000 years ago, agriculture had made inroads into the forest. Only recently, scientists flying over Lac Tele, a remote lake in the heart of the Congo forest, noticed the tell-tale signs of agriculture – raised terraces – thousands of miles from civilization. People had been there, farmers, thousands of years before. Perhaps the forest is not as unexplored as was first thought. Just as remarkable are the finds of 2000-year-old palm nuts in swampy watercourses nearby. The palm nut is not native to the forest but is an agricultural crop used to make palm oil. At some stage there were people here, clearing the forest and planting palm nuts for oil. Nobody knows who they were, where they came from, or even where they went but, whatever the explanation, what is certain is that the idea of clearing the forest is not a new one.

For the most part, the forest climate is unhealthy for people and their livestock. So, populations like this would have been limited and their impact on the forest small. It was not until the Europeans arrived in the sixteenth century, bringing crops like maize and plantain, that the stage was set for massive exploitation of the forest. Slaves, ivory and gold made exploitation of the forest worthwhile and attracted the attention of other colonial powers; soon timber was being exported from West Africa. Foreign-based enterprises built up plantations of cacao and palm oil and established colonies.

Improvements in medicine then sent populations into expansion mode, and by the middle of the twentieth century the forests of West Africa were already hugely fragmented. Those of central Africa were soon to follow and in the 1950s and 1960s, chainsaws, the increased availability of anti-malarial

 ELEPHANTS OF THE FOREST

The forest elephant *Loxodonta africana* (right) is essentially the same animal as the bush elephant that we usually associate with Africa's savannahs, but there are some notable differences. Body size is smaller, tusks are straighter and ears smaller and more rounded, presumably as a consequence of less cooling power being required in the forest (an elephant's ears are its radiators).

Three million years ago the predominant elephant of the African savannah was a relative of the Indian elephant, called *Elephas recki*. *Elephas* had out-competed *Loxodonta africana* on the savannahs and rendered it extinct. However, during the last ice age, about 20,000 years ago, *Elephas recki* vanished, probably as a result of severe climate change and possibly with the help of early humans with a penchant for elephant. As quickly as it went it was replaced by *Loxodonta africana* once again. But where did *Loxodonta* come from, if all its ancestors had been wiped out? Most likely, whilst *Elephas* was roaming the open savannahs *Loxodonta* had its refuge deep in the African forest. Today's great herds of bush elephants are the direct descendants of animals that emerged from the protection of the forest to conquer the wide spaces of the savannah – very much like our own ancestors.

treatments and rapidly expanding European markets for tropical hardwoods made forest clearance much easier and more rewarding. As a result, the tropical forests of Africa have suffered more radical change in the past 40 years than throughout their 10,000-year post-glacial history. More than one-third of the original forest has already gone, this time never to return.

The Bayaka pygmies

Deep in the heart of the central African rainforest the sound of gentle voices – chatter, laughter and yodelling song – carries clearly through the trees. As you follow the sound, the smell of resinous wood smoke mixes with the voices and, like a spirit weaving its way around the trunks and branches, draws you on. In a forest clearing, shafts of soft, filtered sunlight, colouring the smoke blue where they touch it, pick out the forms of what look like compost heaps, arranged in a neat circle. But as you approach, the illusion resolves itself. The heaps are not compost but huts, the voices not those of spirits but of people. This is a forest village and these leafy igloos are the wet season homes of a group of Bayaka pygmies.

Ever since their stories can relate, the Bayaka have had an extensive knowledge of the forest. From these camps they hunt for monkeys and forest antelopes. They gather wild yams and honey. They also collect a whole range of leaves and barks to be used as poisons, medicines and for magic. Here there is no electricity, no alcohol, no cigarettes, not even any litter. In a modern world of money and technology it is a delight to see.

But even the Bayaka need the outside world. This encampment is only a temporary base, a seasonal hunting camp in the forest. Though they are perfectly at home here, they spend the larger part of their lives in

1. Pygmies are expert tree-climbers. They often climb 20 m (65 feet) or more into the canopy in order to collect energy-rich, sweet wild honey.

At present, 4 million hectares (nearly 10 million acres) of Africa's rainforest are destroyed each year.

1. A Bayaka pygmy group, Central African Republic. Their intricate knowledge of the forest world is second to none.

sedentary villages by the side of a permanent road. Here they practise basic subsistence agriculture and trade meat, honey and medicine from the forest for metal and manioc. The forest is a hard place in which to live and the Bayaka are the first to admit it – they are not sentimental. When a logging company arrives for the timber, a cheap resource that can boost a Third World economy, they naturally sign up for a job at the sawmill, one of the few ways they have to ease their cash-flow problems. And the young would rather learn the modern ways, learn to speak English or French, go to school and forget about the lore of the forest. Where survival is hard it is difficult to be sentimental – that is the privilege of the rich.

Africa's laboratory of life

Some would say that wanting to conserve rainforests is simply a Western luxury, something that appeals to our romantic notion of wilderness. It is, after all, nice to know that somewhere out there is an unexplored forest world, untainted by the trappings of modern life.

Some of the older Bayaka are more adamant. They understand that their knowledge is important. Here there is a plant for everything. A liana is squeezed for its sap to make poison for an arrow, a bark is collected and ground to treat diarrhoea, tree saps and resins are used on wounds for their antibiotic qualities. Their intricate knowledge is testament to the crucial importance of plants. Quinine, strychnine, morphine, codeine, pyrethrin, the contraceptive pill, muscle relaxants, cardiac glycosides, now used extensively in surgery, are all compounds derived directly from plants, and so far science has only scratched the surface. The facts speak for themselves. Of all Africa's natural habitats, rainforest is the most vitally important, containing 8000 different plant species, 84 per cent of Africa's primates,

68 per cent of passerine birds, and 66 per cent of butterflies. A one-hectare plot of forest may contain several tens of thousands of species of insect – nobody knows the real number. Although about 1.5 million species have already been described by science it is estimated that another 60 million are yet to be found in the rainforests alone.

The green heart of Africa

What is more, the forests themselves regulate the continent's climate. They cool it down and help to stem the advance of the desert. They lock water and nutrients into the land and are also a massive sink for carbon, which is bound up in the fabric of the forest. If the forest is cleared and large areas burned, this carbon returns to the air as carbon dioxide, a greenhouse gas that warms the climate further. Without forests the centre of the African continent would be a parched dust-bowl, rife with poverty and famine. These are the real reasons for wanting to keep the forest. It is not a luxury.

In Bayaka Jengi ceremonies, the artificial divide between people, forest and animals becomes blurred and the three come together as part of an inextricable whole. The Bayaka know that they are part of the forest and could not survive without it. They need the forest and so do we all. The forest is Africa's life laboratory – it would be foolish in the extreme to ignore its plight. After 60 million years of experimentation it could now be simply a matter of decades before the green heart of Africa beats its last.

A future for the forest

The African rainforest is being utilized largely for short-term gain, without the reinvestment of resources that might ensure that it can regenerate and be re-used in the future. In many cases, this is an easy-fix solution to obtain cash quickly and help to alleviate overwhelming foreign debt. To make matters worse, the forests are often let out as concessions to foreign companies that have little or no interest in the home country itself, and the timber is sold in foreign markets for foreign profit. Very rarely does the revenue for these concessions find its way back to give the forest a value on a local level.

This is a recipe for disaster. A rainforest tree may take hundreds of years to regenerate so it is obvious that the exploitation of timber in Africa needs careful planning. And most importantly, it needs to be economically sustainable over the long term – not a priority for most governments, First or Third World. But things are changing.

Local governments are now liaising with international organizations like WWF and IUCN to formulate tropical forest action plans, or 'TAPS', which look into the best way to manage forests for wildlife diversity, timber production, indigenous people and tourism. There are now many reserves that, following the 'biosphere reserve' model, incorporate a core pristine forest – a reserve for biodiversity – surrounded by concentric zones dedicated to tourism, use by indigenous peoples, game hunting, and on the outside, forestry. There are also well-funded research programmes focusing on the improvement of timber extraction techniques, to minimize the effects of logging and maximize profits by combining selective extraction with regeneration.

In 1999 the heads of state of all the central African countries met to plan the future of the last remaining tracts of undisturbed forest. Their priorities were clearly set out: 'to promote conservation of the forests of the western Congo Basin and their biodiversity'. Things are looking up. It is not too late for Africa's forests. The will is now there, but at what price?

 WHAT IS MOKELE-MBEMBE?

The pygmy tribes of the Likouala swamp region of the Republic of Congo talk of a monster called Mokele-Mbembe, 'the one that stops the flow of rivers'. It is a giant lizard with the neck of a giraffe, the legs of an elephant and the head of a snake, some say with a frill on the neck or a horn on the head. It is 5 to 10 m (16–30 feet) long. It lives in the water and is wholly vegetarian but does not like hippopotamuses and will kill them on sight. It will overturn boats and kill people by biting them, though not eating them.

Like the Loch Ness monster, there are various ideas about what it is. When the locals draw a picture of it in the sand they draw what looks most like a sauropod dinosaur. When shown a picture of a sauropod they say that is Mokele-Mbembe. Others think that, with the horn on its head, it might simply be a rhino. A Japanese expedition in 1992 claims to have photographed the monster in Lac Tele in northern Congo. Clearly, people are seeing something. If there are large animals still to be discovered on Earth, then this has got to be one of the best places to look.

THE HEAVENS

Flying in a light aircraft over the African rainforest is a rare treat. What you see below is an endless carpet of undulating, spongy green stretched out from horizon to horizon under a tropical sun. It is not until you get above the forest like this that it all starts to make sense. This is what it is all about. This is where the real business of a rainforest happens. The forest canopy is, quite simply, a giant solar factory, absorbing the sun's energy and processing the chemicals of life. You can almost feel the lush, green leaves drawing in the water, sucking in the air and soaking up the sun's rays to make the precious food on which the rest of the forest depends. For those that make this place their home, things could not be more different from the dark, dank underworld below.

Previous page:
Riverine forest like
this has been an
important refuge for
many rainforest
species in the past.

1. The forest canopy is like a giant solar panel, absorbing energy from the sun.

THE HIGH-RISE ROOF GARDEN

At first glance, this is the high-rise roof garden of the forest, where the climate is fresh and the living is easy. Though the sun here is hot – tropical hot – there are cooling breezes and an infinite variety of fruits and flowers available to eat pretty much all year round. There are even views.

But, like every home, there is a downside. The heat of the sun and the waft of the breeze combine to make the conditions here more like those of a savannah, especially in the dry season and, ironically, drought is a problem. Though it rains often in the rainforest, there is little surface water up here. The epiphytes (plants that live high above the ground, attached to tree branches) do their best to catch all the water they can, and monkeys and birds sip from reservoirs of water in the hollows of tree trunks. When the rain comes, it comes hard and there is little shelter from the violent winds and lightning that accompany tropical storms. One slip of a foothold or a misjudged leap and gravity hands out a one-way ticket to the underworld.

Leaf power

The canopy is really all about leaves. Myriad leaves spread in an endless green carpet 30 metres (100 feet) above the ground. Each leaf is a highly sophisticated photo-chemical laboratory, intricately designed to maximize its potential for making food out of water, carbon dioxide and light. For some leaves this even includes special motor cells at the leaf base that enable the leaf to track the arc of the sun as it moves across the sky. For any would-be herbivore the canopy might well appear as a giant salad bowl of fresh green leaves free for the taking. However, every leaf in the rainforest invests a large proportion of the energy it creates into self-defence. They literally lace themselves with a whole host of poisons that make them at best indigestible and, at worst, deadly. Tannins, strychnine, cyanide are all

chemicals designed by leaves over millennia of herbal warfare. Some of these chemicals are so powerful that in humans they can cause anything from indigestion to bursting of the blood vessels and even cardiac arrest. But over the millennia the animals of the African forest have counter-attacked. Colobus monkeys have evolved special bacteria-filled guts to help break down some of these chemicals, and can safely digest as much cyanide in a day as would kill a human several times over. Some insects take use of this chemical weaponry even further. They concentrate the plant poisons in their own tissues, in turn becoming toxic to animals that might eat them.

A blushing forest

Even though rainforest trees are evergreen, a leaf has a finite lifespan and so a tree must continuously grow new ones. Young, juicy leaves, no matter how well protected, are particularly vulnerable to predators. If the trees of the forest produced these leaves all year round they would not stand a chance, so they have come up with a behavioural response to herbivore pressure. They resort to safety in numbers. All the trees produce their new leaves at the same time, swamping potential predators, who cannot possibly eat them all. The odds for survival are increased dramatically.

Since the new leaves are too young to have the green chlorophyll needed for photosynthesis, they are bright red and orange when they emerge. As a result, once a year at the beginning of the rainy season, the forest flushes pink and red with fresh leaves – a spectacular, African rainforest version of autumn.

1. A forest tree in Cameroon blushes pink with new leaves.

SLAVES

Plants are remarkably resourceful. They battle with each other for a place in the sun so they can photosynthesize. They wage chemical warfare with those that would eat them in order to hang on to their hard-won energy. But one thing they cannot easily do is move. They are firmly and quite literally rooted to the spot.

But why move yourself when you can get animals to do the moving for you? To this end, plants release tiny amounts of energy in sweet-smelling, irresistible drops of nectar – pure, bottled sunshine. Bees, sunbirds, ants, bats and primates come flocking to do the work of plants – anything that has wings or can climb has a need for nectar. And in getting their fix of the sweetness of the forest they inadvertently pick up pollen on a tongue or a beak, on a leg or a whisker, and carry it sometimes many miles away to fertilize another plant. In this way, trees use animals to reproduce.

Forest on the move

Once fertilized, trees produce seeds. For a seed to germinate directly beneath its parent would mean competition for light, minerals and water. This is good for neither parent nor progeny. So the incentive for most trees is to disperse their seeds as far and wide as possible. Giant bean-like pods like Pentaclethra explode with a rifle-like crack, loud enough to send elephants running. They hurl their seeds over 30 m (100 feet). Others send battalions of winged seeds spiralling down like mini helicopters to the forest floor or cast them into the canopy breeze in soft, fluffy bundles. The trees use their height to cast their descendants to the skies – capsules of genetic material sent on a mission from base, with instructions to colonize new ground.

But, again, it is in their manipulation of animals that the trees have really excelled, relying on nothing less than pure temptation – fruit. The trees offer their best, and animals come from miles around to reap the bounty, and in the process are hoodwinked into serving the plant. For gorillas, chimps, monkeys, bats, rodents and birds, fruit is the principal food source in the canopy, and all play their part in seed dispersal.

There are myriad designs, perfectly marketed to appeal to and tempt every kind of potential disperser. By themselves, trees can throw or drift their progeny at most a few hundred metres, but with animals on their side, it becomes tens of kilometres. And over many generations of trees, when the climate is favourable for forest expansion, this is how the African forest moves.

 FIGS

Because figs fruit all year round, they can be a life-saving food source for animals (right) outside of the main fruiting season.

The way a fig reproduces is one of the intricate marvels of the forest. For every species of fig there is an equivalent species of fig wasp, about 1 mm (⅒₀ inch) long, the female of which flies around the forest looking for a fig tree in flower. When she finds the right kind of fig, she crawls through a tiny opening in the end and finds one of three types of inward-facing flowers, the gall flower, specially designed for her.

Here, she lays around 300 eggs and then dies from exhaustion. When the eggs hatch, two types of adult wasp are released into the interior of the flower case. Wingless males mate immediately with newly hatched females and then they too die, never having left the flower. At exactly the same time, the fig produces pollen from male flowers and the winged female wasps load it onto receptacles on their bodies. They then leave through the hole and fly directly to another fig tree, where they repeat the process all over again. The wasp completes its life cycle at the same time as fertilizing the fig: co-evolution at its rainforest best.

⭐ Larvae of the butterfly, *Danaus chrysippus*, feed on highly toxic milkweeds. The poison is concentrated in their body and they inherit their protection. As adults no predator dares touch them.

IS IT SAFE UP THERE?

One great advantage of rainforest life for a large animal like a mammal is that there are relatively few predators. And that applies particularly to the high forest canopy. Lions and hyenas have recently been discovered in the depths of the Congo forest, but they cannot climb trees. Leopards are about the only real threat, and they are heavy and not designed for climbing that high. There are snakes, poisonous like vine snakes and constricting like pythons, and they can climb trees, but even for them an animal as agile as a squirrel or especially a monkey is difficult to catch.

The canopy world calls for a really specialist predator and that comes in the form of the crowned eagle. This huge bird is the most powerful of the African eagles and nests in the forks of emergent trees, high up above in the canopy. It reigns over up to 10 sq km (4 sq miles) of forest, which it surveys with razor-sharp eyes, its crown of feathers teased by the canopy breeze. The crowned eagle can swoop clean out of nowhere to grab at a monkey in mid-leap. It is so powerful that it will then carry the monkey vertically upwards from the ground and airlift it back to its waiting chicks.

In the forest it is the embodiment of stealth. Where the tangle of trees and foliage would deter other birds of prey with the high risk of breaking a wing, the crowned eagle is the master. With fine control of its short rounded wings, it can dodge and weave through the trunks and lianas for a lightning-fast ambush of its prey, deep in the heart of the forest.

1

Danger from below

Another serious threat to the tree dwellers of the African forest comes from a surprising quarter – the forest floor. In the Taï Forest of West Africa, it is our closest relative, the chimpanzee, that has developed probably the most sophisticated hunting system of all.

Because of the height of the trees here, a single chimp could not possibly catch a monkey like a red colobus alone. The monkeys not only have a system of alarm calls that warn them of the chimp's arrival, they are also much more agile and can retreat to places where a chimp would not dream of following. By hunting together, however, the chimps do stand a chance.

It is only the males that hunt and they have learned to work as a group, each individual

2

1. A crowned eagle eyrie, the penthouse suite of the rainforest – always in an emergent tree, with a spectacular view across the canopy.

2. A lone crowned eagle surveys the forest with its keen eyes. It reigns over a treetop territory of 10 sq km (4 sq miles).

HORNBILL AIRWAYS

Hornbills are the ultimate bulk seed transporter. Large, scrawny-looking birds with big, crested bills, looking remarkably like some latter-day archaeopteryx, they swoop from treetop to treetop in long, bounding glides, punctuated by intermittent bursts of their spread, fingered wings.

They are probably among, if not the, most important seed dispersers of the African forest, being instrumental in the dispersal of the seeds of 22 per cent of African trees. A great number of these trees – at least 30 species – are useful for timber. The aele has seeds that are typical hornbill-attracting designs. They are about the size of a cocktail sausage and contain a thin layer of oily, energy-rich flesh – lightweight but high in energy, just right for airlifting.

It takes at least an hour for the seeds to pass through the hornbill's gut, where the flesh is stripped off and then the seed ejected. In that time, the birds will have visited six or seven different trees and dispersed the seeds of each one far and wide across the forest.

1. By cooperating with one another, chimpanzees can hunt monkeys in the canopy.

2. (opposite) Chimpanzees crack nuts using logs as tools, in the Taï forest, Côte d'Ivoire.

with a specific role, defined by age and experience. The chimps head through the forest in silence, looking and listening for the sound of foraging colobus monkeys. They position themselves underneath a group and wait. One chimp then climbs up to the monkeys in order to flush them out; he is the 'climber', usually a young and less experienced chimp. The colobus head off through the canopy in alarm. Immediately, other chimps take up the pursuit on the ground. Two or three race to either side of the fleeing group of colobus, anticipating their direction of movement. They climb trees, and wait to herd the monkeys into a trap. These are the 'blockers'.

Meanwhile, the most experienced hunter of the group, the 'ambusher', travels on ahead. He takes up a strategic position in a tree in front of the moving colobus. As the climber drives on, the blockers 'funnel' the monkeys together and the trap is sprung. The fleeing monkeys jump straight into the arms of the waiting 'ambusher'. Most will get away but in the confusion that follows, the chimps very often get a catch. Their victim is taken to the ground, where the females and juveniles are waiting. The chimpanzee hunt is over, the catch a triumph of intelligence and teamwork.

Bridging the divide

In the distant evolutionary past, it was the monkeys that so successfully out-competed the apes and drove them from the African forest canopy. But with the resulting increase in size of the apes – in body and especially in brain – the tables began to turn.

Watching a chimp hunt today, it seems that the apes are getting their own back. Chimpanzees follow colobus from the forest floor, they make their catch in the canopy, then they return to the ground with their monkey prey. With their greater strength and especially their intelligence, the direct result of competition with the monkeys, chimpanzees have quite brilliantly bridged the divide between the two disparate worlds of the forest – canopy and forest floor. Today, they are the indisputable masters of both.

THE GREAT GUENON EXPLOSION

Monkeys are brilliantly designed for the canopy. They have opposable thumbs for gripping trees and tails essential for maintaining a fine sense of balance. They are just the right size for a life swinging and springing from branches and they have excellent vision. Their eyes not only face forwards to give binocular vision, enabling them to judge accurately the distance between trees when leaping, but they also see in colour and can process complex information about leaf and fruit ripeness and monkey communication. If there is one group of animals that has truly conquered the African forest canopy, it is the monkeys.

2

1

The cercopithecines

Following changes in the climate about 12 million years ago, a new monkey lineage appeared – the cercopithecines, a group that includes baboons, macaques, mangabeys and guenons. The macaques conquered Asia as far east as Japan but died out in Africa. The baboons stayed out of the forests to become the ultimate monkey of the savannah, as they still are today, and the mangabeys and, most importantly, the guenons, returned to the forest. What followed next shows the power of the rainforest as an environment where evolution can run riot. Within less than 2 million years, a mere blink of an eye in evolutionary terms, the guenons had radiated to fill just about every available niche in the African treetops.

The guenons

Guenons are little monkeys, ranging from 1.5 to 10 kg (3–40 lbs) in weight. They live in groups of just a small number of females with their offspring and a single male. Each species is very specialized in the height at which it lives, the type of forest that it likes and the techniques by which it forages for food. As a result, many species can live in the same place. A rich forest can contain as many as six species and a single tree as many as four.

As the African climate dried up about 2 million years ago and the forest retreated, the predominant habitat became gallery forest – the type of forest that lines the courses of permanent rivers. It is thought that at this time an ancestral guenon moved from the drying, drought-ridden savannah into this network of riverine forest, searching for fruit, gum, buds and insects on the ground and in the trees. Even in the driest times, the massive Congo River and its tributaries supported gallery forest and it was along this vast, linear forest network that the first guenons travelled, most likely colonizing gallery forest throughout the entire extent of the Congo Basin.

3

4

Now the stage was set for an explosion. As the climate improved and the full forest cover returned, there was a real advantage for a guenon that could adapt completely to life in the trees and break away from the rivers. Guenons are very adaptive and this did not present too much of a problem. Soon they were spreading far and wide through the canopy across the whole Congo Basin. As a dry phase returned, the forest contracted again and the new, widespread populations were split, surviving in the gallery forests and remote places where the climate remained wet. In isolation in subtly different habitats, separate populations evolved. When they were united again in the next wet phase, they had specialized so much that they were no longer able to breed and thus formed separate species.

In this way, over repeated cycles of change, 24 species of guenon evolved in just 2 million years – the most vibrant radiation of one group of monkeys in the world. They are varied, beautiful and colourful, with striking, sharp body markings. Many of the guenons of the deep forest have evolved elaborate facial and body signals by which they 'talk' to each other through the dense foliage. Subtle flashes of blue, cream, red and yellow, with nodding, shaking and weaving of their heads, all messages of greeting or interest in prospective mates. The wrong signal – the wrong mate. It is not difficult to see how even these subtle nuances of communication can lead to speciation.

1. Diana monkey
(*Cercopithecus Diana*).

2. De Brazza's monkey
(*Cercopithecus neglectus*).

3. Blue monkey
(*Cercopithecus mitis*).

4. Greater white-nosed guenon (*Cercopithecus nictitans*).

◆ TOPIC LINKS

2.3 Special Feature: The pied colobus of tropical Africa
p.78 The pied colobus of East and North Africa

5.1 Special Feature: The pulsing forest
p.163 Africa's green heart

5.3 THE UNDERWORLD

There is no such thing as a truly evergreen leaf. The leaves that do the work of the rainforest canopy all have a sell-by date and, when they have served their useful life, the tree draws back a few key minerals, cuts off supplies of water, salts and sugars and discards them.

A large, broad sheet of a leaf drifts calmly down through the countless levels of the forest – 30 m , 40 m (100–130 feet) down. Here, the air is still and saturated, almost like falling through water, and as more and more of the African sun is excluded by the other leaves above, the forest gets darker, until only two per cent of the light makes it through.

As the leaf comes gently to rest on the musty forest floor, a welcoming committee awaits. For every life form that exists in the forest, survival is all about getting a share of the sun's energy. For the creatures that live in the forest underworld, this leaf is a rare gift from the heavens.

1. Even before an old leaf is discarded by a tree, fungi are already at work reclaiming what nutrients they can.

LITTLE CREATURES THAT RULE THE WORLD

Bacteria, blue-green algae, mushrooms, toadstools, yeasts, moulds, slime moulds, insects and mammals make up the community commonly known as decomposers. The forest floor seethes with them, but of the millions in every square metre only 1 per cent is known to science.

These are the great recyclers and they specialize in extracting every last drop of energy from the waste of the forest – and not only from dead leaves. Termites, for example, are responsible for breaking down the indigestible cellulose of fallen trunks and branches, whilst scavenging beetles tuck into dead flesh. We are familiar with the fruiting bodies of fungi, such as mushrooms and toadstools, but the working part of a fungus is an intricate net of microscopic hair-like hyphae cast far and wide across the forest floor. When a leaf, twig, flower or even a dead animal falls from the world above, the fungal network embraces it and starts to break it down. It feeds by digesting dead organic matter with special enzymes and, in doing so, releases nutrients back into the system. Nothing is dead for long in the rainforest.

Some fungi have an even more important role. Their mycelial strands interlock with the roots of canopy trees in one of the most important relationships of the forest. In exchange for a discrete supply of sugars from the tree, the fungus pumps nutrients back into its roots. In this way, the fungus gets its tiny part of the sunshine and the tree gains vital nutrients from the bodies of the dead.

The relationship between fungus and plant is a cornerstone of the forest. But it is only one of an almost infinite number of intricate relationships that, over the millennia, have been forged between the inhabitants of this forest underworld and the trees they live in and amongst. With the same sleight of hand that allows trees to entice animals into pollination and seed dispersal in the canopy, the trees forge partnerships here. They even play the same trump card – sugar, sweet elixir from a world above – though here, with effectively no sunlight at all, their hand is even stronger.

It is no coincidence that we dislike rotting food. The bad smell and taste are a decomposer's way of putting us off so it can claim the energy for itself.

Partners of plants

A jet-black, shiny ant, about 1.5 cm (⅗ inch) long is looking for a home. She is a barteria ant queen and predictably she chooses a barteria tree in which to make a start on her new colony. She cuts out a tiny hole in one of the tree's lateral branches and climbs inside. Here, the queen finds a network of hollow chambers, perfect for her requirements, and soon she has set up a colony of ants, united in their unquestioning industriousness and their excruciatingly painful sting. Inside the hollow branches they are protected and they eat sugar solution milked from tiny-scale insects that feed on the sap of the tree. Perfect for the ants, but the relationship is not all one way.

Like all trees, the barteria needs every advantage it can get to compete for light.

Little do the ants know that they are there to help it. The slightest sign of disturbance is the ants' call to arms. They pour out of the now many stem openings in their hundreds and swarm all over the tree. Anything in the vicinity is viciously attacked. Herbivores are driven back, and even the climbing stems of other plants trying to get a hold on the barteria are cut up and methodically dispatched. This is the barteria's private army and it misses nothing. When there is no emergency the ants spend their time chiselling mould and lichens off the barteria's leaves, leaving them shiny and clean so they can make best use of what little light there is here in the underworld. For the ant, full board and lodging; for the plant, at the expense of a little sugar, its own personal security force.

1. Weaver ants make their homes in living leaves of rainforest plants – one of the many relationships between ants and plants.

2. There are many strange, shy animals that eke out a living scuttling around on the forest floor, such as this giant elephant shrew. 1

Rich pickings from the forest floor

Not all animals are restricted to eating the dead or existing in direct servitude to trees. The forest is the ultimate in multidimensional food chains and so, for everything living at the bottom, there is something that will eat it. Again, ants are the specialists. For the termites that spend their time recycling the limbs and trunks of trees, everyday life is routinely upset by *Pachycondyla analis* ants. Some call them 'Sa Sa', because of the way they hiss when breathed on. Regular as clockwork, at the same time every day, orderly single-file columns of raiders set out to find termite nests, which they systematically pillage of larvae and eggs.

Less precise but even more impressive are the huge carpets of army ants that sweep across the forest floor, dispatching to their

2

COMMUNAL SPIDERS

Because it rains so much in the rainforest, spiders' webs are constantly being broken and much hard-earned energy in silk production is wasted. Though *Agelena consociata* (right) is a small spider, it lives in colonies of hundreds of individuals and together they combine web-building power. With many spiders, webs can be built and repaired very quickly – they are also massive. A good example can stretch for tens of square metres, from the forest floor high up into the canopy. As a moth or butterfly drifts through the forest, it first hits vertical web strands that run from high anchor points down to a series of hammocks lower down. It is knocked out of the air and spirals downwards until it eventually lands in one of the hammocks. Here the spiders use strength in numbers to herd the insect down, sometimes even chasing it around like a pack of dogs.

The web also provides protection for larger animals. The tiny woolly bat, *Kerivoula muscilla*, is one of the strangest. The wings of these bats resemble dried leaves whilst resting and their hair is long and frizzy. It is thought that by flying inadvertently through the webs of *Agelena*, bats may pick up a cargo of spiders and help create new colonies through-out the forest.

⭐ The 'miracle plant' gets little light on the forest floor, so it cannot manufacture sugar. Instead, it produces a protein with no nutritional value that tastes 100,000 times sweeter.

encampment any unfortunate individual that blunders into their path. But even the ants do not get it entirely their own way. Not many things have a penchant for ants; they are tough and acidic, and they bite and sting. But as long as there have been ants in African forests, there have been pangolins. The giant pangolin weighs over 30 kg (66 lbs) and is from an ancient lineage of ant and termite eaters that look more like reptiles than mammals. They have armoured scales as protection and lap up their tricky prey with a long, sticky tongue. Ants and termites are difficult to digest, but the pangolin has a gizzard-like stomach, full of sand, which

makes short work of their tough bodies. There are birds too that live exclusively off the small creatures of the forest floor. The shy and extremely rare picathartes from Cameroon and Gabon hops delicately around on the forest floor with its beautiful red and blue head and exquisite creamy belly, picking insects and grubs from the leaf litter as it goes. The picathartes does not need to fly since here it is protected from predators. However, to keep its eggs and chicks safe from tree-climbing snakes, it builds mossy nests that cling to the under-hangs of rocks and thereby wins its common name, the rock fowl.

1. For everything that gains a living from plants, there is something that in turn feeds on it. Here, a female lynx spider preys on a bee.

2. (opposite) A gaboon viper amid the leaf litter. It is an ambush predator and uses its remarkable camouflage to hide in wait for unsuspecting prey.

1

THE BIG ANIMALS

Walking in the African forest, guidebook to mammals in hand, expectations are bound to run high. Ants and termites are all around, as are tree trunks and decomposing leaves, but a sighting of an elephant, a leopard, or perhaps a gorilla would really make the day. Many of the big mammals that make the African forest so unique do live on the ground; but where are they to be found?

The bizarre leaf-eating forest relative of the giraffe, the okapi, is found only in the northeast of the Congo river basin, in the far reaches of the Ituri forest, and even there it is hard to find – at most there is just one animal per 2.5 sq km (1 sq mile). Shy and well camouflaged, it picks its way fussily through the best of the new, green leaf shoots, reaching as much as 2 m (6½ feet) above the ground with its long neck.

Leopards are widespread throughout the rainforest but, being mainly nocturnal and very shy, are extremely difficult to see, and though lions and even hyenas have been recorded occasionally, they are rare. Even common antelopes like the yellow-backed duiker are glimpsed only as they attempt to escape your noise or smell.

The only time it is easy to see the real richness of the forest floor fauna is when there is some kind of draw – an event that animals just cannot afford to miss. And there is no better draw than a fruiting tree. Trees generally bear their fruits high up in the canopy. There they are proudly displayed for all to see. But, once ripe, they fall from the canopy to the forest floor and that is when you do get lucky.

2

1. The shy and elusive forest relative of the giraffe – the okapi.

2. The red river hog, *Potamocherus porcus*, roots through the forest floor, sometimes in groups of up to 100 or more.

Manna from heaven

The moabi tree is one of Africa's most spectacular and beautiful trees. It is strong and straight, with a wide umbrella of a crown spreading thick with epiphytes, almost 70 m (230 feet) above the ground – a true rainforest giant. For centuries it has been prized by humans for its green avocado-like fruit, mainly for the valuable oil that can be heated and squeezed from its seeds. In villages where the surrounding forest has been cleared for agriculture, moabi trees are left standing, proud and tall in a landscape of grubbed and burned-out forest pastures. In these days of deforestation, the moabi's fruit has been its saviour – a fortunate coincidence of evolution. For an animal of the forest floor, January and February – the moabi fruiting season – is a time of plenty. Avocado-sized fruits rain down from 60 or 70 m (200–230 feet). The thud as they hit the ground and the irresistible sweet yeasty smell draws animals from miles around.

Staking out such a tree is the best way to catch a glimpse of the shy characters of the forest underworld. Small antelope, like duikers, pick at the fruit on the ground. Charismatic red river hogs – red, gremlin-like forest pigs – root their way through the leaf litter in groups of 100 or more, hoovering up fruits as they go. Fruit is also a major part of an ape's diet and gorillas and chimpanzees are quick to cash in on fruiting season bounty. The great apes are more than happy on the ground, tucking into succulent, fleshy fruits. You might even be privileged enough to see one of the most impressive sights of the African forest, a troop of mandrills. It is the mandrills' contact calls of continuous barks, grunts and squeals as they move through the forest that first alert you to the coming of an army. Out of the forest, lines and lines of these monkeys emerge, as many as 1000 in a troop. They can take hours to pass by.

The fruit race

Because fruit is such an important investment for the tree, it is very important that it does not rot before its animal dispersers have eaten it. A whole range of special fungicides and antibiotics have evolved in fruits that help to avoid premature rotting. But, in the warm, wet conditions of a tropical forest, the decomposers soon get a hold. Bacteria and fungi begin to decompose the fruit to claim its energy for themselves. As they do so they too produce toxins and evil-smelling compounds that are designed to put the animals off.

1

GUARDIANS OF THE FOREST

One of the most important animals for the forest loves fruit too. It is quite amazing how easy it is for such a huge animal to move unnoticed and unheard behind a veil of leaves in the forest. Often the soft, dinner-plate prints of its feet are the sole evidence of its passing. But then, without warning, you look up and there it is, in front of you, a grey, wrinkled wall of an animal, rumbling with a voice below any human register. Before you know it your heart has jumped out of your mouth and you are running for your life, chased by all 5 or 6 tonnes (4½–5½ tons) of African forest elephant.

Wherever there is a moabi tree in fruit, elephants are not far off. The elephant is the only animal big and strong enough to be able physically to remodel the forest. They can, and frequently do, pull and knock down quite large trees. But, much more importantly for the trees themselves, just by moving around fruiting trees they literally stamp out any plant competition and leave a perfectly maintained clearing at the bottom of the tree. After only a few days of fruiting, a moabi tree has a cleared area around its trunk, a shop window in which to display all its fruit.

Doughnuts

Some trees can reproduce only with the help of elephants. The Omphalocarpum is a medium-sized tree with flaky, grey bark, scarred and swollen from elephant damage. Countless years of gouging with tusks and butting with heads has caused the bark to swell into great knotty swirls and, where the damage is recent, white sap oozes from the trunk to sterilize and protect the wound. But the tree puts up with all of this for the benefit of a partnership with elephants.

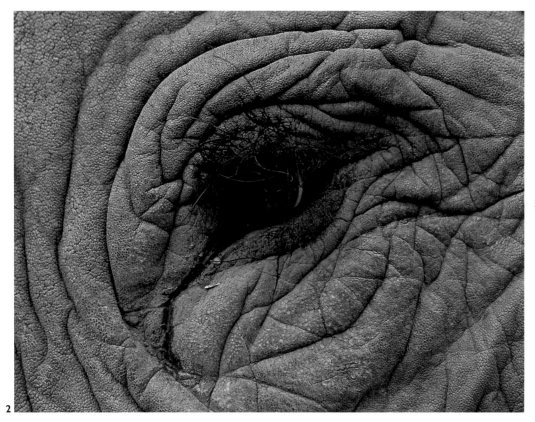

1. Mandrills look like multicoloured baboons, but are more closely related to mangabeys. This young male's facial colours enable visual communication in the thick forest. As he matures, yawns, lip or eye flips and displays of strength will mark his status in the group.

2. In spite of their huge bulk, elephants are remarkably silent. Many rainforest trees have fruits that are dispersed exclusively by elephants.

3. For an elephant, the large doughnut fruits of the Omphalocarpum tree are irresistible.

For the elephants the attraction is not so much the bark but the fruit. Omphalocarpum fruit are unmistakable and can only have been designed for elephants. They are big, about the size of a melon, and are round and brown, with a dimple in the middle like a doughnut. Locally they are called 'the moon's breasts'. They appear not on the ends of branches but on the side of the trunk and drop with the resounding thud of 2 kg (4½ lbs) or more of fruit hitting the forest floor. It can only be worth investing so much energy in a fruit if the tree can be sure of trapping an elephant and, sure enough, elephants cannot resist. With their remarkable low-frequency hearing, they can probably hear the fruits fall from miles away.

Elephants wrap their trunks around the fallen fruit and scoop them into their mouths, eyes watering with delight. Some stab the hard outer covering with their tusks to puncture it open; they are the only animal strong enough. Inside the fruit is a copious amount of sticky sap like chewing gum, and round, flat seeds that slip easily past the elephant's teeth. After a short stay in the elephant's gut they are passed out the other end, totally unharmed and deposited in a pile of ready-made fertilizer.

Elephants are the major dispersers of seeds in the forest. It has recently been found that the network of elephant paths that criss-crosses a healthy forest leads directly from one fruiting tree to another. But in areas where years of poaching have eliminated elephants, doughnut fruits rot on the ground, the trees unable to reproduce. Trees and elephants are inseparable partners in the African forest – remove one and upset the balance of the whole.

The salt road

There are certain minerals and salts, essential for animals, that cannot be obtained from plants. Plant-eating animals must therefore get them directly from the ground itself. In a rainforest there are precious few places where this is possible. That is why it is common to see butterflies gathering on the exposed sand at the sides of rivers. Here they are licking up salts. As elephants walk, they urinate and essential compounds from their urine are concentrated on the ground. So, butterflies also gather on the trails of elephants. In some places, the paths look as though they are made of butterflies. Elephants need these precious compounds too but in much greater quantities and over the centuries they have learned where to find them.

1. Minerals are hard to come by in the forest. Butterflies lick the salts from elephant dung.

2. The western lowland gorilla reminds us of our beginnings in the African rainforest. **1**

2

In Central African Republic there is a place called Dzanga-Sangha, where generation after generation of elephant feet have trodden the paths that lead to a clearing in the forest. At any one time 50 or 60 elephants visit the waterholes at the centre of the clearing. They blow air down their trunks and froth up the water to help dissolve the minerals. Then they drink it like a tonic. There is kaolin here that helps neutralize toxins from plants in the elephants' stomachs but nobody quite knows what other chemicals they are finding. What is known is that they are essential for elephant survival.

Whatever the prize, the elephants' need for this place has ensured another thing. With the continual trampling of feet and rubbing of trees, the elephants have kept the clearing open for others – rare antelope like the beautiful stripy bongo, red river hogs, forest buffalo, African grey parrots and lowland gorillas. Here, canopy world meets underworld, as even black-and-white colobus monkeys come down to the ground to sample the goodness.

Free

In Odzala National Park in Congo, a vast network of these clearings has recently been discovered, some of them huge. From the air they are light-green, grassy oases in a sea of dark-green trees. On the ground they are little Edens, where the large animals of the forest can be seen together. For the newcomer, stepping into the African rainforest for the first time, coming across a clearing like this is a great relief. In the forest underworld there are no views, no horizon, no sunsets or sunrises. Here, the suffocating claustrophobia is lifted.

It is tempting to think that the animals, though perhaps nervous of leaving the protection of the forest, find a sense of relief here too – a place where they are briefly released from the age-old grip of plants. And as you watch lowland gorillas venturing out from the trees in family groups, sometimes momentarily on two legs, you cannot help but be reminded of our own ancestors escaping from the forest to walk upright in the open savannahs for the first time.

6

SAVANNAHS

SAVANNAH STORY

Grass waves gently in the wind on a rolling plain, studded with acacia trees. Lions lie, creamy-white bellies exposed to the sun, eyes tightly shut. Way in the distance, where the silhouettes of delicate lace-canopied acacia trees break the horizon, Thomson gazelles graze, rich chestnut coats broken up by black and white stripes sharp in the sun.

To many of us, this is Africa. But, however familiar the savannah landscape may seem, there are many surprises below the surface. This ecosystem is a newcomer, the latest habitat to emerge from the melting pot of geological and climatic change. An environment modified first by large herbivores, and then by hominid and human activities over the millennia.

Savannahs have unique ecological features, several of which were crucial in our own development as a species. The story opens with the destruction of an ancient order.

Previous page: Apart from females with cubs and mating pairs, leopards are essentially solitary animals and fighting between individuals is rarely seen.

1. Lions spend, on average, 23 out of every 24 hours conserving their energy and doing as much of nothing as possible.

IN THE BEGINNING

The broad swathe of rainforest, maintained by steady rainfall, stretched right across the African continent for millions of years. Then the climate began to change. Less rain fell. Parched trees died and forests fragmented; but this was not a disaster. Change sits uneasily with us but it is a powerful engine for evolution. In this case, the stage was set for the entrance of an unlikely looking hero. Grass. An epic figure in the savannah saga.

There is evidence to suggest that some primitive grasses may have existed 80 million years ago in forest clearings or straggling over rocks where nothing else could survive. As the climate became drier some 25 million years ago, thick forests thinned into thickets, and grasses seized the chance to expand. Today, they are the most successful visible terrestrial life form. Equally good at hanging on to a living in what appear to be the most dire circumstances, grasses are unrivalled at the speed with which they can increase.

The spread of grasses coincided with the increase in savannahs, which today snake their way across Africa from west to east and down to the south. Bordered by forests and deserts, they cover a third of the land surface in a mosaic of grasses, trees and bushes, for 'savannah' is a term that describes a rich range of environments, ranging from tangled woodlands to treeless grassy plains.

In scientific terms, a wooded savannah is different from a rainforest since it has an open tree canopy as opposed to the closed canopies of the forest. A semi-arid savannah has an annual rainfall of over 500 mm (20 inches), making it slightly wetter than a desert. Between these two extremes, savannahs can be treeless grassland, open grassland with a scattering of trees, or woodland of varying density; it depends on local differences in topography, soils, rainfall and fire. But one main distinguishing feature of all types of African savannahs – woodland or grassland – is the combination of distinctly dry and wet seasons coupled with constantly high temperatures. Within a few days of rain, the landscape changes colour from the tawny lion hues of the dry season to an evanescent emerald – and life takes off.

The energy flow

Dark cloud shadows race over rolling green plains dotted with the bright coats of antelopes and gazelles. Horns clash as males wrestle in a cloud of dust. Fawns suckle whilst their mothers nervously scan the skyline. No other environment can match savannahs for the sheer numbers of large mammals that thrive here permanently. The reason such herds are here and nowhere else lies in the energy flow. And, once again, the bottom line lies with the grasses.

The life cycle of grasses dictates a rapid turnover. Unlike long-lived trees, which may survive for 500 or 1000 years, grasses can shoot and produce seed in just one. Seeds can lie dormant for a long time but when conditions are right, they grow fast – so fast that the growing shoots support a huge horde of grazers, which, in turn, feed the largest array of meat-eaters found in the world today. As lions reluctantly leave their kill, scavengers

move in. Hyenas, vultures and jackals strip off every morsel of flesh. A wildebeest carcass disappears in a very short time, leaving only a few bones to whiten in the sun. Little is wasted for there are even moths whose larvae feed on the horns.

Dung beetles speedily deal with immense quantities of animal waste. So-called army worms which are, in fact, caterpillars can clear entire areas of grasses in a very short time. Harvester termites live underground and are also avid collectors of grasses. Aardvarks and aardwolfs feed on termites. There are swarms of locusts and flocks of quelea, a seed-eating bird, whose numbers can build to staggering proportions. All this activity means that, on average, savannahs can recycle 30 per cent of the total living material every year compared with 8 per cent measured in rainforests. And, since the basic nutrients are recycled so fast, this means the ecosystem can support large herbivore populations of grazers and browsers.

HERBIVORES

The first grass-eating animals made their appearance some 25 million years ago, just as grasslands began to expand. Herbivore teeth had to adapt to cope with the hard crystals of silica contained in grasses. At about the same time, one of the greatest evolutionary revolutions in the history of life on Earth – the modification of the stomach into a four-chambered organ – took place between 58 and 25 million years ago. It opened the door for herbivores to change from small, solitary forest occupants, and was to have major consequences, both in the development of the savannah ecosystem and in our own history.

Plant tissue is composed of cellulose. Since multicellular animals cannot process cellulose, most of this potential energy is denied them. However, in ruminants the half-chewed grass is first stored in a compartment of the stomach called the rumen.

 ## GRASS AND THE GRAZERS

Scientist Sam McNaughton reveals that the long period in co-evolution between grass and grazer may have had a very exciting pay-off. He discovered that nitrogen and sodium were at much higher levels in the soils of highly grazed sites compared with nearby areas where animal densities were lower. Despite this difference, the soils had similar fertility, so McNaughton concluded that animals promote sodium and nitrogen availability through urination. And the effects of the grazers are even more complex. Grazing leads to an increase in nitrogen in the leaves, which speeds up the decomposition of leaf litter.

So the mammalian grazers of the Serengeti, like these Thomson gazelles (right), actually accelerate grassland nutrient cycling and, in particular, the two minerals which are especially important in their own nutrition, both sodium and nitrogen being needed by pregnant females and their growing young – the first evidence that terrestrial grazers modify an ecosystem to alleviate nutritional deficiency.

1. Wild dogs depend on stamina, running out in the open for some 5 km (3 miles) at a steady 48 km per hour (30 miles per hour), snapping at the rear and sides of the prey until it eventually tires.

Here, bacteria and protozoa break down the cellulose into fatty acids, which pass into the blood stream. After several hours, the resulting mash is regurgitated into the mouth and thoroughly ground – an activity known as chewing the cud. Only then does the plant matter pass to the third chamber of the stomach and digestion proceeds as in other animals.

This process allows much more fibre to be processed – ruminants' dung is finer-grained than that of non-ruminants such as elephant, rhino and zebra. However, there is a sting in the tail. Ruminants need time to process their food and when the protein content of their food falls below 6 per cent, they are on a

losing streak. Unable to process their food fast enough, they lose weight quickly. As well as acting as a fermentation chamber, the rumen is a storage vessel, giving ruminants the chance to quickly gather food in an area that may have good forage but is full of predators. They can then retire to a safer patch of ground to ruminate.

The evolution of the rumen laid the foundation for the herds of large, gregarious herbivores that munch unselectively on the common but less nutritious grasses of the ever-increasing expanses of the savannah. The result of this is that some herbivores have evolved particularly fascinating aspects to their social behaviour.

The total amount of meat eaten in the Serengeti by lions, leopards, cheetahs, hyenas and wild dogs is estimated to be in the region of 9 million kg (8100 tons) every year.

LIFE IN A CROWD

Thomson gazelles are small and vulnerable to a wide range of predators, from lions and cheetahs to wild dogs and jackals. When these gazelles spot a hunter on the prowl, the response is immediate. Snorting with alarm, heads held stiffly up and striped flanks twitching, the group moves closer to the danger. Gradually attracting more and more gazelles from the neighbourhood, the staring mob gets quite close to the source of danger but maintains a crucial flight distance. They will 'escort' the predator for some distance and, by drawing attention to it, spoil any chance it might have had of ambushing the unwary.

There are some definite benefits to herd life. First, there is safety in numbers. Not only are there many pairs of eyes to keep a look out for danger, but there is a lot of choice for the predator, so the odds against being selected as the victim are much reduced. In addition to reducing the risk of predation, living in large aggregations also means that the chances for both males and females of finding a suitable mate are increased. And there is a third advantage. Thorough research, carried out by Professor Herbert Prins on the African buffalo, shows that their high numbers also result in more efficient foraging on certain types of resources.

The buffalo is the power of Africa personified. In the words of Laurens van der Poste: 'The buffalo's powerful head darkening the yellow grass has more quintessential Africa in it for me than any other manifestation of all the scores of animals that I love and know. It's as if in the buffalo the very stones and earth of Africa have turned magically into a living design of life'. For some people, the

 BUFFALO BULLS

Just a few thousand years ago, a giant buffalo with an enormous span of horns was abundant. Today, the horns of the one-tonne (2250-lb) bulls (left) on the savannah are small in comparison but still very impressive.

As the savannah habitat increased, forest buffalo moved out and slowly grew bigger. Unlike the females, mature bulls only enter a herd when they are in tip-top condition. During their stay, they slowly lose weight and, at a certain point, drop out to regain condition. Now they run a greater risk of being attacked, so to increase their security, they congregate in small bachelor groups where they stand a better chance of getting more top-quality food and building up their strength before re-entering the same herd, or a different one.

To be successful, bulls must mate with as many females as possible. Since the strongest wins the most mates, they are adept at assessing the condition of any potential rivals by eye. When dominance is in doubt, they will tussle in relatively friendly sparring contests. Serious fights are so rare that only three have ever been fully described. In each, both contestants looked as though they were about the same size and condition. All three ended with both winner and loser dying from their injuries.

head with its massive horns shining darkly in the sun was, and still is, the only hunting trophy worth taking home; for others, the formidable bulk of the buffalo is handy meat. Commercial meat poaching has wiped out the vast herds in Mozambique in a mere two decades. Throughout the continent their numbers are in drastic decline, a sad reflection since there is so much more to buffalo than first meets the eye.

Buffalo business

Herds of buffalo move across the plains. From a distance, they form a solid, living wall of black and tan. Their heads held low, their pace is slow and measured. White dust billows from hundreds of hooves.

The herd is faithful to a home range for generation after generation, unless there are severe droughts or floods. It is a highly organized social entity made up of cows, which stay with their natal herd, calves, juveniles and bulls. And when the herd is on the move, each female often occupies the same position.

However, animals at the rear suffer severe social inequality. They get much less food and also suffer from an increased risk of parasite infestation since they are usually grazing close to droppings from the animals in the front. And rarely are they in good enough condition to breed. But despite these serious disadvantages, these animals remain loyal to the herd. The reason lies in the relatively complicated art of grazing. Only a few plant species have enough protein, and only some of these occur in swards sufficiently dense to satisfy buffalo requirements. In addition, competing grazers may deplete some patches and, furthermore, different plants re-grow at varying speeds and with varying quality. Over a year, many of the suitable patches are just not good enough. So each day the question of where to graze is critical.

Buffalo cows are mature females, and they have their own views on where it is best to go next to get the best food. About an hour before the herd moves off, some of them get up and adopt a special posture for a minute or so, before lying down again. Averaged out, the orientation of their bodies overlaps with the compass bearing of the area to which the herd moves. A communal decision has been taken and it is this pooling of opinion, or 'voting', that works so well.

A buffalo herd is, therefore, an information centre on the best way of getting enough to eat. This sophisticated development in ▷▷

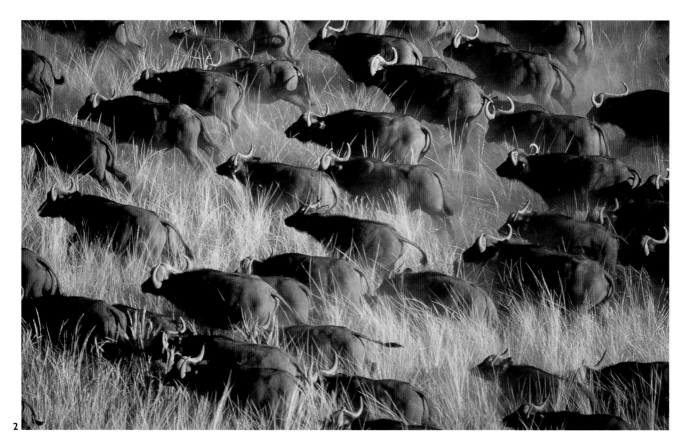

2

1. A herd of impala makes good use of their many ears, noses and eyes to detect danger in their surroundings.

2. Herds of buffalo graze, break and trample grasses, which stimulates rapid regrowth and encourages intense and repeated foraging.

THE SERENGETI/MARA ECOSYSTEM

There is one very special savannah in Africa. It is found in the east, and today it is known as the Serengeti. It is almost impossible to visit this amazing landscape without being moved either by beauty beyond words, or harshness that is hard to understand. Many visitors revisit time and time again. George Schaller, one of the world's greatest naturalists, wrote: 'To witness that calm rhythm of life revives our worn souls and recaptures a feeling of belonging to the natural world. No-one can return from the Serengeti unchanged, for tawny lions will forever prowl our memory and great herds throng our imagination.'

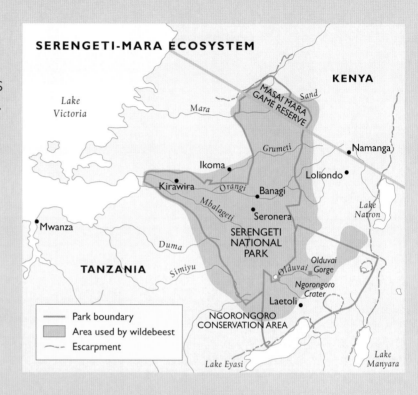

SERENGETI-MARA ECOSYSTEM

KENYA

Lake Victoria

Mara

MASAI MARA GAME RESERVE

Sand

Namanga

Grumeti

Ikoma

Loliondo

Kirawira

Orangi

Banagi

Mbalageti

Lake Natron

Mwanza

Seronera

SERENGETI NATIONAL PARK

Duma

Simiyu

Olduvai

Olduvai Gorge

TANZANIA

Ngorongoro Crater

Laetoli

NGORONGORO CONSERVATION AREA

Lake Eyasi

Lake Manyara

—— Park boundary
▨ Area used by wildebeest
-·- Escarpment

1

Serengeti wildlife

The Serengeti/Mara is, indeed, a place where superlatives are hard to avoid. Stretched across the plains and dotted through the woodland are vast herds of migratory grazers, resident grazers, browsers, predators, prey, recycling agents and an extraordinary diversity of herbivores.

On the plains are Thomson gazelles that, with their constantly flicking tails, manage to convey an air of being busy, even in the heat of mid-day. There are the massive herds of white-bearded wildebeest and smaller groups of wise-looking topi and kongoni. Looking every bit like nursery toys, tight knots of zebra quarrel and bicker, while in the woodland glades, herds of wide-eyed impala and rather stately waterbuck are found. In quiet corners lurk pairs of dik-dik and family groups of oribi.

A frisson of danger is provided by carnivores like leopard, cheetah and lion, plus serval, caracal, wild cat and genet. Vibrant flashes of colour light up the scenery from a variety of birds. There are the exotic electric blues and purples of lilac-breasted rollers and the vivid greens and orange of the Fischer's lovebirds. Lovebirds like company and, as they dart off in panic, the tight, chattering flocks catch the light like bright handfuls of jewels carelessly tossed into the air.

Serengeti history

The seeds for this particular ecosystem were sown some 10 to 12 million years ago. The prevailing winds, which picked up moisture from the Indian Ocean and blew across the African continent, sustaining the wide swathe of forest, were interrupted by a

2

barrier – the uplift associated with the Great Rift Valley. The first effect was that slowly the climate became drier. The second was much more dramatic. Volcanic eruptions from a long chain of volcanoes threw out vast quantities of dust that covered the plains below in a fertile blanket of ash. One, Ol Doinyo Lengai, is still active today.

At the base of these formidable mountains lies an exciting collection of hominid remains. There are the famous footprints of Laetoli, which were made 3.6 million years ago by three hominids walking upright across the savannah landscape. And in Olduvai Gorge there are a huge variety of stone tools and fossilized bones from several other hominid species. Allan Earnshaw talks of the Serengeti as 'a window in time taking us back to our beginnings' and, in fact, the vista has remained

virtually unchanged over the past 3.5 million years. However, many of the animals that shared the savannah with our distant ancestors are now extinct. It is a sobering thought that the spectacular numbers and variety of animals around today are actually a pale vestige of what used to be.

Despite this, the Serengeti/Mara is still one of the most intact savannah ecosystems left in the world today. Even at the end of the nineteenth century, many game migrations were still common throughout Africa. Today, there are only three large-scale migrations left – the white-bearded wildebeest of the Serengeti and Mara, and the migration of the tiang and white-eared kob in southern Sudan. Elsewhere, in Kenya, Tanzania, Namibia, Botswana and South Africa, traditional routes have been severed by game management fences and agriculture.

1. Wild cats are some of the more unusual, rarely seen small carnivores that live in woodlands and out on the grassy plains.

2. Wildebeest and other herbivores feed and move at night as well as during the day, especially on bright, moonlit nights when their vision is good.

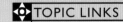 TOPIC LINKS

1. Spotted hyenas form big clans whenever plenty of prey gives them the opportunity, but they spread out or commute whenever their prey disperses.

2. Hunter-gatherers like the Bushmen of the Kalahari and the Hadza, who live near the Serengeti, also form larger groups when prey is abundant.

1

social organization is paralleled in the social lives of some carnivores.

Hyena politics

The teeming herbivore numbers building up throughout the savannah habitats also gave carnivores an opportunity to develop social groups. There are packs of wild dogs, prides of lions and affiliations of male cheetahs, but probably the most elaborate social structure of them all is found amongst the clans of spotted hyenas.

Unusually for mammals and unique amongst social carnivores, spotted hyenas live in a world dominated by females. Power resides with just one matriarch, an alpha female, although there may be 80 to 100 individuals within a clan. Males are subservient

to all the females and, unlike females who stay with their natal clan for life, they leave around puberty, often wandering hundreds of kilometres before finally being accepted into a new clan. The alpha female dominates clan life, taking absolute precedence at kills. Next in rank are her cubs and, below them, her sisters and their offspring. The newest born cubs of the alpha-female immediately take precedence over their older siblings. A mother often stays on her own at the birthing den to build up a close relationship with her cubs. After about two weeks, she then brings them to the communal den where the rest of the clan members greet them all with intense excitement.

In hyena society there is a range of ritualized body language to show submission, respect and aggression, plus the range of

subtleties in between. These social skills are vitally important in this matrilineal society, as the alpha female's power depends on a network of complicated alliances. Old alliances can be broken and new friendships formed in the blink of an eye. Loyalty can be rewarded by a move up (or a slide down) the hierarchy, depending on who is successful in the power struggle. However, being at the top pays, since the offspring of high-ranking females enjoy more food, grow faster and bigger and have automatic entrance into the higher echelons as their birthright.

Hyena politics is not far removed from the day-to-day life of another social species that was to romp ahead in the race for life within the savannah system – a species that was to have a profound effect on the very fabric of the ecosystem itself.

HOMINID EVOLUTION

Savannahs have the fastest energy turnover, the highest numbers of resident and migratory herbivores, and an array of social carnivores. It was also in this habitat that one species was able to hone its hunting skills, reasoning power and communication abilities to such a degree that it quickly became the top predator all over the world.

The history of hominid evolution is complicated and controversial. However, the discovery by Mary Leakey of fossilized footprints at Laetoli, on the edge of the Serengeti National Park, was a major breakthrough. About 3.6 million years old, the footprints are the first evidence so far that some apes had become bipedal. At this time, this area of East Africa probably looked much the same then as it does today. Savannah grasslands interspersed with clumps of acacia thickets and woodland. Because the forests had been cut back by drier weather, some tree-loving apes might have ventured out onto more open ground in search of food. The ability to walk upright may have come about by these apes trying to keep an eye out for predators, or as a way of leaving their hands free to carry food back to safe forest havens. Or perhaps an upright posture simply meant that less of the body's surface area was exposed to the sun. Whatever the reasons, this single development laid the foundation for *Homo sapiens*. Along the way, and well before the advent of *Homo sapiens*, many other hominid species lived, and died.

But, for the future of savannahs, it was the hominids' use of fire that was so crucial. Fire was probably first used as a defence against predators some 1.8–1.6 million years ago. It may well have caused huge conflagrations, reducing thickets and woodlands, and encouraging the spread of grasslands. Latterly, in the hands of *Homo sapiens*, using and controlling fire became a skilled accomplishment. Today, many pastoralists use fire as a tool to promote fresh shoots for their herds.

The biomass of termites has been measured at densities more than double that of the largest herds of vertebrates on Earth.

2

ACACIA WOODLANDS

At first glance, acacia woodlands seem to be a mad tangle of trees and thickets. In the early morning, the low sun gives them a touch of magic. The fawn-coloured grass is shot through with silver as countless strands of cobweb catch the sun and the bodies of an impala herd are rim-lit with dusky gold.

For a breathless few minutes, there is not a hint of wind and all around an infinity of ring-necked doves call out to the new day. Animals can be hard to spot in the dense undergrowth, but acacia woodlands are rich in woodland species as well as providing vital dry-season refuges for many savannah animals. Apart from acacia, which is the archetypal savannah tree featured at sunset on many a postcard, there are many other types of trees in the savannah woodlands, including commiphora and baobabs. However, acacias are a dominant element in the vegetation of the arid to semi-arid African savannahs.

Previous page: Lions hunt most successfully on moonless nights or at dawn and dusk when their prey's night vision has not completely adjusted to the lessening light.

THE TREES

The classification of acacias is complex. There are some 1200 species worldwide and by far the majority grow in Australia. However, 129 are found in Africa, whilst the rest are distributed throughout Asia and the New World. In Africa, the acacias' stronghold lies in the east; 43 per cent of acacia species are found there and nowhere else.

Acacia woodlands and thickets are rich in life and home to some resident species that never make it out into the plains. Dik-diks are members of the dwarf antelope family and rely on the shelter of bushes and fallen trees to hide from predators. They are territorial and monogamous, with pair bonds maintained by close proximity and coordinated activities such as social grooming.

The woodlands are vital for many other herbivores. Acacia foliage and pods provide welcome food in the dry season since the pods reach maturity when other food is short. The seeds contain over three times more protein than the pods, so this availability of high-quality food during a period of general shortage is particularly welcome. The smell and sound of falling pods will bring animals from several hundred metres away. But a bull elephant does not wait for pods to fall – he has enough strength to shake the tree and let the pods rain down around him, which quickly brings antelopes like impala and the tiny dik-dik to the scene. In addition to the pods, many herbivores also feed on the highly nutritious leaves; however, the trees have evolved an array of defences that help them to repel these attacks.

1. Baboons, like other primates such as ourselves, have very poor night vision, so seek the refuge of tall trees to sit out the hours of darkness in relative safety.

Acacia armaments

African acacias absolutely bristle with long, sharp thorns. It seems amazing that any browser could attempt to penetrate such wicked-looking defences. However, elephant and giraffe seem completely undeterred. Elephants use their tusks to strip bark and are happy munching entire branches, including the thorns. However, studies show that although the thorns do not prevent giraffes from feeding on the leaves, they do slow down the feeding rate and therefore protect the tree to some degree. In fact, giraffe, their extinct relatives and other browsers are thought to have shaped the biology of their food trees, including the evolution of thorns and galls. When giraffes have reduced the foliage to a certain critical level, seeking out shoots between the spines involves too much movement between bites and is no longer energy efficient. So they move to another tree. And then acacias have another weapon up their sleeve.

The more an animal browses on a tree, the less tasty it becomes. Under attack, a tree can increase the levels of phenols in its remaining leaves quite quickly, which makes them far less palatable. It also emits ethylene, which stimulates other trees as far as 50 m (160 feet) away to increase their production of phenols, so generally a giraffe only feeds on one acacia in ten, avoiding trees downwind of those on which it has already fed.

Acacias have also entered into a contract

1. Many species of giraffe were widespread and diverse in Africa and southeast Eurasia between 15 million and 1 million years ago.

2. Kirk's dik-dik are able to have small home ranges since the woodland offers them fairly consistent cover as well as food.

with independent mercenaries to bolster their defences. Lethal-looking whistling thorns grow in soils that become saturated with water in the wet season. These floods prevent ants from foraging on the ground during the rains. However, the branches of whistling thorns produce round swellings, called pseudo-galls, which are used by the ants as homes in which to raise their young, to store their dead, or to tend fungus gardens. The trees give a bonus too, by providing extra floral nectaries at the shoot tips and small glands that develop on the leaves of many species – all of which exude copious sugary secretions of which the ants are very fond. In return, ants crowd around the growing tips of the branches as soon as a browser begins feeding. A horde of angry ants will often deter, if not prevent, further attack. ▷▷

2

 IMPALA, TERMITES AND ACACIA

There is a neat relationship between impala, termites, and acacia. The ripe pods of *Acacia tortilis* are big and heavy and do not burst when they hit the ground. They are rich in carbohydrates and form a staple diet for impala, amongst others, in the dry season.

In turn, the acacia is dependent on animals like the impala for the dispersal and germination of its seeds. The pods are chewed but the hard, smoothly rounded seeds are not crushed and pass unharmed through the gut. In fact, the chances of germination are improved.

Like impala, termites, too, are often dependent on the acacia for food and, in some areas, dead thorntrees are the most important part of their diet. Some termite species build enormous mounds, which are dotted through the woodlands. As the mounds grow bigger and become less active, or are even deserted, star grass starts to grow on their sides. Impala feed on the shoots and their droppings further enrich the soil, encouraging the grass to grow even more strongly.

And so a satisfying cycle is born. *Acacia tortilis* feeds impala and termites, termites help star grass to get a footing in the woodland, the grass feeds the impala, and a healthy population of impala helps to nourish the grass and spread the acacia.

ELEPHANTS – SAVANNAH ARCHITECTS

Spreading its ears wide and standing tall, a bull elephant is built to impress and when he towers above you, he certainly does. Elephants are the largest surviving land mammals and, with the rhino, the only mega-herbivores left from prehistory. It is a testament to their survival skills that, despite almost continuous persecution by people, two elephant species are still alive and well. One is found in Asia and the other is the magnificent African elephant, *Loxodonta africana*.

2

1

Heroes or villains?

Aristotle described them as being 'the beast that passeth all others in wit and mind' and that was over 2400 years ago. Anyone who spends time with elephants soon realizes that they are not just intelligent but each animal is an individual, capable of experiencing fear, joy, tenderness, happiness and excitement.

Their social structure is highly complex, extending well beyond the immediate family unit and displaying a high degree of altruism, which puts many humans to shame. Sisters are quick to reassure younger siblings who are frightened by thunder or get themselves into trouble; and the whole group will rush to the aid of a wounded family member. Despite the danger to themselves, they will support a fallen comrade with their tusks and trunks in a desperate effort to help it escape. And they effectively bury their dead by throwing dirt, leaves or branches over the bodies.

However, bush elephants are also the subject of much impassioned debate between differing factions in the conservation arena. Elephants consume some 5 per cent of their body weight every 24 hours, which means a big bull can need up to 300 kg (660 lbs). They eat grass and succulent herbs, as well as the leaves, stems and bark of trees. They are adept at pulling down branches, uprooting saplings, seedlings and, particularly in the dry season, pushing over trees. Big bulls can fell quite large acacias using a powerful combination of tusks, trunk and sheer weight. Large numbers can have quite an impact on woodland in a relatively short time and some people are alarmed by the disappearance of savannah woodlands in various parts of Southern and East Africa. Others are quick to point out that elephants are playing a vital role in the unique dynamics of the savannah ecosystem, which continuously cycles

3

between open grassland and dense woodland.

Elephants are also the only agents capable of releasing energy locked up in wood and, via their abundant droppings, redistributing it back into the system as well as dispersing seeds over huge areas. By rolling and wading in puddles, they seal the soil and create larger, more impervious waterholes that benefit others. They also open up thickets and trample long, rank grass, encouraging the growth of sweeter, more palatable vegetation within the reach of smaller browsers. In this way, bush elephants create habitats for others. If bush elephants disappear from the ecosystem, many other species of plant and animal may follow them into oblivion. So what does the future hold?

The future

There are three basic threats facing bush elephants and all of them stem from people.

First, there is our apparently insatiable desire for their teeth. Despite the ivory ban, some 8000 elephants are killed by poachers every year. Even worse, our ever-increasing population competes with elephants for land in many African countries which leads onto the third pressure, the intensifying calls to increase culling and manage elephant numbers to our own satisfaction.

To date, our ancestors have already directly or indirectly caused the extinction of several elephant species in less than half a million years. It will be a sad indictment if we cannot give the last remaining species a little space to live undisturbed; as the writer, V.S. Pritchett, says:

'If the elephant vanished
the loss to human laughter,
wonder and tenderness would
be a calamity.'

1. Trunks are very versatile, able to draw up columns of water or dust; or even to burrow down into sand or soil.

2. Elephants use their tusks to strip bark or simply to prop up their heads on a handy support and snooze.

3. Trunks and tusks are not just used as tools; they are also weapons used in ritualized or serious fighting with their own species.

TOPIC LINKS

⭐ Elephants are important agents of seed dispersal and as many as 12,000 seeds of the umbrella thorn have been counted in just one ball of dung.

WOODLAND CARNIVORES

Dappled with shade, a leopard lies on the broad branch of a tree, paws dangling, green eyes shut against the bright light. Velvet, black rosettes decorate the warm, bronze hues of the leopard's coat, which flushes through to apricot, then to white-gold on the stomach. In the heat of mid-day, the leopard is very much at home high up off the ground where the warm breezes play. Fast asleep, only the tip of the tail twitches and curls with a restless spirit all its own. Bold and versatile, consummate masters of conceal-ment, leopards seem to embody the heart and soul of the woodlands. In fact, they thrive wherever there is enough cover and even survive in city suburbs.

Adults are solitary but pair up briefly to mate. Females bring up cubs on their own and the bonds are strong – they will often share kills with offspring for some time after separation. They will eat anything from beetles to antelopes twice their own weight, for, like most carnivores, they are generalists, able to hunt and feed on a wide variety of prey. This ability has ensured the leopard's survival, as even throughout the most dramatic series of environmental upheavals, the generalized sets of teeth retained by carnivores have allowed them to take advantage of whatever prey is available. In contrast, herbivores tend to be specialists, adapted to life centred around certain types of vegetation, and they flourish only as long as that particular vegetation remains abundant. Evidence from the fossil record shows that leopards have not changed much in 3 million years, whereas 30 species of antelope have come and gone.

Apart from leopards, other carnivores find woodlands a place of refuge. Unlike the open plains, there are always some resident prey dispersed throughout the trees. For example, the rate of survival for woodland lions is

1. Servals are active either at night or during the day, depending whether their predominantly rodent prey is nocturnal or diurnal.

2. Young cheetah cubs have extraordinary colouring, with an impressive mantle of pale fur that only disappears when they are about a year old.

1

generally higher than for those restricted to life on the more open plains. In a run of wet years, lions may establish a pride in an area of the plains where none existed before. But these prides are subject to the vagaries of the climate and movements of their prey. A run of dry seasons can kill them all. The prides in the woodlands can, therefore, be seen as 'source populations', with the potential to supply the rest of the Serengeti ecosystem with lions. And woodlands are even more important for cheetahs, surely the most elegant of the big cats.

Cheetahs

A pair of male cheetahs stride shoulder to shoulder through a stand of tall grass. Their heads turn to scan the distant skyline, and the evening sun colours their eyes a deep, deep amber. Cheetahs are wonderful to watch but, alarmingly, they are also the most endangered of the big cats in the whole of Africa. Once widespread across much of the continent and the Middle East, they are now almost entirely restricted to eastern and southern Africa. The decline has been caused by hunting and persecution by people which still continues in many places. Today, there are only some 10,000 left and the numbers are still dropping.

One of the African 'hot spots' for cheetah is the Serengeti/Mara ecosystem. The Serengeti National Park is also the focus for the Serengeti Cheetah Project, the only ongoing, long-term study of wild cheetahs. The results of this project have great significance for cheetah conservation and there have been some surprising revelations. The Project has discovered that, despite their image as supreme hunters of short-grass plains, the plains are actually far from paradise for cheetahs. Out here they face major problems. They are highly visible to

2

1. The high kicks of impala send out puffs of scent from fetlock glands which may help scattered animals to regroup after a fright.

2. (opposite) Overall, leopard diets reflect what can be caught most easily close to the margins of thick cover.

other carnivores, and their cubs are vulnerable to predation. New-born cubs are blind and helpless, and need to be hidden for safety. Their eyes open at 4–14 days old and, to protect them, the mother frequently carries them to new refuges.

Cheetah females have sole responsibility for the cubs and seek hiding places in long grass, reeds or thickets. Unfortunately, lions and hyenas also tend to concentrate in these areas, which are few and far between. In fact, observers have noticed that lions go out of their way to comb likely areas, apparently on the search for cheetah cubs, although pythons, eagles and jackals are all potential dangers. Lions are some four times the size of a cheetah female so, once her cubs have been discovered, there is little she can do to protect them.

The Cheetah Project has discovered that only one in every 20 cubs survives to independence. Lions, followed by hyenas, are the biggest killers of small cubs. It follows that, with such high mortality, the population on the plains is actually maintained only by immigration from the surrounding woodlands, where cheetahs have far more hiding places to choose for their young.

THE WOODLAND EDGE

Nervously stepping through the woodlands, with ears spread wide and ready to flee, an impala herd is full of graceful movement. Few antelope are so beautiful as the females with their long, slender legs and gentle, expressive heads. The males are equally impressive, standing proud to advertise their territorial status, or roaring loudly with white tail flashing to display dominance.

As a species, the impalas are browsers, perfectly adapted to live at high densities on an abundant but unstable food supply. They favour woodland margins, where the trees are more scattered and open. During the rains they feed almost wholly on grass, but as it becomes drier this drops to a mere 30 per cent, when they turn to browsing on shrubs, herbs, pods and seeds. Female imapalas live in clans, which number up to about 130 individuals and show loyalty to traditional home ranges. Juveniles often play together, forming loose crèches, which shows that maternal bonds are relatively weak. Active, territorial males spend a lot of energy and about 25 per cent of their time rounding up females,

chasing out bachelor males, searching for oestrous females and trying to forestall any female's departure.

The woodland edge is also a favourite haunt of servals, a species of small cat that is slender and a little taller than the average house cat. Servals are long-legged experts at catching grass rats. With huge ears tuned to the slightest rustle, a hunting serval stalks almost silently, freezing mid-stride at the hint of any movement. When a rat is pinpointed, the serval leaps into action – a series of athletic jumps and pirouettes. When the rodent is cornered, the serval's long legs come into service, probing through grass clumps to flush out the victim. But servals are feisty animals, able to do a lot more than just hunt rodents. Individual servals have been seen driving jackals off kills and they will even catch large prey such as storks or fawns.

The border between woodland and grassland offers many animals the best of both worlds. And over the years, it moves back and forth as grasslands increase and woodlands retreat. There is no such thing as stability within the savannah ecosystem, for here change is the order of the day.

SAVANNAH DYNAMICS

Generally speaking, forest is the most stable and longest-living type of vegetation in any area where trees can grow. Wherever the climate or other circumstances are less favourable, grasslands tend to become established. And when forest is destroyed, successive waves of vegetation begin. First, plants that are adept at colonizing bare ground take hold, followed by other stages of less robust vegetation, until eventually the original forest takes over once again. This is called the 'climax community'.

Unlike a climax community, which results from conditions of long-term stability, savannah vegetation is subject to long-term cycles or transitions between different stable states. The dynamics are complex and continually changing, and far more rapid than previously assumed. The first catalyst for change is climate. The second comes in the shape of the animals, and in the past there were many more species and considerably bigger animals. Just a few million years ago, when the savannah climate was a little wetter, there were three species of elephant, a baboon the size of a gorilla, giant pigs the size of hippos, and an enormous relative of the buffalo with horn spans exceeding 2 m (6½ feet). Apart from the effects of browsing, constant trampling by all these animals would have prevented many young tree seedlings from reaching maturity. Heavy trampling also compacts the soil, which favours grasses since their roots can romp ahead on the surface.

Today, giraffe maintain browsing pressure on immature *Acacia tortilis* – the flat-topped trees that are so characteristic of East African savannahs – and prevent trees maturing to their full size. Other animals also have a detrimental effect on saplings. Wildebeest energetically rub their horns on small trees and bushes as they wander through the woodland, whilst Grant's gazelle, Thomson gazelle, dik-dik and impala browse on trees less than a metre high. These small browsers have a substantial impact on woodland regeneration and are largely responsible for the slow growth rates in saplings of this size. However, there is another modifying agent at large in the savannah ecosystem. And it increased markedly with the rise of our own ancestors.

Fire

A raging bush fire can sound like an angry beast. When fire sweeps through dead grass, little can be heard above the roar of the

THE UNDERGROUND AGENTS

There is one highly social animal that is usually ignored by the eager safari traveller. Individuals feed, groom, and protect each other, and they help their parents to raise the next generation. They are termites and they have a major impact on the whole landscape.

Each termite colony has a queen and king with workers that can be of either sex. There are also soldiers and descendants of the royal family, the latter capable of reproducing in their own right. Each colony can number over 7 million individuals and they can consume up to a third of the total annual production of dead wood, leaves and grass. The secret of their success lies in their ability to digest cellulose by entering into associations with protozoa, bacteria and fungi, which produce the enzymes needed to digest the plant material.

In the Congo savannah, about 30 per cent of the soil surface is occupied by termite mounds. Excavations on such a massive scale are bound to have effects and, on the negative side, termites can accelerate soil erosion by clearing off plant cover. On the positive side, the mounds are often highly fertile, high in organic matter and rich in vital plant nutrients, and cheetahs (right) enjoy using them as high vantage points.

1. Fire encourages certain grasses and suppresses woodland regeneration by destroying tree seedlings.

flames. Clouds of acrid smoke pour high into the sky and the immense heat distorts bushes and the distant skyline into surreal waves. Lines of marabou storks often move slowly along in the fire's wake, jabbing at fleeing beetles and small reptiles. Piles of dung lie smoking on the coal-black ground, and ghostly skeletons of white ash are left behind where fallen trees have burned and smouldered.

The land can be set alight by lightning strikes, but today, most fires are lit by people. Dead growth may be burned off in anticipation of the rains bringing tender, fresh shoots of green for livestock. Some fires may be started to make antelope easier to find and hunt. Fires also bring safety from large predators and poisonous snakes, which no longer have a refuge in which to hide.

It is a controversial point as to which hominid species first began to make use of fire, even as a haphazard means of manipulating the environment, but it could have been as much as 1.8–1.6 million years ago. Since then, the cumulative effect of fire has been colossal. A big, hot fire kills mature trees over a wide area, and suppresses the growth of tree seedlings. But it is a little more complex than that, since herbivores also have an effect. As their numbers rise the effects of fire decrease, since there is less vegetation to burn. In contrast, as herbivore numbers fall, and the vegetation flourishes, the severity of fires increases. With infrequent fires, woodlands have the chance to expand. As fires increase, so too do certain types of grasses.

There are, however, some areas in a few savannahs where trees just cannot grow. In the Serengeti, it is on the ashy soils of the short-grass plains.

6.3 SERENGETI GRASSLANDS

On leaving the forest in the Congo, Stanley – the famous Victorian explorer – eulogized: 'To our undisguised joy, we emerged upon a rolling plain, green as an English lawn, into broadest, sweetest daylight and warm glorious sunshine, to inhale the pure air with uncontrolled rapture'.

In the Serengeti, there are kilometres of grasslands where the plains appear to unfold forever, undulating in a series of apparently infinite curves to a shimmering horizon lost in a smudge of violet haze. In fact, the Masai tribe say: 'There is place where the grass meets the sky, and that is the end'.

When the grass is green, the plains are full of promise and birdsong. At the beginning of the dry season, winds howl across the open grasslands, sucking out moisture. Later on, these hot winds die, and the desiccated lands are still and silent, almost as if they are holding their breath, listening for approaching thunderstorms.

1. Elephants are able to forage as far as 80 km (50 miles) from water, which means that, before the human population expanded, they could live in most areas of Africa, with individuals migrating long distances all over the continent.

THE RAW MATERIALS

These dramatic, virtually treeless grasslands of the eastern and southern Serengeti were born out of intense environmental upheaval. Some 3.6–2 million years ago, volcanoes were active, throwing out huge amounts of ash onto the surrounding lands. Today, the soils nearest the volcanoes are coarse and sandy since these were too heavy to be carried far by the wind. Further away, the soils are lighter and more finely textured. The ash closest to the volcanoes is highly porous. Over centuries, the rain has trickled through, forming a calcrete layer just below the surface, which is so hard that even roots cannot penetrate, barring the growth of deep-rooted plants like trees. Further away, the soil can hold more moisture and is also comparatively deeper and less salty. This variation in soil texture, moisture retentivity and salt concentration is reflected in the vary-ing height and luxuriance of the grass.

The grasses on the plains of the southeast are as smooth and short as the proverbial bowling green. Here are the dwarf forms of drop-seed and star grass. Further west flourish rich stands of red-oat and bamboo grass which, when the rains are good, can grow as high as the backs of the grazing animals. And it is over these plains that both resident and migratory herbivores range.

The grass eaters

A plain dotted with thousands of grazing animals is a fantastic sight, and at root level there are plenty of smaller details, which are equally fascinating. As the animals move slowly through the grass, a host of busy wagtails catch insects stirred up by hooves, and sulphur-yellow butterflies gather on heaps of warm dung generated by thousands of herbivores.

Most of these grazing animals are migrants and consist of some 1.6 million wildebeest, 450,000 Thomson gazelles and 250,000 zebra. During their annual migration, the large herds move twice. Round about December, when the first rains start to fall, the herds leave their dry-season woodland refuges in the north and west of the ecosystem, and move towards the short-grass plains in the southeast, where the females give birth in February and March. The herds leave the plains at the end of the rains in May, returning to the dry-season areas. Amongst these vast numbers are smaller herds of eland and buffalo plus, here and there, a sprinkling of hartebeest. Then there are lower numbers of stalwart residents, for in some areas a few wildebeest, zebra and gazelles manage to find enough food in a much smaller home range.

Migration is vital in maintaining high pop-ulations since long-distance movements reduce grazing pressure. Therefore, migratory herbivores dominate the animal biomass wherever they occur. Added to this, the actual variety of herbivores is also high. They all feed differently, which reduces competition between species. It is called the grazing succession.

Elephants and buffalo trample and pull at long grasses, stimulating the regrowth of finer grasses suitable for zebra and wildebeest. Zebras eat drier and tougher grass by shearing it between their upper and lower incisors whereas wildebeest, like other antelope, only have incisors on the bottom of their jaw and a hard, tough biting pad on the top, so prefer grasses that are less tough. Gazelles and warthogs graze on really short grass, whilst Egyptian geese nibble at the leftovers. However, surprisingly, huge numbers of the tiny termite are responsible for the greatest consumption of grass (▷ p. 216).

Grasses

Unlike herbivores that can move when the going gets tough, grasses have to stay put in the hardest of droughts. Grasses on the open plains are perennials with the shortest growth and the finest of leaves. They form tiny cushions and can cope with prolonged dry spells. Even in the lightest of showers, the drops splash dust off the dry herbage and trickles of water are dammed up between the tiny hummocks. The grasses flower quickly and their roots are adapted to make use of the condensation created by cool nights and long, hot days. Encased in sand, each absorbs the moisture lodged between every grain.

Perennial grasses grow, live and spread by runners or rooting at the joints so seeds are quite incidental to their long-term survival. Starchy food reserves are stored underground in rhizomes or bulb-like corms. When it is too

dry or too cold, the above-ground parts of the plant wither, but the roots remain alive with their store of starch. So perennial grasses are well equipped to survive drought, and fire.

Annuals can complete their life cycle in a single year and are perfectly adapted to short-term success. Their seeds can lie dormant for years, waiting for the very best time to grow and flower. Annual grasses are great opportunists in the reproduction stakes. So much goodness is stored in the seed head at maturity that it can weigh as much as the rest of the plant. These adaptations enable annual grasses to be great colonizers and effective modifiers of the soil. They have comparatively deep water-searching roots and add nutrients to the soil when they die.

Grasses have adapted to a life of feast and famine, forcing herbivores to follow their lead; thus some carnivores have also come up with interesting solutions to the same problem.

1. Male impala have short, muscular necks that are essential in the frequent horn fighting necessary in a high-density, intensely competitive society. **1**

2. Hyenas are the most important predator in terms of numbers and have a big effect not just on prey, but also on other carnivores by stealing food or killing offspring.

THE COMMUTERS

In the Serengeti, spotted hyenas have a problem since their principal prey, which are wildebeest, Thomson gazelle and zebra, all migrate long distances in search of food. The hyenas have evolved an interesting lifestyle as a result. They commute – shuttling between the herds and their cubs.

In the Serengeti, hyenas combine a territorial clan life with long-distance foraging outside this territory. While large numbers of herbivores are within their borders, all of the 50 or so members can hunt close to home. However, when the herds move, many members regularly go on commuting journeys, which can last several days. An individual may travel as far as 140 km (87 miles) in a round trip, travelling a total of some 2800–3700 km (1800–2300 miles) per year.

Large cubs accompany their mothers on these journeys, and in doing so learn the major routes and become familiar with commuting destinations. Spotted hyenas spend 46–62 per cent of their whole year commuting. This regular traffic means that intruding hyenas are constantly passing through the territories of other clans so certain rules of engagement must be observed. Commuters in transit are tolerated by the residents so long as they are on recognized routes. However, residents will determinedly attack intruders on kills. Hyenas are adept at spotting kills from over 3 km (2 miles) away so, to avoid conflict, it pays commuters to forage at a discreet distance from the residents' den.

Various morphological and physiological traits enable spotted hyenas to be highly mobile, and behavioural adaptations in maternal care mean that mothers can risk being absent for as long as 3 or 4 days. Hyenas den communally, which lessens the chances that cubs are left unguarded. Dens are often accessible only to cubs to reduce the risk of predation, which means the cubs have to come out to be suckled and cared for by their mother. Also, although hyena cubs are kept at the communal den and dependent on their mother's milk for the first 12 months, they can survive for as long as 9 days without food.

For spotted hyenas, this unique adaptation to a particular set of problems has paid a handsome dividend. It has enabled them to become by far the most abundant large carnivore in the whole Serengeti ecosystem.

SOCIAL CATS

Hyenas may be the most numerous carnivore in the Serengeti, but most tourists still consider the lion to be the royalty of the plains. It is hard to disagree when you come face to face with a triumvirate of male lions standing tall, blond manes flowing in the wind, and yellow-green eyes fixed on far horizons. Or lion cubs wrestling in a tangle of tawny, spotted bodies while their mothers lie fast asleep, their power masked in indolence.

The African lion is the only member of the cat family to live and hunt in stable social units. Lion prides consist of closely related animals, and advances from outsiders are strongly resisted. In the Serengeti, the long-running Lion Project has tracked the changing fortunes of different prides, and explained various aspects of lion behaviour. Sociability in female lions, for example, is closely related to defence of the cubs against new males, who often kill them, and to maintaining the territory against larger prides.

Work done in the semi-arid savannah woodlands of Chobe National Park in northern Botswana reveals another element that is crucial in the story. The African lion has evolved in the presence of a powerful competing carnivore – the spotted hyena – and this may have had a greater effect than previously thought. The study showed that adult male lions on kills, and the females with them, were virtually immune to takeover bids by hyenas. However, females feeding alone were mobbed in over 80 per cent of cases. Females in groups of five could repel the invading hyenas over 40 per cent of the time, whereas those in groups of ten or more were completely safe.

Although their bellies are often full of food when lions lose their kill, they have to hunt

1. Despite the label 'king of the beasts', lionesses are far more important than males to the basic social structure, being longer-lived and more numerous.

2. Male lions form strong alliances, but their membership of a pride seldom lasts for more than three to four years.

3. (opposite) Lionesses provide the continuity in a pride, though large prides can only exist in areas where there are big enough herds of large animals to support them.

again sooner than would have been the case had they not lost the carcass. The losses, therefore, result in a constant energy drain. Thus, it may be beneficial, even for lions that are unrelated, to band together in order to repel hyenas and keep their kill.

The social lives of cheetahs

The cheetah has also been the subject of long-term studies in the Serengeti. In these studies, the cheetah's social life has been under scrutiny and this is quite intriguing, since social groupings are particularly varied.

Some cheetahs are solitary whereas others live in small groups, some of which are permanent, others less so. The groups include cubs staying with their mothers for a full year after weaning, adolescent littermates of both sexes remaining together as a temporary unit, and some males forming permanent coalitions. In this way, cheetahs bridge the gap in the cat family between two extremes: lions, who live in more or less permanent groups, and leopards, who only associate with one another at mating.

What are the benefits of group living? Mothers benefit from the presence of older cubs in two ways: vigilance is shared amongst the group so mothers can spend less time watching out for danger, and predators tend to avoid cheetah families containing older cubs.

The pay-off is that mothers with large cubs do not get as much food as single females, although this does not seem to affect their condition unduly. Cubs benefit from staying with their mother for a full year after weaning. The long period of dependency is apparently needed for them to gain the minimum skills required to catch their own food.

After independence, the main reason that cheetah adolescents stay with their littermates is that they are less likely to be harassed by spotted hyenas or male cheetahs, though, once again, they have to share food in return. Male cheetahs that live alone find it hard to defend a territory against encroachment by other male cheetahs. However, the main reason males

1

form coalitions is not to deter predators or to get more food, but to increase their chances of reproductive success. A coalition of males is able to defend a much larger territory, and with a bigger range, the chances of meeting females are much improved. In contrast, females lead relatively nomadic lives, wandering over home ranges that can be as large as 800 sq km (300 sq miles). ▷▷

1. Female cheetahs and their young cubs can be very vocal, using a wide variety of purrs, chirps, hums and yelps as contact calls.

2. Cheetahs prefer to stalk close (within 50 m/160 feet or so) to their prey before racing flat-out at about 60 km (40 miles) per hour.

▷ KEEPING COOL

As the equatorial sun blazes down on the open, grassy plains of the Serengeti, many mammals face the problem of keeping cool (left). Between 11 a.m. and 4 p.m., ground and air temperatures can soar to over 40°C (104°F). The body temperature of some antelope species also rises to over 45°C (113°F) but, despite this, their brains do not become overheated.

Long muzzles are the key. Heat is lost by the evaporation of water from the moist lining of the nasal chambers. This cools blood that is collected near the base of the cranium and acts as a heat exchanger to cool the brain's own blood supply. However, this method limits brain size, so until the development of a more efficient system, larger-brained animals could not evolve.

Homo sapiens has the most effective body cooling system of any living mammal. Our muzzles are short, so we developed other ways to keep cool. An upright stance only exposes 7 per cent of the body to the sun and avoids up to 60 per cent of the direct solar radiation received by four-legged animals. In addition, brains lose heat 33 per cent faster simply due to the cooling effects of elevation. It is just conceivable that finding a new way to keep cool led to our unique upright stance.

THE WILDEBEEST MIGRATION

In the Serengeti and the Masai Mara, migration is a way of life for many animals and it is, perhaps, the main distinguishing feature of the whole ecosystem. Many herbivores such as Thomson gazelle, eland, zebra and wildebeest migrate but, undoubtedly, the most spectacular is the wanderings of the wildebeest, single herds of which are larger than any other left on Earth. Migration is a word that conjures up vivid pictures of hordes of animals cantering across plains and plunging into rivers. But that is the superficial picture; there is much more to this migration than first meets the eye.

1. Wildebeest males are efficient fighters, helped by heavy necks, heads and horns.

Wildebeest

Wildebeest first appeared on the scene some 1.5 million years ago and are members of a fast-evolving and very successful group of animals that includes kongoni, topi and impala. All grazers, they have evolved to live at high densities on an unstable food supply and have always been at their most abundant and diverse in East Africa.

However, a disease known as rinderpest, accidentally brought over by Europeans from India in the 1880s, decimated the population. Luckily, a cattle vaccination programme in the 1950s and 1960s allowed the numbers to recover and today their population, although it fluctuates from year to year, is some 1.6 million animals – a staggering 60 per cent of the total number of animals. It is a vital statistic since this species is the keystone herbivore in the Serengeti and Mara. Enter

the magnificent western white-bearded gnu, *Connochaetes taurinus*.

Why migrate?

These animals range over a vast area of some 25,000 km (15,500 miles), and it is the movements of the wildebeest that actually define the Serengeti/Mara ecosystem. They can travel in small groups or bunch together in herds that defy description. Occasionally, they will ford rivers, braving the onslaught of crocodiles, or gallop through gorges. More often, they will spend several days in one place, grazing peacefully. Averaged over a whole year, they travel some 10 km (6 miles) every day but this travel takes its toll, increasing their mortality by some 3 per cent. To counterbalance this negative effect, the benefits brought about by migration are significant. First, far higher populations can accumulate compared with more sedentary

systems since migration avoids over-exploitation of food resources. Second, rainfall in the north is typically more than twice as heavy as that further south. However, in a good year, during February and March, the dry short-grass plains in the southeast become a lush, verdant lawn thickly dotted with hundreds of thousands of wildebeest. In some cases, the density is over 1000 animals per square kilometre (2500 per square mile).

But the trigger for mass movement may not, as might be supposed, be a shortage of food or water but of vitamins. Unlike the grass in the north, the short-grass plains are rich in phosphorus, needed by the females for lactation and by the young, growing calves. The grass may also contain higher concentrations of protein.

It is on these short-grass plains that thousands of females gather on traditional calving

2

grounds. As many as 90 per cent of calves are born in a flurry of activity that lasts as little as 3 weeks. In fact, very few other tropical mammals have such a restricted birth season. It is a successful strategy since there is safety in numbers and it results in another spectacular wildebeest display – a short and intense breeding season.

The march northwards is triggered by the build-up of salts in the surface waters, but if the rainfall in the south is particularly meagre during April and May the wildebeest gather early in the western arm of the ecosystem. And here, for a couple of weeks or so, the excitement, especially amongst the males, builds to a frenzy in the annual rut.

3

2. Wildebeest are members of a family that is adapted to live at high densities on a very abundant but unstable food supply.

3. During the short but intense rutting season, wildebeest males engage in frantic, frenzied leaping, cavorting and head-shaking.

◆ TOPIC LINKS

6.3 Serengeti Grasslands
p.219 The grass eaters

1

'I SPEAK OF AFRICA AND GOLDEN JOYS'

When Shakespeare wrote, 'I speak of Africa and golden joys', he was not alone in his enthusiasm. The African continent has enticed and enthralled artists, poets, explorers and colonists of different nationalities throughout the ages. Recent research into animal behaviour confirms just how fascinating this continent is and how truth really is stranger than fiction, for who would have imagined that we live in a world where buffalo vote and hyenas engage in power politics?

The research results are interesting as they stand, but they also serve as a mirror in which we can look at our own place in the world. As research and information accumulates, we now know that other species are close to us in social organization, communication and tool use. The notion that only humans think and feel is outmoded but basic to our anthropocentric view of the world, where there is a lack of understanding and sympathy with the other living things on this planet.

For hundreds of thousands of years, our species teetered on the brink of extinction. However, today, our population is over 6 billion and is still rising. We consume almost 50 per cent of the planet's net primary productivity, which does not leave much for the millions of other species living on Earth. And in only the last 30 years, we have consumed an estimated 30 per cent of the planet's non-renewable natural resources.

It is a pure accident of fate but, for now, chance has decreed that we dominate much of the world. So where does this leave savannah – the land that was instrumental in our rise? Agriculture is certainly no friend to this habitat, swallowing entire savannah systems whole. Out of the patchwork of fragments remaining, the Serengeti may be

CHANGE AND EXTINCTION

Once, we believed that our species represented the pinnacle of evolution. But now we are beginning to accept that this is not true.

Scientists have discovered a pattern of mass extinctions in the fossil record dating back to the beginning of life on Earth. So far, there have been five mass extinctions on this planet where some 65 per cent of all species became extinct in a brief geological instant. In one instance, about 225 million years ago, more than 95 per cent of marine animal species vanished. The scientist David Raup has remarked that 'global biology (for higher organisms at least) had an extremely close brush with total destruction'.

Recovery is slow and, as the palaeontologist Richard Leakey writes, 'it is a time of evolutionary opportunity offered to the lucky few'. Importantly, after studying the pattern of ecological communities that assemble afterwards, scientists have shown that it is really a matter of luck as to which organisms survive the catastrophe and which ones thrive in the new set of circumstances. All life, past and present, is an accident of fate shaped by many forces, some chaotic, some random. Chance and change lie at the very heart of our own existence.

the most intact but even it is a pale vestige of what it was one million years ago and the future is still far from rosy.

The future

Since the 1960s, poachers have all but eliminated the black rhino and 90 per cent of the elephants have been killed. In the northwest of Africa, meat hunters have reduced the buffalo population by 90 per cent as well. Every year, meat poachers kill about one quarter of a million wildebeest within the Serengeti National Park and the Masai Mara Game Reserve. Buffalo, eland, zebra, warthog, topi, zebra, impala, Grant's and Thomson gazelles are also targets. Often, wire snares are used which are highly unselective and trap lions, cheetahs, giraffes, ostriches and hyenas. For the unlucky few that escape with a snare embedded around a neck or leg, death is slow and torturous. Game-meat hunters may already be significantly affecting hyena populations since the average clan size is in decline. For now, the wildebeest population may be holding its own. But the situation can change fast, as shown by the sudden, precipitous fall in buffalo numbers.

Some people write that conservationists are sentimental romanticists, but it is a simple fact that to lose a world in which wildebeest cavort and cheetahs stride free is to lose something infinitely precious in its own right. And this loss destroys our own biological roots. There are solutions that can prevent this; all that is needed is the will. Although we seem to be retreating from the world in which we evolved to seek solace in artificial trivia, maybe more of us will discover the simple truth that the novelist, Jostein Gaarder, sums up so succinctly: 'people would have gone absolutely wild if the astronomers had discovered another living planet – they just don't let themselves be amazed by their own'.

2

1. Grasses have replaced a lot of woody vegetation, surviving in all kinds of habitats, but they are at their best when they can spread over vast areas – savannahs.

2. Living African rhinos were, until the heavy poaching of the last few decades, widespread, abundant, advanced and successful species.

Overleaf: Grasses can grow fast in good conditions, as well as endure long, dry periods and fires. They are heroes in a world in which so many fascinating herbivores and carnivores thrive.

Useful organizations

CONTINENT-WIDE

African Elephant Conservation Trust
http://www.elephanttrust.org
The goal of the African Elephant Conservation Trust is the successful conservation of Africa's elephants within the context of human needs and pressure.
African Elephant Conservation Trust, 65 Valley Stream Parkway, Malvern, PA 19355, USA
Tel: +1 610 415 9601
Email: webmaster@elephanttrust.org

African Wildlife Foundation (AWF)
http://www.awf.org
African Wildlife Foundation (AWF) is dedicated to helping wildlife thrive and people prosper, working principally in East and southern Africa.
AWF Office of African Operations, PO Box 48177, Nairobi, Kenya
Tel: + 254 2 710 367/8/9 Fax: + 254 2 710 372
Email: awfnrb@awfke.org

African Wildlife Foundation, 1400 16th Street, NW, #120, Washington, DC 20036, USA
Tel: 202 939 3333 Fax: 202 939 3332
Email: africanwildlife@awf.org

Born Free Foundation
http://www.bornfree.org.uk
Born Free Foundation is an international wildlife charity working with compassion to prevent cruelty, alleviate suffering and encourage everyone to treat all individual animals with respect. Born Free believes wildlife belongs in the wild and is dedicated to the conservation of rare species in their natural habitat, and the phasing out of traditional zoos.
Born Free Foundation, 3 Grove House, Foundry Lane, Horsham,
West Sussex RH13 5PL
Tel: +44 (0)1403 240170 Fax: +44 (0)1403 327838
Email: wildlife@bornfree.org.uk

Conservation International
http://www.conservation.org
CI's mission is to conserve the Earth's natural heritage, our global biodiversity, and to demonstrate that human societies can live harmoniously with nature.
Conservation International, 2501 M Street, NW, Suite 200, Washington DC 20037, USA
Tel: + 1 202 429 5660
Email: newmember@conservation.org

The David Shepherd Conservation Foundation
http://www.dscf.demon.co.uk
Actively raising funds and working for the survival of tigers, elephants, rhinos and other critically endangered mammals in the wild.
61 Smithbrook Kilns, Cranleigh, Surrey GU6 8JJ
Tel: +44 (0)1483 272323 Fax: +44 (0)1483 272427

The Dian Fossey Gorilla Fund
http://www.dianfossey.org
The Dian Fossey Gorilla Fund works internationally to save the mountain gorillas from extinction and ensure the local people benefit from their unique natural heritage.
110 Gloucester Avenue, London NW1 8JA
Tel: +44 (0)20 7483 2681

ECOFAC
http://www.ecofac.org
A European Union-funded forest conservation programme, dedicated to conservation and rational use of forest ecosystems. The programme works to promote biodiversity, conservation and sustainable development throughout the forests of several African countries.
ECOFAC, BP 15115, Libreville, Gabon
Tel: + 241 732343/44 Fax: + 241 732345
Email: coordination@ecofac.org

International Fund for Animal Welfare
http://www.ifaw.org
The IFAW works to improve the welfare of wild and domestic animals throughout the world by reducing commercial exploitation of animals, protecting wildlife habitats, and assisting animals in distress. IFAW also seeks to motivate the public to prevent cruelty to animals and to promote animal welfare and conservation policies that advance the wellbeing of both animals and people.
HQ: IFAW US, 411 Main Street, PO Box 193, Yarmouth Port, MA 02675, USA
Tel: +1 508 744 2000 Email: info@ifaw.org

UK: IFAW UK, 87–90 Albert Embankment, London SE1 9UD
Tel: + 44 (0)20 7587 6700

IFAW South Africa, 147 Buitenkant Street, Cape Town 8002, South Africa
Tel: + 27 21 465 7300

IUCN – The World Conservation Union
http://www.iucn.org
To influence, encourage and assist societies throughout the world to conserve the integrity and diversity of nature and to ensure that any use of natural resources is equitable and ecologically sustainable.
Eastern Africa Regional Office, PO Box 68200, Nairobi, Kenya
Tel: + 254 2 890 605 Fax: + 254 2 890 615
Email: mail@iucnearo

Save the Rhino International
http://www.savetherhino.co.uk
Save the Rhino International has been the leading non-profit rhino organization since 1990. They are committed to ensuring the survival of the rhinoceros in the wild by working closely with local communities and providing support for wildlife managers and game rangers.
Save the Rhino International, 16 Winchester Walk, London SE1 9AQ
Tel: +44 (0)20 7357 7474

Worldwide Fund for Nature
http://www.wwf.org (International site)
http://www.panda.org (UK site)
WWF's mission is to conserve nature and ecological processes by preserving diversity; to ensure sustainable/renewable resources; to promote actions that reduce waste/pollution; to stop and eventually reverse the degradation of our planet's natural environment.
WWF – South Africa, 116 Dorp Street, Stellenbosch 7600
Mail: PO Box 456, Stellenbosch 7599
Tel: + 27 21 887 2801 Email: userid@wwfsa.org.za

WWF – UK, Panda House, Weyside Park, Godalming, Surrey GU7 1XR
Tel: +44 (0)1483 426 444
Email: userid@wwfnet.org
(where userid = first initial and full name)

WWF Cameroon Programme
Tel: + 237 217 083 Email: rmekeng@wwfnet.org

WWF Central African Republic
Tel: + 236 614 299 Email: wwfcar@intnet.cf

Wildlife Conservation Society
http://www.wcs.org
The WCS uniquely combines the resources of wildlife parks in New York with field projects around the globe to inspire care for nature, provide leadership in environmental education, and help sustain our planet's biological diversity.
Wildlife Conservation Society, 2300 Southern Blvd, Bronx, NY 10460, USA

BOTSWANA

Okavango Lion Conservation Project
http://www.bornfree.org.uk/okavango
Aims to collect detailed biological information in order to develop a comprehensive conservation programme

for Northern Botswana, which will also assist in developing programmes in other key areas.
Lion Conservation Project, Born Free Foundation, 3 Grove House, Foundry Lane, Horsham, West Sussex RH13 5PL
Tel: +44 (0)1403 240170

ETHIOPIA
Ethiopian Wildlife and Natural History Society
The society is a non-profit-making association whose purposes are: to study and promote the interests of the fauna, flora and natural environment of Ethiopia; to disseminate the knowledge gained; and to support legislation to protect these resources.
Prof. Shibru Tedla (Hon. Chairman), PO Box 13303, Addis Ababa
Tel: 251 1 183 520 Fax: + 251 1 552 350
Email: ewnhs@telecom.net.et

GHANA
Ghana Wildlife Society
Prof. Yaa Ntiamoa Baidu (Exec Director), PO Box 13252, Accra
Tel: + 233 21 663 500 / 665 197 Fax: + 233 21 670 610
Email: wildsoc@ighmail.com

KENYA
African Butterfly Research Institute
Steve Collins, PO Box 14308, Nairobi, Kenya
Tel: + 254 2 884 972 / 884 973
Email: steve.c.collins@ea.monsanto.com

Amboseli Trust for Elephants
Cynthia Moss, PO Box 15135, Nairobi, Kenya
Tel: + 254 2 891 191
Email: cmoss@elephanttrust.org

The Colobus Trust, Diani
http://www.bornfree.org.uk/colobus/ colobus.htm
Colobus Cottage is an office, research base, information centre, primate rescue facility, and home for the Colobus Trust staff. It's also a charity that helps the last remaining black-and-white colobus (Angolan) south of Mombasa, Kenya. In this heavily frequented area of the Kenya coast and the inevitable traffic, the centre aims to reduce colobus road kills by putting up signs along the road, building speed bumps and setting up canopy ladders for the colobus to cross in safety to the forest on the other side.
Julie Anderson, Colobus Cottage, Diani Forest, Kenya
Tel: + 254 1 273 519 Fax: + 254 1 273 519

email: colobus@africaonline.co.ke
Contact via the Born Free Foundation.

East African Wildlife Society
http://www.eawildlife.org
The EAWLS is proud to be involved in a number of programmes geared to the preservation and conservation of the environment. These include species conservation, wetlands and marine resources conservation, education and eco-tourism.
PO Box 20110, Nairobi, Kenya
Tel: + 254 2 574 145 / 171 Fax: + 254 2 570 335

The Green Belt Movement
The Green Belt Movement is a grassroots Non-Governmental Organization (NGO), based in Kenya, that focuses on environmental conservation and rehabilitation.
Prof. Wangari Mathai, PO Box 67545, Nairobi, Kenya
Tel: + 254 2 603 867 / 571 532
Email: gbm@iconnect.co.ke

Kenya Wildlife Service
http://www.kenya-wildlife-service.org
On behalf of the Government of Kenya, Kenya Wildlife Service holds in trust for present and future generations locally, nationally and globally the biological diversity represented by its extraordinary variety of animals, plants and ecosystems ranging from coral reefs to alpine moorlands and from deserts to forests. Special emphasis is placed on conservation of large mammals found in few other places on earth.
PO Box 40241, Nairobi, Kenya
Tel: + 254 2 501 081 / 506 671
Email: kws@africaonline.co.ke

Save the Elephants
http://www.save-the-elephants.org
It is our mission to secure a future for elephants and to sustain the beauty and ecological integrity of the places where they live; to promote man's delight in their intelligence and the diversity of their world, and to develop a tolerant relationship between the two species.
Iain Douglas-Hamilton, PO Box 54667, Nairobi, Kenya
Tel: + 254 2 891 673 / 890 596/7
Fax: + 254 2 890 441

SWARA magazine
PO Box 20110, Nairobi, Kenya
Tel: + 254 2 574 145 Fax: + 254 2 570 335
Email: eawls@kenyaweb.com

NAMIBIA
The AfriCat Foundation
http://www.africat.org
The overall goals of The AfriCat Foundation are to create short, medium and long term solutions for the conservation of predators in a predominantly livestock farming community. While there are many aspects to the conservation of endangered species, the AfriCat Foundation is focusing on release and relocation, improving farming methods and education.
PO Box 1889, Otjiwarongo, Namibia
Tel + 264 (0) 67 304 566/ 306 585
Fax: + 264 (0) 67 304 565
Email: africat@natron.net

NIGERIA
Nigerian Conservation Foundation
Dr Muhtari Aminu-Kano, PO Box 74638, Victoria Island, Lagos
Tel: + 234 1 264 2498 Fax: + 234 1 264 2497
Email: ncf@hyperia.com
or aminukano@infoweb.abs.net

RWANDA
Association pour la Conservation de la Nature au Rwanda (ACNR)
Mr Serge Joram Nsengimana, PO Box 4290, Kigali
Mob Tel: + 250 8530015 Fax: + 250 77845
Email: ldgl@rwandatell.rwanda.com (c/o Noel Twagiramungu)

SEYCHELLES
BirdLife Seychelles
http://www.seychelles.net/birdlife
This branch of Birdlife International in the Seychelles aims to monitor and conserve the island bird species, and implement management programmes for threatened species. They are also involved in education.
Mr Nirmal Jivan Shah (Chief Executive), PO Box 1310, Suite 202, Aarti Chambers, Mont Fleuri, Mahe
Tel: + 248 225 097 Fax: + 248 225 121
Email: birdlife@seychelles.net/birdlife

SIERRA LEONE
Conservation Society of Sierra Leone
Dr Sama Banya (Hon. President), PO Box 1292, Freetown
Tel: + 232 22 229 716 Fax: + 232 22 224 439
Email: cssl@sierratel.sl

SOUTH AFRICA
BirdLife South Africa
Part of BirdLife International.

Dr Aldo Berruti, PO Box 515, Randburg 2125,
South Africa
Tel: +27 11 789 1122 Fax: + 27 11 789 5188
Email: info@birdlife.org.za
or aldo@birdlife.org.za

Peninsula Baboon project
http://www.scarborough.org.za/
baboon.html
The Cape Peninsula Baboon Project (CPBP) aims to
maintain a sustainable baboon population in the Cape
Peninsula, whilst minimizing conflict between people
and baboons.
Ruth Kansky or Dave Gaynor, PO Box 44009,
Scarborough, 7975, South Africa

TANZANIA
The Cheetah Project in the Serengeti
http://www.londonzoo.co.uk
The longest-running study of cheetahs in the wild.
Zoological Society of London, Regent's Park,
London NW1 4RY
Tel: +44 (0)20 7722 3333

Frankfurt Zoological Society
Dr Markus Borner, Serengeti National Reserve,
Tanzania
Email: fzs@africaonline.co.ke

The Jane Goodall Institute for Wildlife
Research, Education & Conservation
http://www.janegoodall.org
The Jane Goodall Institute advances the power of
individuals to take informed and compassionate action
to improve the environment of all living things.
Jane Goodall, 15 Clarendon Park, Lymington,
Hampshire S041 8AX

The Lion Research Project in the Serengeti
http://www.lionresearch.org
The lion research centre has two main goals: to
promote research into the basic biology and

conservation of African lions; to make our research
findings available to the public.
Under the direction of Dr Craig Packer at
University of Minnesota, Dept of Ecology,
Evolution and Behaviour, 100 Ecology Building,
1987 Upper Buford Circle, St Paul, MN 55108,
USA
Tel: + 1 612 625 5700
Email: info@lionresearch.org

Red Colobus Society
Jozani Forest Natural Resources, PO Box 3526,
Zanzibar
Tel: + 24 223 6089 / 223 8628

Roots and Shoots
http://www.wcsu.ctstateu.edu/
cyberchimp/roots/rsindex.html
A charity set up by Jane Goodall for improving wildlife
awareness in Tanzanian schoolchildren.
Roots & Shoots Program, The Jane Goodall
Institute, PO Box 599, Ridgefield,
CT 06877, USA
Tel: + 203 431 2099
Fax: + 203 431 4387

The Tanzania Forest Conservation Group
http://www.easternarc.org
The TFCG was formed with a mandate to work
towards improved conservation of natural forests
through community-based projects and promoting
sustainable forest conservation management practices
amongst the local forest edge communities.
PO Box 23410, Dar es Salaam, Tanzania

Tazama! Trust
The primary goal of Tazama! Trust is the protection
and conservation of natural resources and wildlife in
Tanzania, East Africa. Creating a forum for dialogue
between Tanzania's indigenous people, farmers,
conservationists, tour operators, developers and the
government, Tazama! Trust succeeds in finely

balancing the needs of people with the survival of
wildlife and their habitat.
PO Box 12644, Arusha, Tanzania, East Africa
Tel: + 255 741 512345 or + 255 742 401234
Email: ellis-josch@habari.co.tz

Tanzania Land Conservation Trust
The Tanzania Land Conservation Trust is a non-profit
organization whose objective is to acquire or buy
threatened conservation areas and manage them for
conservation and benefit to local communities.
Tanzania Land Conservation Trust, PO Box
2658, Arusha, Tanzania
Email: JKahurananga@awf-tz.org
or CDouglis@awfke.org

The Wildlife Conservation Society of
Tanzania
Mr MYC Lumbanga (Chairman), PO Box 70919,
Dar es Salaam
Tel: + 255 22 211 2518 Fax: + 255 22 212 4572
Email: wcst@africaonline.co.tz

UGANDA
Nature Uganda
Dr Pantaleon Kasoma, PO Box 27034, Kampala,
Uganda
Tel: + 256 41 540 719 Fax: + 256 41 533 528
Email: eanhs@infocam.co.ug
or muienn@imul.com

ZIMBABWE
The Zambezi Society
The Zambezi Society is the only conservation group
devoted solely to looking after the Zambezi, the finest
and wildest river in Africa.
Mukuvisi Environment Centre, Glenara
Avenue, Harare, Zimbabwe
Mail: PO Box HG774, Highlands, Harare,
Zimbabwe
Tel: + 263 4 747002/3/4/5
Email: zambezi@samara.co.zw

Acknowledgements

Working in Africa over the past three years, we have visited some of the most beautiful places on Earth and witnessed spectacular wildlife events. All along the way we have been hosted with untold warmth, friendship and good humour, and our greatest thanks go to the people and governments of Botswana, Cameroon, Central African Republic, Chad, Congo, Djibouti, Ethiopia, Equatorial Guinea, Gabon, Kenya, Libya, Malawi, Mauritania, Morocco, Namibia, Rwanda, South Africa, Sudan, Tanzania, Uganda, Zambia and Zimbabwe. Without your help, this book, and the television series it accompanies, would never have been possible.

We are indebted to the work and advice of countless scientists and field workers, whose discoveries and insights form the backbone of this book. In particular we would like to express our thanks to Jonathan Kingdon, a guiding light whose comprehensive understanding of African biogeography has given us endless inspiration. We are also extremely grateful to a host of other contributors who have generously shared their scientific knowledge, field experience and hospitality with us. These include:

Kate Abernethy, Ali Aghnaj, Conrad and Muriel Aveling, Bruce Anderson, Luis Arranz, Vernon Baillie, Marco Barbieri, Simon Bearder, Janice and Richard Beatty, Nigel Bennett, Roger Bills, J.P. Botha, Charles Francois Boudouresque, Chris Bowden, Tom Butynski, David Bygott and Jeanette Hanby, Peter Byrne, Pierre Campredon, Stephano Cannicci, Alan Channing, Colin and Lauren Chapman, Tim Clutton-Brock, Mike Coppinger, William and Emma Craig, Robert Crawford, Jeremy David, Jenny Day, Bruno Di Giusto, Tamara and Alex Double, Edmond Dounias, Angela and James Drysdale, Louis du Preez, John Fa, Chris Fellowes, Anmarie and Faan Fourie, Colin and Rocky Francome, Jean-Mark Froment, Dave Gaynor, Berihun Gebre, Aadje Geertsema, Tom Gillespie, Charles Griffiths, Jean Hartley, Andre Hartmann, Mark Harvey, Gail Hearn, John Henschel, Hamid Herraf, Oliver Höner, Hassan Houmed, Chadden Hunter, Tim Jackson, Tania Jenkins, Jan van der Kamp, Ruth Kansky, Jeremy Kemp, Bakary Kone, Margaret and Per Kullander, Alain Laurent, David Leathborough, Brian and Mandy Leith, Colin Little, Penn Lloyd, Michael Lock, Barry Lovegrove, Colin and Karen McConnell, Neil MacGregor, Doyle McKey, Chris Magin, Emmanuel de Merode, Bethan Morgan, Paul Morkel, Chad Morze, Tracy Morze, Mike Moser, Gilles Nicolet, Juliet Nightingale, David Obura, Bruno Pardigon, Anton Pauw, Fiona and Nigel Perks, Liz Pimbley, Olivier Pineau, Joand Robin Pope, Elaine and Barry Pryce, Dyreen and Peter Quinn, Ian Redmond, Matt Richmond, Susan Riechert, Jean Michael Roux, Jean Paul Roux, Louis Sarno, Nicky Sayer, Ute Schmeidel, Kirstin Siex, Claudio Sillero-Zubiri, Rob Simmons, Martin Skov, Cor Smit, Tom Smith, Gary Stafford, Jay R. Stauffer Jnr, Chris and Tilde Stuart, Stephen Swanson, Andrea Turkalo, Leshia Upfold, Delulu Upson, Marco Vannini, Peter Vine, Bettina Wachter, Hartmut Walter, Hilary and Geoff Welch, Lee White, Louise and Paul White, Ingrid Wiesel, Chris Wild, Liz Williamson, Wim Wolff, Graham Wood, Bongo Woodley and Jean Worms.

In making the television series we have been fortunate to work with highly skilled and dedicated wildlife photographers, many of whose outstanding pictures also feature in this book. An enormous thank you goes to Martyn Colbeck, Simon King, Richard Kirby, Alastair MacEwen, Owen Newman and Peter Scoones who formed the core of our team, and to John Brown, Gil Domb, Mark Gottlieb, Mike Holding, Chris Hooke, Phil Lovel, Ian MacCarthy, Rebecca MaGahey, Justin Maguire, Rolando Menardi, Michael W. Richards, Warren Samuels, Phil Savoie, Michael and Rita Schlamberger, Phil Sharpe, Toby Strong, Gavin Thurston, Simon Wagen and John Waters who all contributed excellent sequences to the series. Thank you also to our highly talented and endlessly resourceful field assistants James Aldred, Andrew Barrel, Natasha Breed, Paul Brehem, Hamish Hofmeyer, Paul Liechte, Jamie MacPherson, Samson Teshome and Jo Walker.

Working in 22 countries and conducting over 50 separate filming trips to Africa has been no easy task. We are indebted to our brilliant production team at the BBC Natural History Unit, notably Richard Chambers, Adam Chapman, Loulla Charalambous, Charlotte Cross, Katie Cuss, Glenys Davies, Clare Flegg, Ros Gillions, Christina Hamilton, Julian Hector, Bernadette John-Lewis, Emma Jones, Pip Lawson, Jo Lester, Anna Mike, Anuschka de Rohan, Miranda Sturgess and our executive editors Neil Nightingale and Keith Scholey. We are particularly grateful to Charlotte, Pip, Adam and Anna for helping us far beyond the call of duty with sorting photographs, checking text and providing information, and to Joanne Osborn, Sarah Lavelle, Susannah Parker and Marian Thornley at BBC Worldwide for their support and faith in us.

A last word must go to the animals, into whose lives we briefly intruded, and to whom we wish to dedicate this book.

Patrick Morris
Amanda Barrett
Andrew Murray
Marguerite Smits van Oyen

Bibliography

Adams, W., Goudie, A.S. and Orme, A.R., *The Physical Geography of Africa* (Oxford Regional Environments).

Bearman, G. (ed.), *Ocean Circulation* (Open University, Pergamon Press, 1989).

Bramwell, M. (ed.), *Atlas of the Oceans* (WWF, Colour Library Books, 1977).

Brown, L., *East African Mountains and Lakes* (East African Publishing House, 1971).

Brown, L., *The Mystery of the Flamingos* (East African Publishing House, 1973).

Caro, T.M., *Cheetahs of the Serengeti Plains* (University of Chicago Press, 1994).

Cloudsley-Thompson, J. (ed.), *Sahara Desert* (Pergamon Press, 1984).

Coe, M. and Beentje, H., *Acacias of Kenya* (Oxford University Press, 1991).

Coppinger, M. and Williams, J., *Zambezi: River of Africa* (New Holland, 1994).

Cowling, A. and Pierce, S., *Namaqualand – A Succulent Desert* (Fernwood Press, 1999).

Cowling, R. and Richardson, D., *Fynbos – South Africa's Unique Floral Kingdom* (Fernwood Press, 1995)

Denslow, J.S. and Padoch, C., *People of the Tropical Rainforest* (University of California Press, 1988).

Eltringham, S.K., *The Hippos* (T & D Poyser Ltd, 1999).

Estes, R.D., *The Behaviour Guide to African Mammals* (University of California Press, 1991).

Fleagle. J.G., *Primate Adaptation and Evolution* (Academic Press, 1999).

Gargett, V., *The Black Eagle: A Study* (Acorn Books and Russel Friedman Books, 1993).

Hanby, J., *Lions Share* (Houghton Mifflin Company, 1982).

Hedberg, O., 'Afroalpine plant ecology.' *Acta Phytogeographics Suecica* 49 (1964).

Hofer, H. and East, M.L., 'The commuting system of Serengeti spotted hyenas: how a predator copes with migratory prey.' *Animal Behaviour* 46 (1993): 547–89.

Hogarth, P.J., *The Biology of Mangroves* (Oxford University Press, 1999).

Hughes, R.H. and Hughes, J.S., *A Directory of African Wetlands* (IUCN, UNEP and WCMC, 1992).

Kingdon, J., *Island Africa: the Evolution of Africa's Rare Animals and Plants* (Collins, 1990).

Kingdon, J., *The Kingdon Field Guide to African Mammals* (Academic Press, 1997).

Knight, M. and Joyce, P., *The Kalahari – Survival in a Thirstland Wilderness* (Struik, 1997).

Lawson, G.W., *Plant Ecology in West Africa* (John Wiley & Sons, 1986).

Leakey, R. and Lewin, R., *The Sixth Extinction* (Weidenfeld & Nicolson, 1996).

Letouzey, R., *Manual of Forest Botany: Tropical Africa* (CTFT 1982, 1983).

Lindblad, L. and Lindblad, S.-O., *The Serengeti, Land of Endless Space* (Rizzoli International Publications, 1989).

Little, C. *The Terrestrial Invasion, an Ecophysiological Approach to the Origins of Land Animals* (Cambridge University Press, 1990)

Louw, G. and Seely, M., *Ecology of Desert Organisms* (Longmans, 1982).

Lovegrove, B., *The Living Deserts of Southern Africa* (Fernwood Press, 1993).

McNaughton, S.J., 'Ecology of a grazing system: the Serengeti.' *Ecological Monographs* 55 (1985): 259–94.

Mimms, W.J., *A Geography of Africa* (Macmilllan Education Ltd, 1984).

Moss, C., *Elephant Memories* (Elmtree Books, 1988).

Open University Course Team, *Ocean Circulation* (Butterworth Heinemann, 1998)

Pauw, A. and Johnson, S., *Table Mountain* (Fernwood Press, 1999).

Payne, A.I.L. and Crawford, R.J.M. (eds), *Oceans of Life off Southern Africa* (Vlaeburg, 1989).

Pringle, L., *Rivers and Lakes* (Time Life Books, 1985).

Prins, H.H.T., *Ecology and Behaviour of the African Buffalo* (Chapman & Hall, 1996).

Reader, J., *Wild Africa* (Penguin Books, 1998).

Reader, J. and Croze, H., *Pyramids of Life* (William Collins and Sons, 1977).

Richmond, M.D. (ed.), *A Guide to the Seashores of Eastern Africa and the Western Indian Ocean Islands* (SIDA Department for Research Cooperation, SAREC, 1997).

Ross, K., *Okavango: Jewel of the Kalahari* (BBC Books, 1987).

Sayer, J.A., *The Conservation Atlas of Tropical Forests, AFRICA* (Macmillan, 1992).

Seely, M., *The Namib* (Shell Namibia, 1987).

Silcock, Lisa, *The Rain Forests: A Celebration* (Barrie & Jenkins Ltd, 1989).

Sillero-Zubiri, C. and MacDonald, D., *The Ethiopian Wolf* (IUCN, 1997).

Sinclair, A.R.E. and Arcese, P. (eds), *Serengeti II: Dynamics, Management and Conservation of an Ecosystem* (University of Chicago Press, 1995)

Smith, A., *The Great Rift – Africa's Changing Valley* (BBC Books, 1988).

Spinnage, C., *Elephants* (Poyser Natural History, 1994).

Struhsaker, T.T., *Ecology of the African Rainforest* (University of Florida Press, 1997).

Stuart, C. and Stuart, T., *Africa – A Natural History* (Swan Hill, 1995).

Sutton, S.L., *Tropical Rain Forest: Ecology and Management* (Blackwell Scientific Publications, 1983).

Swift, J., *The Sahara* (Time Life, 1975).

Vaniini, M., Cannicci, S. and Ruwa, K., 'Effect of light intensity on vertical migration of the tree crab, *Sesarma leptosoma* Hilgendorf (Decapoda, Grapsidae).' *Journal of Experimental Marine Biology and Ecology* 185 (1995): 181–9.

Vesey-Fitzgerald, D., *East African Grasslands* (East African Publishing House, 1973).

White, L. and Abernethy, K., *A Guide to the Vegetation of Lope Reserve, Gabon* (Ecofac 1997). Available from ECOFAC, Gabon. BP 9352, Libreville, Gabon.

Willcock, C., *Africa's Rift Valley* (Time Life, 1974).

Picture credits

BBC Worldwide would like to thank the following for providing photographs and for permission to reproduce copyright material. While every effort has been made to trace and acknowledge all copyright holders, we would like to apologize should there have been any errors or omissions.

Ardea London 62 Jean-Paul Ferrero; **BBC Natural History Unit** 11 Marguerite Smits van Oyen, 17 MSvO, 18 MSvO, 22 MSvO, 24 MSvO, 26b MSvO, 36r MSvO, 37 Film Grab, 41 MSvO, 42t MSvO, 43 MSvO, 47 Martyn Colbeck, 52 Chadden Hunter, 57 Natasha Breed, 63 Natasha Breed, 64 Natasha Breed, 65 Natasha Breed, 71 Jamie McPherson, 74/5 Miles Barton, 78 Jamie McPherson, 83 Richard Kirby, 86 Pip Lawson, 99l Pip Lawson, 158 Andrew Murray, 164 Andrew Murray, 166 Andrew Murray, 171 Richard Kirby, 172 Richard Kirby, 173 Richard Kirby, 183b Andrew Murray, 189r Andrew Murray, 195 Owen Newman, 198t Owen Newman, 198b Owen Newman, 202 Owen Newman, 203 Owen Newman, 209 Owen Newman, 221 Owen Newman, 223 Owen Newman, 227b Owen Newman, 228 Owen Newman; **BBC Natural History Unit Picture Library** 1 Torsten Brehem, 8 Rod Haestier (Rotman), 12 Victoria Keble-Williams, 14 Jeff Rotman, 15 Jürgen Freund, 30/1 Georgette Douwma, 32 Doc White, 35 Roger De La Harpe, 39 Simon King, 53t Anup Shah, 53b Bruce Davidson, 54 Richard Du Toit, 55 Ian Redmond, 60 John Cancalosi, 69l Bruce Davidson, 70 Keith Scholey, 72l Peter Blackwell, 73 Barrie Britton, 76/7 Bruce Davidson, 79 Anup Shah, 80 Tony Heald, 84 Neil P. Lucas, 89 Pete Oxford, 92/3 Anup Shah, 95 Bruce Davidson, 101 Peter Blackwell, 102t Anup Shah, 102b Peter Scoones, 104/5 Pete Oxford, 110 Bruce Davidson, 121 Tony Heald, 125 Eliot Lyons, 128 Richard Du Toit, 129 Tony Heald, 133 Jason Venus, 141 Tony Heald, 142 Owen Newman, 148/9 Francois Savigny, 151 Vincent Munier, 152 Richard Du Toit, 157 Michael W. Richard, 160 Bruce Davidson, 162 Anup Shah, 165 Bruce Davidson, 174 Michael W. Richards, 175 John Downer, 177 Michael W. Richards, 178t John Waters, 179l Bruce Davidson, 179r Pete Oxford, 183t Bruce Davidson, 184 Prema Photos, 186 Bruce Davidson, 188 Bernard Walton, 190 Richard Du Toit, 192 Richard Du Toit, 197 Bruce Davidson, 201 Anup Shah, 207 Anup Shah, 208 Anup Shah, 210b Anup Shah, 212 Owen Newman, 214 Richard Du Toit, 215 Owen Newman, 220 Peter Blackwell, 224 Anup Shah, 226 Tony Heald, 229 Anup Shah, 230/1 Richard Du Toit; **Stefano Cannicci** 26t, 27;

Bruce Coleman Collection 19 Atlantide snc, 44 Bruce Coleman, 49 Rod Williams, 85t Bruce Coleman, 99r Gunter Kohler, 122 Dr Hermann Brehm, 123l MPL Fogden, 123r HPH Photography, 144 John Cancalosi, 150t MPL Fogden, 150bl MPL Fogden, 150br MPL Fogden, 154 Gunter Ziesler, 185 Joe McDonald, 225t Gunter Kohler; **DRK Photo** 176 Kennan Ward; **Georgette Douwma** 29, 33; **Focal Point** 97 Peter Pickford; **Gallo Images** 38, 42b, 109b Anthony Bannister, 126 Heinrich Van Den Berg; **Robert Harding Picture Library** 96 Liaison, 216 Minden Photos; **Images of Africa** 51 David K. Jones, 61 Vanessa Burger, 67 Eric Patrick, 69r David K. Jones, 72r David K. Jones, 145 Friedrich Von Hörsten, 217 Carla Signorini Jones; **Monique Le Sueur/apexpredators.com** 40; **NHPA** 16 Martin Harvey, 36l Nigel Dennis, 120 Anthony Bannister, 124 Martin Harvey, 127 Nigel Dennis, 132 Daniel Heuclin, 138 Hellio & Van Ingen, 159 Stephen Dalton, 161 E. A. Janes, 163 Daniel Heuclin, 182 Daniel Heuclin, 187 Daniel Heuclin; **National Geographic Image Collection** 168/9 191 Michael Nichols; **Nature Photographers** 91 John Karmali; **OSF** 21 Mark Deeble & Victoria Stone, 25 Mark Deeble & Victoria Stone, 28 Nick Gordon, 107 John Downer, 108 Liz & Tony Bomford, 109t Mark Deeble & Victoria Stone, 113 Frank Schneidermeyer, 136 Richard Packwood, 139b P.&W. Ward, 189l Martyn Colbeck; **Planet Earth Pictures** 2 P Ravaux, 48 Anup Shah, 66 Elio Della Ferrera, 135 Alain Dragesco, 143 Thomas Dressler, 147b Peter Lillie, 153 Johan Le Roux, 178b Anup Shah, 196 Richard Coomber, 200 Wendy Dennis, 204/5 M.&C. Denis-Huot, 211 Peter Lillie, 213 M.&C. Denis-Huot, 219 Jonathan Scott, 222r Angela Scott, 225b Jonathan Scott; **Science Photo Library** 103 Adam Jones, 116 Bernhard Edmaier, 119 Nigel Dennis, 131 Tony Buxton, 137 Geoff Tompkinson 147t Bernhard Edmaier; **Raoul Slater** 23; **Tony Stone Images** 59 John Lamb, 90 Darryl Torckler, 98 Manoj Shah, 114 Hugh Sitton, 115 Manoj Shah, 199 Nicholas DeVore, 222l Kevin Schafer, 227t Johan Elzenga; **Jan Vermeer** 181; **John Warburton-Lee** 139t, 210t; **Jumbo Williams** 85b; **Woodfall Wild Images** 111.

Index

ISBN 0-7894-7830-7
First US edition 2002
Published in the US by DK Publishing, Inc.,
95 Madison Avenue, New York, New York 10016

First Published 2001 by BBC Worldwide Limited, Woodlands, 80 Wood Lane, London W12 0TT

Artwork on page 22 based on originals © Cambridge University Press 1986, from The Botany of Mangroves by Tomlinson.

Commissioning Editor: Joanne Osborn
Project Editor: Sarah Lavelle
Art Editor: Lisa Pettibone
Designer: Dominic Zwemmer
Copy Editor: Marian Thornley
Picture Researcher: Susannah Parker
Cartographer: Olive Pearson
Illustrator: Wildlife-Art Limited/Robin Carter

Printed and bound in Britain by Butler & Tanner Ltd, Frome and London
Colour separations by Radstock Reproductions Ltd, Midsomer Norton
Jacket printed by Lawrence-Allen Ltd, Weston-super-Mare